Behind the
Silken Curtain

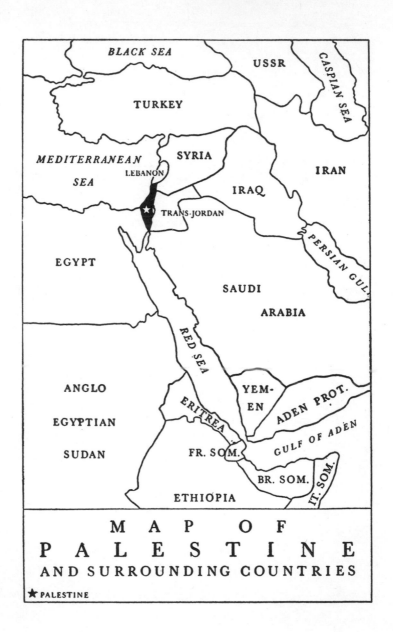

MAP OF PALESTINE
AND SURROUNDING COUNTRIES

★ PALESTINE

Behind the
Silken Curtain

A PERSONAL ACCOUNT
OF ANGLO-AMERICAN DIPLOMACY
IN PALESTINE AND THE MIDDLE EAST

BY

Bartley C. Crum

KENNIKAT PRESS, INC./PORT WASHINGTON, N. Y.

IN TRIBUTE TO
WENDELL L. WILLKIE

Acknowledgments

I owe a deep debt of gratitude above all to Gerold Frank for his brilliant assistance in the preparation of this book.

I am deeply indebted, as well, to Winthrop Martin, Olive Neick, Irita Van Doren, to Ted and Dorothy Thackrey, and many, many others for countless suggestions and helpful criticisms.

Preface

THIS *is in no sense a disinterested book. I am proud it
is not. As I look through the pages of the manuscript, I
find it difficult to recall the detachment with which I once
viewed the issues dealt with here. But I do not believe that
anyone, having seen what I have seen, having been exposed to what I was exposed to, could have come to a conclusion far different from mine.*

*The four months I devoted to the Palestine question
and that of the displaced persons of Europe (which is an
integral part of it) were, in a way, the most rewarding
spiritually—as they were the most affecting emotionally—
that I have ever known. Somehow, in the displaced-persons
camps of Europe and in the Palestine* Kibbutzim, *I had the
sense of coming to grips with reality, which eludes most of
us in the hustle and artificiality of modern living. I do not
wish to burden the reader with an excursion into mysti-
cism: perhaps my reaction was the normal reaction of a
rather matter-of-fact person suddenly catapulted into a
basic experience. I do not know.*

*This book is, essentially, the record of one American's
opportunity to look behind the scenes of current history
and to learn for himself what forces shape the disturbed
world in which we live. When I was appointed one of the
six American members of the Anglo-American Committee*

of Inquiry on Palestine, I was brought face to face with a problem which superficially might seem of a very special character, but which, I was to learn, presents the greatest issues of our time in microcosm. I was to learn much about how governments govern; about the prejudices that underlie the thinking and the decisions of the leaders of nations; about the way democracy must go if it is to survive; and, particularly, about one of the great social and national experiments of our time, the tangled, tragic, yet deeply promising twentieth-century history of the Jews. I was to find, on what is commonly called the highest level, instances of duplicity and intrigue which would seem almost incredible to the ordinary masses of decent citizens everywhere, and I was to come to know far more intimately than I had ever dreamed one of the chief battlefields in the struggle for world-wide freedom.

When I began, I had the usual American ignorance of Palestine. The word had had its magical connotations through my youth. It was the Holy Land, of course. But when I thought of it, it was in terms of stained-glass windows and pilgrimages. I had a vague idea that Great Britain had done something rather reprehensible in issuing a White Paper in 1939, but I had no definite knowledge as to the terms of this document. I knew next to nothing of the seventeen previous inquiry committees which had probed this problem. I realized that Palestine is the historic crossroads of the Middle East, but I certainly did not appreciate fully the extent of its strategic importance: that today it is the key to power in the Middle East; that, indeed, much in the Palestine problem has to be understood in terms of the vast struggle for power between the western democracies and Russia.

If Palestine were a detached trouble spot on an other-

wise tranquil planet, there would be no excuse for this book. The literature on Palestine is enormous. But Palestine is not an isolated phenomenon. Politically and physically, the world today is shrinking with frightening rapidity. Wendell Willkie, whom I was proud to count as a good and a wise friend, developed his thesis of One World out of his growing conviction that domestic and foreign issues cannot be separated: that what happened to an untouchable in far-off India had ultimately a direct relation to the sort of life his son and my son would live. In the experience out of which this book grew, I saw Wendell Willkie's conviction proved time and again.

It is because of this that I contend that one of our great errors in thinking through our problems has been to relegate the tragedy of the Jewish people to the realm of special pleading. Even some Jewish groups have fallen into this pitfall of treating their problem as a question apart. It is not separate: it is a part of the struggle of democratic forces everywhere to make real the freedom to which our victory over the Fascist forces entitles us. The settlement of the Palestine question is basic to the settlement of the problem of the Middle East, which, as one of the underdeveloped areas of the world, invites intervention and power conflicts.

This country, then, has no choice: it can neither stand aside and say it has no formulated policy for Palestine nor say that Palestine is a special case for which it has a special policy. It must treat Palestine, as it should treat China or India or Latin America, by the dictates of a foreign policy based on the twin concept of freedom and progress on which the United States itself was built. In Palestine, as I have tried to point out in this book, the issue is sharply drawn and the necessity for a solution is urgent.

I think it clear that the history of our foreign policy proves that every time we fail to stand for freedom, we meet with disaster, as in the shipment of scrap iron to Japan, as in our failure to back the republican government of Spain. I have written this book because I believe so strongly, and because I want my fellow Americans to share my belief, that Palestine is an essential part of this stand for freedom. If you are a Catholic, perhaps Irish by background, you need only to read County Mayo for Rehovoth; if you are a Negro, you need only substitute for the concentration camps of Cyprus and Eritrea a county in Mississippi; if you are a Protestant, or an "Okie," you will understand the struggle. What our American forebears fought for in the eighteenth century, the Jewish pioneers are fighting for today. That they are prepared to die for their freedom is significant. That they intend to live and to fight for their lives and their children's lives is even more significant.

What we here must know is that we cannot stop the fight. We can delay, but we cannot prevent a democratic Middle East and a free Palestine. The failure to help work out a democratic solution, the continued evasion and delay, Britain's prolonged refusal—with, I fear, the connivance of forces in our own country—to place world morality above expediency, all these set a grim and strangling pattern for the world.

The fate of our committee's recommendations is one of the scandals of this postwar period. There is absolutely no question that every American member of the committee— and I think the British members—believed that, as Mr. Ernest Bevin had promised, our recommendation would be carried out. I find it painful now to admit that Dr. Albert Einstein, Dr. Abba Hillel Silver, the American

Zionist leader, and others who characterized the committee's appointment as a device to postpone action were correct.

If we who stand for freedom win, I am convinced that neither Palestinian Jewry, nor the surviving fragment of European Jewry, nor the greater interests of the Arabs will lose. I am convinced that democratic forces ultimately will triumph in the Middle East and bring freedom for millions of the oppressed. When that happens, the world will see a new and broadened concept of justice in actual operation.

Palestine is the proving ground. It will test our intelligence, our courage, and our good will. It will prove whether our civilization can survive.

Table of Contents

xiii

BOOK FOUR

CONCLUSION

BOOK ONE

The Curtain
Rises

CHAPTER 1

Washington: Briefing

"MR. CRUM," drawled the soft voice at the other end of the telephone, "this is Judge Joseph C. Hutcheson, Jr., of Houston, Texas. The President asked me to call you and invite you to serve with me as one of the six American members of the Anglo-American Committee of Inquiry on Palestine."

Judge Hutcheson's call from Washington to my office in San Francisco was not the first time I had heard that Mr. Truman wanted me to serve. But the story of this Palestine mission properly begins with that telephone call. When I put down the receiver the world had suddenly become more complicated. I had become involved in "the Palestine affair." I had no idea that so many persons were so profoundly interested in the subject. From the very hour, almost, that my appointment became known, I was given little peace. The British Information Service was ready to help. So was the Zionist Organization of America. So were the United States Army, the Institute for Arab American Affairs, the American Christian Palestine Committee, the American Jewish Committee, the Arab Office, the American Refugee Service, UNRRA, and the American Red Cross. Jewish and Arab groups of every persuasion were prepared to explain the issues to me in from

1000 to 100,000 words. Letters, telegrams, speeches, books, and even prayers began to descend upon me. My office staff, which until now had been living in a comparatively sedate world of corporation law, began hurriedly typing file indexes under such headings as *Absorptive Capacity; Balfour Declaration; Jordan Valley Authority; Kibbutzim; King-Crane Commission; Weizmann, Dr. Chaim,* and *Yishuv.*

Actually, though, there was a preface to the full story of my introduction to this far-reaching problem. I had indicated previously that if I were appointed to the committee, I would accept; but when the list of appointees was issued in Washington, my name was not on it. This was the first suggestion of that strange atmosphere of intrigue which was to make itself felt so frequently throughout the course of our investigation over four continents and through a dozen countries. The State Department—or at least someone in the State Department—preferred not to have me on the committee. From other sources in government I learned that the President himself had sent in my name, but that it was rejected three times. Only through the insistence of Mr. Truman, who found it necessary to cable Mr. Byrnes in Moscow, was I finally appointed.

I have tried to analyze why I was *persona non grata.* The only key I can find is my association with liberal causes. I had been active in "Fight for Freedom." I believed that the moment Lend-Lease was passed we were really in the war. I took the matter of free speech and freedom of belief seriously. I had been interested in many causes that I considered would help make real the things for which the United States was founded. As special counsel for the President's Committee on Fair Employment Practices; as one who fought to compel Southern railroads to re-employ Ne-

4

groes; as a firm believer in job equality for all, I assume that I was viewed with some alarm by certain persons. I believed our policy toward Franco Spain was a dangerous one and threatened our own democratic institutions. I said so publicly. When I went East from San Francisco I was greeted by men on street corners selling a pamphlet attacking me for having been chairman of a Spanish Refugee Rally at Madison Square Garden. In fact, when Judge Hutcheson telephoned, I was preparing to leave for Spain, where my help had been enlisted for two anti-Franco underground fighters in danger of execution in a Madrid jail.

My record was clear. Perhaps for these and other reasons still unknown to me, the State Department was not happy about having me a member of the Anglo-American Committee of Inquiry. Yet, after all, I do not think their fears were justified. I was not a radical: I was a corporation lawyer. I was not a member of the Communist Party: I was a West Coast Republican. The danger represented by me, I felt, might possibly have been exaggerated.

In Washington an office awaited us on the first floor of the old State Department building. There the six American members of the committee met for the first time, under the chairmanship of Hutcheson. I had known Judge Hutcheson, judge of the Fifth Circuit Federal Court at Houston, by reputation. I knew that as a United States district judge, he had singlehandedly broken the Ku Klux Klan in Houston. Salty, independent, self-described as an "Old Testament Christian," he would enter this investigation, I knew, with a profound desire to find a solution both just and workable. There, too, I met the other four American members of the committee: Dr. James G. McDonald, who had been League of Nations High Commissioner for German Refugees; Frank W. Buxton, veteran editor of *The Boston Herald,* and a one-time Pulitzer Prize winner; Dr. Frank Aydelotte, Director of the Institute for Advanced Study at Princeton, American Secretary of the Rhodes Trust; and William Phillips, former Ambassador to Italy. It was Phillips, lean and distinguished in appearance, so perfectly the diplomat that he could have walked on any Hollywood set type-cast for the part, who arranged our protocol in meeting the six British members. We went in a body to welcome them when they arrived by train from New York: Sir John Singleton, who as Judge of the King's Bench, London, was Judge Hutcheson's opposite number; Lord Robert Morrison, Labour peer; Richard H. S. Crossman, Labour Member of Parliament; Major Reginald Manningham-Buller, Conservative Member of Parliament; Wilfrid Crick, adviser to the Midland Bank; and Sir Frederick Leggett, a labor conciliator. My first impression of the British contingent, there in Washington's huge, drafty Union Depot, was perhaps a naïve one: they looked, indeed, as British as I had expected them to look.

The following day we held our first formal gathering as luncheon guests of Dean Acheson, Acting Secretary of State, at Blair House, across Pennsylvania Avenue from the White House. I had been wondering, going East, what sort of reception I would get from State Department officials. Dean Acheson greeted all of us warmly, and he and I both acted as though we knew nothing about the earlier rejection of my name.

At this luncheon, Sir John, as British chairman, emphasized the need for Anglo-American co-operation. "We must endeavor to capture, in peace, the wartime partnership of Mr. Roosevelt and Mr. Churchill," he said. "This,

I think, is perhaps the most important phase of our joint mission: to demonstrate that Great Britain and the United States can together solve the problems before them."

It was an atmosphere of hope in which we met, and I am sure all of us subscribed in full measure to that wish.

Later we made an official call upon President Truman. He told us that never before in the history of the White House had there been such a tremendous volume of mail as that dealing with the displaced persons. There was no problem which concerned him more deeply, he said: he stressed the obligations of the democratic world to give these people who had wronged no one a chance to rebuild their lives; and he told us that he and the American government would do everything in their power to carry out a solution. He hoped, he said, that we would be able to complete our investigations and present our recommendations within 120 days.

There were the usual pleasantries. One of my British friends ventured to remark, "Mr. Truman, I have often wondered how it feels to be President."

Mr. Truman looked up from the President's chair, in which he had sat only a few months since Franklin Roosevelt's death, and said very simply, "I don't feel that I am. I feel that I am trying to carry on for someone else."

It was said with such disarming honesty that I am sure the British were touched as deeply as we by the words of this man who had been so suddenly catapulted into perhaps the most difficult job in the world.

If there had been pressures in San Francisco, there were new pressures in Washington. Everyone to whom I was introduced seemed eager to explain the Palestine situation to me. But it was not until I met Loy Henderson, Chief of the Near East Division of the State Department, that I received my sharpest and clearest briefing. He took me aside and told me, "There is one fact facing both the United States and Great Britain, Mr. Crum. That is the Soviet Union. It would be wise to bear that in mind when you consider the Palestine problem." I thought this was a most interesting observation to hear from an official of our State Department, and tucked it away for future consideration. I was to hear this same view expressed by a representative of the British Foreign Office aboard the *Queen Elizabeth* en route to Europe, and later again, in Europe itself. It was this same British gentleman who was to unburden himself completely in Lausanne, Switzerland, where we wrote our report, by assuring me that British policy was based on the protection of British interests against Russia, and explaining that it should be in our interests to fall in with that policy.

In the jockeying about of our first days in Washington, in the give-and-take of our meetings, I grew to know and. I think, to understand some of my British colleagues on the committee. The night before I left for Washington, I had spent an evening with several of Richard Crossman's wartime associates in New York. They told me of his brilliance and of the extraordinary work he had done during the war as Deputy Director, Psychological Warfare Division, SHAEF. A former Oxford don, an associate editor of the liberal *New Statesman and Nation,* at thirty-nine Crossman was a Labour Party M.P., considered by many the party's left-wing spokesman on foreign affairs, and a socialist theoretician of recognized influence. He came of an old, conservative family; his father was a high-court judge in England. That his background was so eminently conservative and that as a socialist he had been guilty of

8

what might be termed class treason made such persons as Major Manningham-Buller, who was thoroughly devoted. to the Kipling idea of empire, regard him with some coolness. Perhaps this attitude—that of the Conservative toward the Socialist—was best expressed by a Britisher who told me, "You know, it isn't that I object to Dick having the point of view he does. It is simply that a person with his background ought not to have it."

I had looked forward to meeting him. We were, each of us, the youngest members of our respective groups on the committee. Both of us had been, as it were, censured now and again for our "dangerous" radicalism. Crossman, his eyes sharp behind shell-rimmed spectacles, greeted me with a hearty handclasp. "I have quite a dossier on you, Mr. Crossman," I said.

He countered, "Ah! You should see *our* dossier on you!"

There are persons with whom you feel *en rapport* at once. So it was with Dick Crossman and myself. Meeting him here in person, I found him most refreshing, with an agile mind, a quick sympathy, and a gift for striking swiftly at the nub of complicated questions.

Crossman's wit—and Judge Hutcheson's delightful ability at riposte—were exhibited at our first committee meeting. Judge Hutcheson read to us the statement he proposed to make at the opening of the hearings a few days later. It was quite lengthy. Under the circumstances, none of us knowing the others very well, there was hesitation about being critical. Finally, Crossman looked about him and delivered himself in deliberate, measured phrases somewhat as follows: "Mr. Chairman, had it fallen to me to say the things which you, Mr. Chairman, propose to say, I venture to think that I should have said, Mr. Chairman, precisely what you propose to say. But, as I listen to your

9

remarks, I am struck with the remarkable unity of what you said, and such is the unity of your proposed opening statement that in my opinion it would be quite impossible to alter or remove even a single paragraph or amend a single sentence without destroying the unity of the whole. And therefore, Mr. Chairman, I venture to suggest that the real question is should anything be said at all?"

There was silence. Judge Hutcheson, whose face had been an impassive mask while Crossman spoke, carefully arranged his papers and then said, in his salty Texas drawl: "Those are the first kind words I have ever heard from a Britisher, and I thank you for them. Yet, as I sit here, having listened to what you have said so eloquently and well, I am afraid to shake my head, because I think"—and here he paused—"I think you have cut my throat from ear to ear."

Touché!

Lord Morrison was an elderly, reserved, pipe-smoking Scotsman with an unmistakable burr in his voice, who had been raised to the peerage as a representative from Tottenham, the heart of cockney London. He had been an outstanding union leader in his younger days.

Wilfrid Crick was a banker's banker, precise, self-contained, and thorough. Sir Frederick Leggett had had great success conciliating management and labor and was one of Bevin's intimate friends. Sir John was a bachelor in his sixties, lean, pink-faced, and as British in appearance as a character out of Dickens. One could scarcely imagine him other than in his silver wig of office. The contrast between our two chairmen, one British, one American, was marked. This was amusingly shown one afternoon when we paid a courtesy visit to members of the United States Supreme Court. As our committee walked into the enormous building, we were greeted solemnly by guards and escorted in dignified silence down what seemed interminably long marble corridors. It was an atmosphere in which one found oneself whispering. Suddenly, from an open door, boomed a great voice shouting, "Where the hell are you, Texas Joe?" It was the then Chief Justice of the United States, the late Harlan Fiske Stone, looking for his old friend, the Circuit Judge from the West.

Our British colleagues were rather taken aback at this exhibition of uninhibited American mores. It was difficult for them to envisage such a greeting between the Lord Chief Justice of England and a judge from the lower court. From then on I think they were surprised at nothing—not even when, in Vienna, at a dinner given by the American military, and after an orchestra had played a Texas song in honor of the Judge, the latter suddenly threw back his head, opened his mouth, and emitted a rafter-shaking "Yippee—ee!"

President Truman had asked Prime Minister Attlee to allow 100,000 Jewish displaced persons to enter Palestine. Attlee had replied by suggesting the appointment of our committee to examine the entire matter. Our joint terms of reference, therefore, required us to study the position of Jews in European countries where they had been victims of Nazi and Fascist persecution, and to determine what practical measures could be taken to enable Jews, who so wished, to continue to live in Europe free from persecution; and to determine how many wished, or would be impelled, to migrate to Palestine and to other non-European countries. If President Truman was correct, an emergency situation existed in the camps of Europe which might require action by us before we reached Palestine.

We were therefore authorized to make recommendations if necessary for ad interim or immediate handling of the problem. In Palestine we were to examine political, economic, and social conditions, to determine whether further Jewish immigration was feasible and how such immigration would affect the well-being of the peoples living there.

The British brought with them a staff headed by Harold Beeley, a member of the British Foreign Office and an expert on the Near East; our staff was headed by Evan Wilson, of the Near East desk of the State Department.

Together we worked out a general investigational procedure. We would hear the views of competent witnesses and consult representative Arabs and Jews on the problems of Palestine. We would hold hearings in Washington and London; travel through Europe and examine for ourselves the conditions of Jews in and out of the displaced-persons camps; we would hold hearings in Cairo and Jerusalem. Then, after firsthand examination of the situation in Palestine, write a report containing our recommendations. This was to be our task, to be completed in 120 days. In terms of human hopes a vast and somewhat terrifying responsibility rested upon our shoulders.

Our hearings began in an atmosphere of tense expectancy in a crowded chamber on the second floor of the State Department building, where in the course of eight days more than a dozen Jewish, Christian, and Arab organizations in America appeared to outline the question before us.

Our first witness was Earl Harrison, dean of the University of Pennsylvania Law School, who had written the report on the Jewish survivors in Europe on the basis of which President Truman had made his appeal to Mr. Attlee. Dr. Harrison saw this as the problem: we must accept the fact that there are tremendous numbers of displaced persons in Europe for whom there is no solution except resettlement—not repatriation. At least 100,000 Jewish DPs in Austria and Germany need such resettlement, he said, and he urged the quick evacuation of all nonrepatriable Jews in Germany and Austria to Palestine. He had come to Germany believing it desirable to rehabilitate the victims of Nazism on German soil. But after he had seen the situation—and he was sure we would come to agree with him—he realized how very intensely the majority of the Jewish DPs wanted to go to Palestine. It was their first and, for the most, their only choice for place of resettlement. He suggested their swift immigration to Palestine on a purely humanitarian basis, with no reference to ideology or politics. The Polish Jews fleeing Poland to Germany were, he said, fleeing terror. Their lives were not safe in their former home.

Dr. Joseph Schwartz, European director of the American Jewish Joint Distribution Committee, a tall, haggard-appearing man who had just come from four years of overseas relief work, described conditions among the million and a quarter Jews who had survived out of 6,500,000 prewar Jewish citizens of continental Europe. The majority of those in the western democratic countries—France, Belgium, Holland—would be able to reintegrate themselves there. But thousands of Jewish refugees who had been living without any legal status in western Europe since 1933 must emigrate, he said. As to the 100,000 displaced Jews in Germany and Austria, he agreed with Harrison: they must be removed as quickly as possible to the only available haven, Palestine. Under American immigration laws, he pointed out, years must pass before the thousands of Polish Jews in the German camps could be brought here.

In Poland, Hungary, Rumania, and Slovakia, the Jews, destitute, economically uprooted, were faced by recurring pogroms, he reported. Virtually seventy-five per cent of them, or about 600,000, wanted to go to Palestine now.

"I happened to be in Hungary," Dr. Schwartz said, "when Mr. Bevin said he would want the Jews to stay in European countries and help to rebuild their economy. The reaction that I noted among Hungarian Jews was something like this: 'For centuries now we have been building for others. Then, as a reward, we have been murdered; we have been shoved into concentration camps; we have been deported; we have been treated as aliens, even though we were patriotic. Now the time has finally come when we must act and live in our own interest, when we must build something which will mean a future existence for us; when, if we lose, we lose with people whom we understand, with people whom we love.' "

Sir John leaned across the table toward him. "If conditions improved in Europe, would not the number of those wishing to emigrate be reduced?" Dr. Schwartz shook his head. "The unprecedented catastrophe which has happened to European Jewry has left such profound aftereffects that it would take a very long time—and much more than the formal promulgation of laws and decrees—to make eastern Europe livable for Jews again. These people prefer even an unsettled Palestine to their present homes."

Granted that the refugees wanted to go to Palestine, was Palestine economically able to receive them? On this we heard two Washington economists, Robert Nathan, who had done important work with the War Production Board, and Oscar Gass, a former Treasury Department aide,

14

who had spent nearly a year in Palestine studying this problem and analyzing Palestine's industry, agriculture, trade, power costs, and housing possibilities.

Seated before us, a huge, black-haired fellow who looked more like a professional football player than an economist, Nathan reported that in the last twenty-five years the population of Palestine had trebled, manufacturing production had increased sixfold, changing from handicrafts to modern mass production, and electrical consumption—always an index of development—had increased eightyfold. The country, he concluded, could absorb 100,000 refugees within six to nine months: and, depending upon conditions, could absorb from 615,000 to 1,125,000 immigrants within the next ten years.

Nathan and his group had found that the Arabs' living conditions had been improved by the presence of the Jews in Palestine and would be additionally enhanced by further Jewish immigration.

This rather complicated lesson in Middle East economics ended the crammed first day of the hearings. The two next days were devoted to spokesmen for the Jewish organizations—the American Jewish Conference, representing the majority of the Jews of the country; the Zionist Organization of America; Hadassah, the Women's Zionist Organization; the labor and religious groups; and the American Jewish Committee and the Council for Judaism, which did not subscribe to Zionist doctrine. The Zionists defined the Jewish case for Palestine as more fundamental than an answer to refugeeism; they maintained that it involved the security of the position of Jews in a world composed of nationalities each with territorial centers.

Dr. Stephen S. Wise, a veteran leader of American Zionism, described the development of the movement in this country and cited the important part played by the late Justice Louis Brandeis and by Woodrow Wilson.

He quoted President Wilson as having said to him, "I am a son of the manse, son of a Presbyterian clergyman, and therefore I am with you completely and am proud to think that I may in some degree help you to rebuild Palestine."

President Wilson's sympathy was a distinct element in the history of the Balfour Declaration, Dr. Wise asserted. It would never have been issued unless American support had been secured. He quoted from his diary a statement made to him by Lord Balfour: "This means that all Jews who may at any time in the future wish or require to dwell in Palestine shall be free to do so."

In preparation for the hearings, I had boned up on the history of the struggle. I knew of the Balfour Declaration of November 2, 1917, and its pronouncement that the British government "views with favor the establishment in Palestine of a Jewish National Home." I knew that this statement of British policy had become the basis of the League of Nations Mandate for Palestine, and had been incorporated into the preamble of the mandate. I knew, too, that Balfour's phrase "Jewish National Home" had been debated for more than a quarter of a century. Was it a concept for a spiritual and cultural center for Jews, as the Arabs and some Jews themselves held? Or did it, as the Zionists contended, envisage a state in which Jews, not on sufferance but by right, would be free to live under their own government? According to Lord Balfour, the author of the phrase, as quoted by Dr. Wise, the Jewish National Home meant a place where all Jews would have the right to dwell.

Once that right was recognized, the Zionist spokesmen

declared, it followed that the Jewish refugee problem could be solved through immigration to Palestine. The problem of the refugees could not be divorced from the political problem of Palestine. The Balfour Declaration and the Mandate for Palestine had been designed precisely in order to establish a homeland to which persecuted Jews and Jews who found themselves in conflict with their environment might freely go. Such a home, in the natural course of events, as Jews became a majority there, would develop into an independent Jewish state. That, the Zionist witnesses asserted, was implied in the Balfour Declaration, and they cited statements by Lloyd George, Churchill, Smuts, Wilson, and others to support this point of view.

This, in essence, was the main thesis of Dr. Emanuel Neumann, presenting the legal case for Zionism, who contended that the Balfour Declaration, with its assurances that "nothing shall be done which may prejudice the civil and religious rights of existing non-Jewish communities" in Palestine, "implicitly pledged the land to the Jews."

Dr. Neumann added, perhaps with lawyers on the committee in mind:

"You will note further that the Declaration explicitly provides for safeguarding the civil and religious rights of the non-Jewish communities in Palestine. Obviously, this was done to allay any apprehension lest a large Jewish immigration and the creation of a Jewish majority should result in the curtailment of the civil and religious rights of the native Arab population.

"If what had been intended was a relatively small or moderate immigration of Jews who would remain a minority in a predominantly Arab country, then the application of that safeguarding clause should have been reversed. It would have been logical to stipulate that the

17

Jews settling in Palestine should be assured their civil and religious rights rather than the large non-Jewish majority."

The other side of the story was the Arabs' warning that a whole inflamed Moslem world would wage holy war to prevent a Jewish state. Of this, Dr. Neumann said: "It has been pointed out to us that there are hundreds of millions of Moslems and they extend from Casablanca across North Africa through India and Indonesia. The Christian world is equally extensive and more numerous. Yet no one would say that the Christian world is a unit. Neither is the Moslem world. The distance from the Mediterranean to Indonesia is precisely the same mathematically as the distance from Indonesia to the Mediterranean. There is conflict in Indonesia today. There is armed conflict in Java. Forty millions of its population are Moslems. What repercussions has it aroused in the Near East? What difficulties has it evoked in the Near East? So far as I know at the moment, none whatsoever. I think that these dangers are exceedingly exaggerated."

The Jews and Arabs in Palestine could live amicably, he contended, each preserving autonomy in religion, education, and language, as, for example, the French Catholics and English Protestants in Canada and the Walloon and Flemish populations of Belgium. The Zionist program, he said, sought a Palestine which would assure full democratic rights to all its inhabitants.

Did he envisage that in time some of the Arabs in Palestine might be moved elsewhere, Major Manningham-Buller asked.

"There is no need for it," Dr. Neumann replied. "The Zionist movement has never suggested the displacement of a single Arab from Palestine." Then he added, "The suggestion regarding that idea was made by the British Labour Party, as you probably know."

Some in the audience laughed, and Major Manningham-Buller, every inch the Conservative M.P., observed imperturbably: "I am not fully acquainted, I am afraid, with all that party has said."

Dr. Neumann argued that the committee could not use the British White Paper of 1939 as a criterion because, he charged, it was invalid. This was a matter which touched the very roots of our problem: it was the White Paper which closed the door of Palestine to Jewish refugees, and it was our responsibility, under the committee's terms of reference, to determine whether that door should be swung open again.

The White Paper set a five-year quota of a maximum of 75,000 Jewish immigrants into Palestine—after which there was to be no more without Arab consent—and barred the Jews from buying land in ninety-four per cent of the country. The Mandates Commission of the League of Nations had found that it was contrary to the terms of the mandate which required Britain to "facilitate" Jewish immigration and to foster "close settlement" of the land, the Jewish case emphasized.

Therefore, we were told, the refugees now entering Palestine despite the White Paper could not be termed "illegal."

Speaking as the head of the American Jewish Committee, an organization "not identified with the Zionist movement," Judge Joseph Proskauer of New York made it clear that he was not pleading for the establishment of a Jewish state in Palestine, but urged that the displaced-persons camps of Europe be emptied immediately and the

Jews in them be sent to Palestine, "the only place where they can go immediately."

Why, Sir John asked, was Palestine the only place to which the DPs could go at once? Why wasn't it possible to arrange for them to go to other countries?

"If you can do it, then God be with you," Proskauer answered. "But with one exception: I don't believe that the world can force these people to go where they do not want to go and where they would be strangers in a strange land."

I had understood that Judge Proskauer was, at best, lukewarm to the Zionist idea and was surprised at the ardor with which he espoused Palestine as the one haven for the remaining Jews of Europe. Still, his argument was consistent: his appeal was on humane, not on political grounds.

As for the political future of Palestine, he called for a United Nations trusteeship. Britain had interests in Palestine, he said, and no country should have the sole administration as a trustee over another country "whose administration involves considerations foreign to that trusteeship."

As a lawyer, I thought the Jewish case logical. And as a human being, I saw here a challenge to Christian mercy. If this were all, and if the committee's conscience were clear, as far as I could see, its duty also was clear. But, after all, I had not heard the Arabs yet. They, too, had a long history in the land and they were a majority of the people. That there was another side was stressed by a noted historian, Dr. Philip Hitti, professor of Semitic literature at Princeton, who, as the first Arab witness, spoke on behalf of the Institute for Arab American Affairs.

Dr. Hitti, a Christian Arab, explained that there was

actually no such entity as Palestine—never had been; it was historically part of Syria, and "the Sunday schools have done a great deal of harm to us because by smearing the walls of classrooms with maps of Palestine, they associate it with the Jews in the mind of the average American and Englishman."

He traced the history of Palestine back seven thousand years. All that time, he said, it had been the immemorial home of the Arabs. He asserted that Zionism was indefensible and unfeasible on moral, historic, and practical grounds. It was an imposition on the Arabs of an alien way of life which they resented and to which they would never submit.

"Dr. Hitti," Crossman asked, "your view is that anything like a Zionist solution could only be imposed by force on the Arabs?"

"Yes, sir," Dr. Hitti replied.

"And that any Arab solution could only be imposed by force on the Zionists?"

"That is correct."

Crossman: "What you are saying to the Mandatory Power is that it will be all right to suppress one part of the community for the sake of the other because there is no solution?"

Dr. Hitti: "That is up to the Mandatory. The Mandatory brought us into the impasse. The Mandatory has committed herself to many different views along the line."

Crossman: "Your criticism of the British government is the attempted reconciliation of Jews and Arabs?"

Hitti: "Yes, sir, absolutely."

Suppose the goal of a Jewish state were eliminated, asked Judge Hutcheson: would the Arabs then agree to Jewish immigration?

"Frankly, no," said Dr. Hitti. "Jewish immigration seems to us an attenuated form of conquest." Perhaps, he said, if the Western Powers admitted more Jews, the Arabs might be more amenable to the humanitarian plea made by Judge Hutcheson. But they now felt they had taken more than their share of Jews.

The Arabs in Palestine were opposed to the process of industrialization introduced by the Jews, Dr. John Hazam, of the College of the City of New York, told us: they might eventually industrialize the country themselves, but meanwhile they objected to its being turned into a "combination of Pittsburgh and Coney Island."

Dr. Khalil Totah, executive director of the Institute for Arab American Affairs, asserted that there had been trouble ever since Zionism had appeared on the Palestine horizon. He went on to observe that there was "a power maneuvering quite openly in the Middle East and it is catching Arab favor."

One theme repeatedly emphasized in the Arab case, which was to be presented in greater detail in our hearings overseas, was that the Arab people were on the land: that the land belonged to the people who were on it—to rule for themselves, to develop or neglect, to industrialize or not to industrialize, as they preferred. Dr. Hitti had mentioned the name of Frank W. Notestein, director of the Office of Population Research at Princeton. He was introduced to us as the man likely to be able to tell how many people would be at a given spot on the globe at a given time in the future.

Dr. Notestein testified that in view of the high Arab birth rate and the decline in the Arab death rate, it would be difficult to imagine how the Jews could maintain a Jewish majority in Palestine after 1960. In other words, a permanent Jewish majority in Palestine could not be maintained, unless some of the Arabs were moved out, because the Arabs increase twice as fast as the Jews.

Some of the Arab witnesses spoke in a conciliatory vein, ready to grant the Jews any demands except the right to go to Palestine. Others spoke more aggressively. But all emphasized that whatever the British and international promises to the Jews—which they interpreted more narrowly than did the Jews—and whatever the benefits the Jews had brought to Palestine—which they felt were exaggerated by the Jews—those pledges had no moral validity since Palestine is inhabited by an Arab majority and, therefore, ought to become an Arab state.

Were the committee instructed simply to determine the composition and wishes of Palestine's present population, the Arab case might have been unanswerable. But our terms of reference made it clear that we were to consider that certain rights had been internationally guaranteed to the Jews concerning Palestine, that the suffering of homeless and stateless Jews in the displaced-persons camps had to be alleviated, that Jews menaced by persecution had to be protected, and that the world wanted this question solved. I felt, therefore, that we must consider this Arab argument as only one of the elements in a complex and many-sided situation.

On one of the moot subjects which were to plague us again and again—were the Jews a religion or a people—a lively exchange took place between McDonald and Lessing W. Rosenwald, president of the anti-Zionist American Council for Judaism, which, he said, had 10,000 members "who rejected the Hitlerian concept of a Jewish state," and who held that the Jews were a religion and not a people. McDonald quoted Dubnov and Graetz, whom he described as the two greatest Jewish historians. "Graetz," he said, "uses the phrases 'the Jewish people' and 'the Jewish folk' quite commonly. Now I wonder whether he was wrong and whether he should have spoken only of Jews or people of Jewish faith?" Rosenwald said he was not qualified to answer such a question.

Rosenwald suggested in his testimony that the fundamental theories of Zionism raise the question of dual allegiance.

McDonald asked, "Do you agree that men like Lloyd George, Churchill, and Wilson were friends of the Jewish people?" "I have no doubt of it," Rosenwald replied. McDonald went on, "Do you think it likely that these great statesmen would have lent themselves to a program which would have implied, even remotely, divided loyalty?" Rosenwald said, "They probably did not understand all of the implications in Zionism." He spoke of the danger of "Jewish nationalism."

For me the most significant of our Washington hearings came with the appearance of Dr. Albert Einstein as a witness for the Jewish case. It was the first time I had seen him in person. I had thought of him as a small man. He is not. His entrance into the room disrupted our hearing. Although another witness was testifying, the moment the door opened and the audience caught sight of the figure so familiar to them in newsreels, they burst into applause. With his great mane of flowing white hair reaching almost to his shoulders, with his slow step, he looked like a patriarch stepping out of a Biblical tale. Judge Hutcheson rapped sharply for order. Later, when Dr. Einstein's turn came, Judge Hutcheson said, "Now all who feel I have restrained them from giving an appropriate welcome to Dr. Einstein may do so." The room echoed with applause.

Dr. Einstein murmured to a friend beside him, "I think they ought to wait first to see what I say," and shuffled forward to take his place on the witness chair. When he spoke his voice was so soft that those in the rear could not hear. They pushed forward, and within a minute the rigid regulations we had established were forgotten, and committee and witness both were engulfed in a mass of reporters, photographers, and spectators, seeking to catch every word.

"I wish to explain why I believe the difficulties in Palestine exist," Dr. Einstein began, in his slow, halting English. "First, I believe they are artificially created by the English. I believe if there would be a really honest government for the people there, which would get the Arabs and Jews together, there would be nothing to fear."

This was unabashedly twisting the lion's tale. Sir John looked at him as though he hadn't heard correctly, and Dick Crossman, who had been doodling on a scratch pad, stopped and stared at him.

"I shall first state what I think about British colonial rule," Dr. Einstein went on in a calm, professorial manner. "I find that the British rule is based on the native. Do you know what that means? I find that everywhere there are big landowners who are exploiters of that race of people. These big landowners, of course, are in a precarious situation because they are always afraid they will be gotten rid of. The British are always in a passive alliance with those land-possessing owners who exploit the work of the people of the different trades.

"It is my impression," he continued, smiling in friendliest fashion at us, "that Palestine is a kind of small model of India. There is an attempt to dominate, with the help of a few officials, the people of Palestine, and it seems to me that the English rule in Palestine is absolutely of this kind."

He paused, and added mildly, "It is difficult to imagine how it could be done otherwise." He went on to refer to the former Mufti of Jerusalem and said, "How can I explain otherwise than that national troublemaking is a British enterprise?"

By this time even we American members felt a sense of shock. I stole a covert glance at some of my British colleagues. They were obviously deeply pained.

Still in the best of humor, Dr. Einstein proceeded to say, in effect, that the British Colonial Office sponsored Arab-Jewish clashes because if the two peoples united, both might discover they had no need for foreign rule. Our committee, Dr. Einstein declared, was a waste of time—a "smoke screen"—since, in the long run, the Colonial Office would impose its own policies. He was "absolutely convinced," therefore, "that councils will have no effect." The Palestine people under the United Nations would be able to create a better state of affairs, but, "with British rule as it is, I believe it is impossible to find a real remedy."

Crossman bore down hard on him.

"Since the British are, according to your point of view, completely incompetent to rule in the various parts of the world where they have ruled——"

"No, oh, no," protested Dr. Einstein.

"Well, at least in Palestine," pursued Crossman. "You say they should not rule in Palestine. Would you be prepared to advocate publicly that the American people should take over the mandate and assume full military responsibility for unlimited Jewish immigration and thereby prove——"

Dr. Einstein interrupted, laughing, "No, I would not do that. I would be King of Palestine if I did that. God forbid!"

Crossman was not amused. "Your point of view is that you wish to blame the British. You are not prepared to suggest that the other great democracies, since we have failed, should take responsibility for carrying out the job which we have failed to do. We have failed, according to you. Why shouldn't you take the responsibility and show how wrong we are?"

"It should be done under an international regime," Dr. Einstein said.

"Well, what soldiers should go there to Palestine to carry out the American policy?"

"There should be a mixed organization."

"So the officials should be of fifty-four nations, or six, or five, or two?" Crossman demanded.

Dr. Einstein said, "I think it should be arranged. . . . I believe that any enterprise that is not too difficult, if successfully done, could be done by an international organization."

"Well," said Crossman, "we rather felt that inasmuch as we had failed, you Americans should take the executive and perhaps the military responsibility and then prove whether your theory is right."

Judge Hutcheson interrupted with a dry, "I doubt if that is the way you would authorize the Americans to do it." A few moments later, Judge Hutcheson observed to Einstein, "Your views about the British shenanigans are shared by many, not only with reference to Palestine, but

Ireland and many other countries, so we need not debate that matter." There was laughter.

Both Buxton and Dr. Aydelotte wanted to know why Britain should encourage strife in a country which she had to govern. "I do not quite get your idea of why the situation in Palestine is maintained as an advantage to the British."

Dr. Einstein replied: "At the present time the whole situation makes for trouble. A little enmity is good for everybody, but much is not."

All in all, it was not a pleasant afternoon for our British colleagues. My own feeling was that Einstein had perhaps not realized how unfair it was for him, with his great prestige, to state dogmatically that our committee was a smoke screen. I felt I owed it to ourselves to make this clear before he left the witness chair.

"Dr. Einstein," I said, "our British and American colleagues are doing everything in their power to find a speedy solution of the Palestine problem. I, for one, think it is wrong for you, as a citizen of the world, to say that this committee is a smoke screen. Believe me, sir, it is not."

He looked at me benignly. "How can you know it is not?"

"I know it from my own activities," I said.

"Yes, but you *estimate* it is not a smoke screen. I believe the Colonial Office makes it that."

"May I suggest," I said, "that you judge us by the actions following the recommendations of the committee?"

"I would be glad to be wrong," Dr. Einstein said.

Another high light of the Washington hearings was the testimony given us on an engineering plan for Palestine—the Jordan Valley Authority—based on the American model of the Tennessee Valley Authority. Its originator, Dr. Walter Clay Lowdermilk, Assistant Chief of the Soil Conservation Service of our Department of Agriculture, appeared before us with charts and maps. It had been his job for a quarter of a century, he said, to try to learn how we may make "a righteous adjustment of people to their land resources."

In the course of his studies, in 1938 and 1939, he had gone on a long tour of Europe and Asia. Traveling nearly 20,000 miles throughout the Arab lands, he had found erosion and desert waste everywhere among the vestiges of a once-flourishing ancient agricultural system. In Palestine, however, he had found a reversal of the trend: the old lands were being reproductivized by Jewish settlers who loved their soil and cared for it with intelligent application of modern science.

"Now," said Dr. Lowdermilk, "wherever—whether in China or Georgia or Syria or Palestine—I find a man who is conserving the soil, the basic resource which supplies the food of mankind, I am going to speak for him. And so I will speak for these Jewish colonists in Palestine. They are doing something there that has significance for the whole Near East and the whole world."

This had led him to his JVA project, which was based on the unique geological fact that a short distance from the Mediterranean the floor of the Jordan Valley drops to 1300 feet below sea level. Sea water from the Mediterranean would be introduced through a twenty-mile canal and tunnel into the Jordan River. Dropping down the first incline to the Dead Sea, it would generate tremendous hydroelectric power, far more than produced at our Norris Dam. Not only cheap electric power, but adequate water for irrigation would be made possible by the JVA, for the sweet water of the Jordan, above the point where sea water was introduced, would all be diverted for irrigation.

What a challenge this presented, and what such electrical power and irrigation could mean in terms of good to men and women, not only in Palestine but in its neighboring countries with their vast parched and undeveloped lands, he said, we could better visualize when we arrived in the Middle East and looked about for ourselves.

We gathered up the written record of testimony, which included printed documents presented to us by every organization and individual who had appeared, called together our staff of seventeen—experts, court reporters, and stenographers—and proceeded to New York, to board the *Queen Elizabeth* for London and the troubled continent of Europe.

CHAPTER 2

Shipboard: The Secret File in the State Department

With Evan Wilson, of the State Department's Near East desk, I was climbing the stairs of the *Queen Elizabeth* to the sun deck to attend our first meeting aboard ship. As we discussed the ramifications of the Palestine problem, Wilson used the phrase "an aroused Arab world." He spoke of Britain's life line, and as he spoke I heard in my mind again the careful words of Loy Henderson. Wilson, echoing him, was carrying his warning one step further: "If the committee reaches a decision which could be interpreted as too favorable to the Jews, an aroused Arab world might turn to the Soviet Union for support. That," he was saying, "is a matter the committee must consider seriously."

"If your words reflect the position of the State Department," I asked, "how do you square that with all the assurances this government and the Labour Party have made to the Jews? What exactly is the real position of the State Department?"

Wilson looked at me quizzically. "You can't always make the department's confidential records public," he observed. "But I can tell you that our concern is shared by the British Foreign and the British Colonial Office."

I said I thought the only thing, then, was to face the issues squarely. "I don't think there can be a middle ground at this late date," I said, and we went into our meeting.

Only a few days earlier, Winston Churchill, upon arrival in the United States, had stated that he had always been and still was a Zionist. This gave me further reason to doubt the validity of the State Department's stand.

"Surely," I wrote in my diary that night, "if the situation were as grave in British eyes as Wilson indicated, Churchill would not have spoken as he did. There is also the matter of written promises—the Balfour Declaration, the mandate, the exchange between Prince Feisal and Felix Frankfurter. It seems plain to me that we cannot begin *de novo*."

We spent much time trying to state the questions involved. It was clear that the attitude of our State Department, and that of the British Foreign Office and the British Colonial Office, were not consistent either with the statements made by Franklin Roosevelt before the 1944 elections, or with the platforms of the Republican and Democratic parties in 1945 when they called for a Jewish state, or with the declarations and policy statements of the British Labour Party before the 1945 election. In short, the foreign offices of Britain and America appeared to follow a policy certainly at variance with the publicly proclaimed policies of our two governments.

I began to think that perhaps the charges of power politics and imperialism made by Dr. Einstein and others were not as much oversimplification as I had hoped. Was it true that Jewish immigration and development must halt because of fear that Western civilization and social democracy would upset the applecart of British imperial-

ism and Arab landowning feudalism in the Middle East?
Did the British life line really depend upon maintaining
so shaky a *status quo?*

I rather doubted it. I hadn't yet been to the Middle
East. But if, as the Jews said, they could make Palestine
a model for a progressive and industrially expanding
Middle East, this would in turn mean new and larger
markets for the products of the British Isles. So long as
there was an economic problem in the Middle East, the
result would probably be the same as anywhere else in
the world: growing difficulties for the area and the government responsible for that area.

I sought to get an answer from the British secretary of
our committee, Harold Beeley, the Foreign Office man
who had come along as a Near East expert. Tall, rangy,
wearing thick black-rimmed spectacles, Beeley had a
thorough knowledge of the highly complicated political
history of Palestine. One evening in the ship's lounge he
explained his views to Buxton and me. The Palestine
issue, Beeley said, must be seen in the framework of strong
Soviet expansionism. The Soviet planned to move down
into the Middle East. The United States, therefore, would
do well to join Britain in establishing a *cordon sanitaire*
of Arab states. If Palestine were declared an Arab state,
it would be a strong link in this chain.

This proposal to set up the Arab world as a bulwark
to keep Stalin in his lair did not strike me as wise, particularly when one considered the Arab position during the
war. We had heard conflicting reports about the strength
of the Arab world and the elasticity of its loyalties. If the
issues were as clear cut as Beeley saw them, the investigation we were making seemed hardly worth the effort.

Beeley was frankly and forthrightly pro-Arab. It was obvious that he had tremendous influence with the British members of the committee. Now and then I would remark jokingly that he placed the Arabs even ahead of the British Empire. Of course, this was an overstatement, but it had a measure of truth. I had no objection to the point of view of Beeley or of any member of our staff, but I had gathered from the beginning that our experts were presumed to be neutral on the Palestine question. We were a committee of inquiry, charged to find the facts, and surely we should be able to turn to our experts for advice. Yet, if the British brought along an adviser definitely pro-Arab, we were not guiltless either. William F. Stinespring, professor of Old Testament at Duke University, an authority on the Semitic languages and an archeologist, was one of our experts. We had been assured that he had taken no stand on the Palestine question. But among the letters I carried aboard the *Queen Elizabeth* was one that had been sent to my Washington hotel by a local newspaperman. He had enclosed a newspaper clipping reporting a speech in which Professor Stinespring had ascribed Palestine's troubles to the "misguided efforts of the Zionist movement to secure political control of the country for the Jews." The note that accompanied the clipping concluded with a sentence, "You wouldn't say the cards are being stacked, would you?"

As we neared England our meetings grew more intense. Basic differences between the points of view of the American and British members began to emerge. It seemed to me that we, the Americans, began with the assumption that the nations of the world must co-operate. Sir John, speaking for the British, assured us that this was also his view. Yet, I sensed that the British felt they must never compromise Britain's position as a great world power. Thus, not only our points of view on Palestine differed radically from each other, but our national approaches to international problems. I felt, too, a sharp divergence with regard to the general applicability of democratic processes. It expressed itself in differences of interpretation as to the function of the press, as to the obligations of public servants, as to the entire problem of the postwar world. Here, at these shipboard meetings, began a cleavage which grew wider throughout our trip and, during our final deliberations in Switzerland, at times reached a point at which some of us were scarcely speaking to each other.

Despite this, there was much talk of the need for Anglo-American co-operation, in which I was the first to agree. But in the course of the next few meetings, a second underlying position on the British side became evident. Beeley was not a lone voice crying in the wilderness. The majority of my British colleagues were anti-Russian, their attitudes so strong as to be almost a phobia. They saw the Soviet as an evil force dedicated to reducing Britain to a fourth-rate power in the Middle East. It was Anglo-American unity they desired, not so much to solve the problem before us, but rather to establish a bloc against the Soviet.

Naturally, I found my American colleagues much less preoccupied with anxieties over our national security. We realized, I think, that the Soviet and the system it chose to follow were both in the world and that we had to live with both, like it or not. If we traveled different roads, each still had much to learn from the other. The world was large enough for both, and the market place, not the battlefield, should be the testing place of ideas. There might be points at which British imperial and Russian nationalistic interests did not coincide, but surely the United States and Russia had few points at which their basic interests were in conflict.

We were all constantly perplexed by the many threads to the Palestinian tapestry. For instance, Buxton, the newspaper editor, was concerned about the testimony in Washington by Arab spokesmen from other countries who seemed to take a direct interest in the Palestine question. "I want to find that out for myself," he said one day. "I don't know anything about their psychology, but I don't suppose the Arabs are different from any other people. Do you suppose that Arabs in Saudi Arabia or Iraq, a thousand miles from Palestine, are really exercised about the number of Jews in Tel Aviv?" I said I didn't know. Arab witnesses had asserted that Palestinian Arabs didn't want the Jews and resented them; Jewish witnesses countered that the Palestinian Arabs accepted the Jews and as proof pointed out that Arabs flocked to settlements near Jewish towns.

On our third day out we held a session which seemed, in a way, to make academic all our discussions up till now. I was given a document marked, "Contents of file of confidential communications on Palestine supplied by Division of Near Eastern Affairs for use of Anglo-American Committee of Inquiry." It dealt with seventeen items—despatches, cables, correspondence, memoranda of conversations. This was a résumé of the State Department secret file on Palestine, the existence of which apparently not even President Truman had known. According to this file, since September 15, 1938, each time a promise was made to American Jewry regarding Palestine, the State Department promptly sent messages to the Arab rulers discounting it and reassuring them, in effect, that regardless of what was promised publicly to the Jews, nothing would be done to change the situation in Palestine. This file confirmed the charges of double-dealing that had been hurled at both the United States and Great Britain.*

It was a sorry and bitter record for an American to read.

I said, "I think I ought to book passage home as soon as we arrive in Southampton. I don't see that there is any purpose in going on with our work."

Sir John said dryly, "It appears that Great Britain is not the only power who promises the same thing to two different groups."

I made a careful study of this confidential State Department material. It revealed that steadily and successively we had made public promises to the Zionists and private promises to the Arabs. From my reading of the voluminous record I had accumulated back in San Francisco, I was sharply aware of the promises, both actual and implicit, which the Jews had been given throughout the years of the Roosevelt administration. Two of them stood out in my memory because they were so clear and uncompromising, and because, together, they represented both the personal pledge of the President of the United States and the position of his party.

The first was the plank of the Democratic Party adopted at the Chicago Convention in 1944: "We favor the opening of Palestine to unrestricted Jewish immigration and colonization and such a policy as to result in the establishment there of a free and democratic Jewish commonwealth."

The other was President Roosevelt's personal letter in

---

* When I charged last summer that the middle levels of the State Department had sabotaged President Truman's Palestine policy, Under Secretary of State Dean Acheson denied my charges. I challenged him then to make public the communications in this secret file. To this writing Mr. Acheson has remained silent.

October, 1944, to Senator Robert Wagner of New York, to be read before the Convention of the Zionist Organization of America. In his statement—which may be construed as the official foreign policy of the United States government—the President not only reiterated the plank of his party, but also committed himself personally as follows: "Efforts will be made to find appropriate ways and means of effectuating this policy as soon as practicable. I know how long and ardently the Jewish people have worked and prayed for the establishment of Palestine as a free and democratic Jewish commonwealth. I am convinced that the American people give their support to this aim, and if re-elected, I shall help to bring about its realization."

I was further impressed by President Roosevelt's statement, made after his Red Sea visit with Ibn Saud, and less than a month before his death, in which he reaffirmed his pro-Zionist stand. Dr. Wise was authorized to quote him— and I hold this to be a sort of solemn legacy—"I made my position on Zionism clear in October. That position I have not changed and shall continue to seek to bring about its earliest realization."

Now, reading the State Department record aboard the *Queen Elizabeth,* I saw the evidences of our duplicity. Here, for example, was proof that when the Prime Minister of Iraq questioned the authenticity of the statement quoted by Dr. Wise, the Prime Minister received a secret cable from the State Department assuring him that the statement referred to "possible action at some future date," and adding that when President Roosevelt wrote his letter to Senator Wagner he was "of course keeping in mind the assurances made to certain Near East governments regarding consultations with the Arabs."

The chronological story was as follows. On May 26, 1943, a highly confidential note to King Ibn Saud from us asserted that no decision affecting the basic situation in Palestine would be reached "without full consultation with both Arabs and Jews." This, of course, implied that nothing would be done. It was a vitally important message because at that moment delicate negotiations were going on in Europe for the ransoming of Jews. Difficult though it is to say, this note may have helped send to death additional hundreds of thousands of European Jews. As I was to learn, the former Mufti of Jerusalem, then in Berlin, on June 5, 1943, less than a fortnight later, was able to make a successful plea to the Nazi-dominated Bulgarian government not to permit the ransoming of 4000 Jewish children. These children ultimately were killed. On October 26, 1943, in a secret cable to the acting foreign minister of Saudi Arabia, the United States took the position that "we sympathize with the aspirations of the people of the Near East to attain full independence and strengthen the ties between them." While this message may have been designed to offset the pro-Axis broadcasts then being made from Berlin by the ex-Mufti,* it certainly encouraged the Arabs at this critical moment to believe the United States might repudiate the Balfour Declaration and the Mandate for Palestine and accept Britain's White Paper.

Thus, from time to time, as American Jewry obtained Congressional support, our State Department, on February 24, 1944—again on March 4, 1944, and on March 28,

* The mufti reached the high point of his exhortations to the Arabs on March 4, 1944, when the United States Monitoring Service heard him broadcast to the Arab world: "Arabs! Rise as one and fight for your sacred rights. Kill the Jews wherever you find them. This pleases God, history, and religion. This saves your honor. God is with you."

1944—reassured Cairo, Yemen, Baghdad, Beirut, Damascus, and Jidda by secret diplomatic cablegram that President Roosevelt's views remained unchanged and there would be no decision reached without consultation with the Arabs.

Then came Dr. Wise's authorized statement of the President's position. This was followed not only by the reassuring message cited above to the Iraq Prime Minister, but by similar messages to King Ibn Saud of Saudi Arabia, the Regent of Iraq, the Prime Minister of Lebanon, the Emir of Trans-Jordan, and the Prime Minister of Egypt. The only part of this correspondence made public so far is the now-famous exchange between Ibn Saud and President Roosevelt in March and April of 1945, in which President Roosevelt assured Ibn Saud that no decision with respect to the "basic situation" in Palestine would be taken without full consultation with both Arabs and Jews.

It was clear that the State Department continued playing both ends against the middle under President Truman's administration. On August 16, 1945, President Truman revealed that he had discussed Palestine with Mr. Churchill and Mr. Attlee at Potsdam, and that they wanted to let as many Jews into Palestine as possible. But on October 23, in a confidential cable to Baghdad, Cairo, Damascus, Beirut, and Jidda, the State Department explained that President Truman and the Prime Ministers "engaged in exploratory correspondence on this subject and naturally mentioned Palestine as one of the havens for homeless Jews, but there has been no change in this government's previously announced attitude on Palestine." On November 15, 1945, another similar reassurance was given to the Arab world.

No doubt those who drafted these dispatches to the

Arabs and gave contrary assurances to the Jews believed themselves astute. I consider them to have been guilty of dangerous stupidity. I can think of no more perfect illustration of the danger of power politics and secret diplomacy than this "secret file." It exists in our State Department: its counterpart undoubtedly exists in the British Foreign Office. Many are apt to say that open covenants openly arrived at and world government under law are idealistic and not practical. But the results of British and American policy in the Middle East, based upon this cynical belief that one can be all things to all people, has only been to alienate both Jews and Arabs, to bring about among the small peoples of the world a profound disillusionment with the great democratic powers. The conduct of my own country in this matter had been highly questionable, to put it in the best possible light; and I began to realize how badly we needed a decisive, honest foreign policy.

The attitude of some of the British to these disclosures I found painful. Sir Frederick was almost amused. Crossman said he could not understand the stupidity that would permit us to do a thing like that, "but I must say it pleases me to find the British and the Americans are in the same boat."

Sir John consoled me. In his stateroom he explained matters. "Really, the Jews are not the most important factor at all," he said. "The important thing is Anglo-American co-operation. Since these promises of yours have put both nations in the dock together, it only serves to bring us closer in the world ahead."

As one who had fought for the re-election of President Roosevelt in 1944, in fact even bolting my own party to do so—and thus becoming, in the words of Congressman

Rankin's committee, a "renegade Republican"—I think I was more deeply depressed than anyone else. McDonald had supported Roosevelt, but, as former head of the Foreign Policy Association, he was a veteran in the diplomatic business, as was Ambassador Phillips. I am afraid neither of them was very surprised. Judge Hutcheson was most displeased, but felt that as agents of President Truman we should not consider ourselves bound. Buxton, who had been a Willkie man and a Republican, put the best possible face on it. He said, "In spite of all the correspondence, we'll call the shots as we see them."

On the *Queen Elizabeth,* the British generally began to make it clear that they viewed Zionism with anything but favor. Sir Frederick referred repeatedly to Lessing Rosenwald's phrase, "the danger of Jewish nationalism." One British member spoke of Zionism as "Jewish Fascism"; another characterized it as "Communism in disguise," and told me, "Bear in mind that hundreds of thousands of these Jews have been behind the Russian lines for years. We simply cannot afford to have the Middle East go communistic."

I myself had begun with no clear convictions on the issues before us. Some of my British colleagues, on the other hand, undoubtedly had definite ideas about them. While I could understand that a British subject might possibly entertain certain views on a matter intimately involved in his country's foreign policy, I felt most uncomfortable at what certainly appeared to me prejudgment of the case.

The British also brought up the subject of the Jewish Agency for Palestine, which is the representative of both Zionist and non-Zionist Jews all over the world so far as

Palestine is concerned, and the *Haganah,* which had been described to me by a Zionist as the Jewish home guard of Palestine. My British colleagues were, for the most part, strongly incensed over immigration into Palestine outside the White Paper quota. They charged that the Jewish Agency for Palestine not only encouraged this immigration but also supported much of the Jewish terrorism in Palestine. If recognition were withdrawn from the Jewish Agency, and if the *Haganah* were disarmed, this immigration would be slowed up, Jewish terrorism would be weakened, and the Arabs would believe that Britain was on the right path. Beeley said to me, "The matter of Britain's honor is at stake. In the 1939 White Paper we pledged independence to the Arabs of Palestine. We must carry out that pledge."

I do not think this argument impressed me even then. Testimony in Washington had made it clear that the White Paper of 1939 was a unilateral act by Great Britain and had been termed contrary to the meaning of the Mandate for Palestine by the Permanent Mandates Commission of the League of Nations. Whether Britain had or had not made such a pledge to the Arabs of Palestine in 1939 in a White Paper which was of dubious legality, both Britain and the United States, together with fifty-one other nations of the world, had made a prior and unanimous pledge to the Jews. To a lawyer, studying the documents alone, legal justice lay unquestionably on the side of the Jewish case; but I was determined to see the picture whole and judge it whole.

A note in my diary here reads: "Ambassador Phillips suggested today to Dick Crossman and me that it would be wise for our two chairmen to call on King Ibn Saud— to make it as clear as possible that we are not enemies of the Arabs. Phillips feels that the Congressional resolutions on Palestine inflamed the Arab world. I think for us to do this is a bad move unless we simultaneously assure the Jews that we are not their enemies. At any rate, I don't see Ibn Saud's right to be consulted on this matter. I suggested to Phillips that when he reaches Rome, as he expects to, he ask the Pope to send a pastoral letter to Polish Catholics urging tolerance toward the Jews.

"The over-all question," I wrote, "is whether the Western democracies have moral integrity. If they do, we will win out. If they don't, I think the Middle East may become a breeding place of new wars."

CHAPTER 3

London: The Soviet Jitters

ONCE IN LONDON I felt for the first time the strange sensation of being watched. I do not say that I was being trailed day and night. But aboard the *Queen Elizabeth* I had been told that it was not wise to send confidential messages over the ship's radio to Washington. Beeley was in charge of our arrangements in London, and when we arrived I discovered that I was to share a room in the Hyde Park Hotel with one of my British colleagues. It seemed reasonable to suppose that members of governmental committees might have rooms of their own. I was keeping a diary, making and receiving many personal telephone calls, and I preferred privacy. I broached the subject a number of times, and on the third day I was given a room of my own. Nonetheless, a British member of the committee cautioned me to be careful to whom I spoke and particularly to choose my words when I was on the telephone. I took this as a pleasant way of letting me know my conversations were being tapped, that we were under some form of surveillance.

The result of this stage managing was that when a Jewish leader sought to see me my second evening in London he felt constrained to advise me to wait for him to pick me up on a near-by corner. During that evening I discussed with him various solutions of the Palestine problem, including that of a partition of Palestine into Jewish and Arab states. This could be achieved by moving the Palestine-Trans-Jordan boundary to include the Nablus area—almost predominantly Arab—in a greater Trans-Jordan. Thus, the dominantly Jewish area of Palestine that remained would become a Jewish state, and Trans-Jordan plus the Nablus area would become a new Arab state. The next morning one of my British colleagues met me with a smile. There was almost a chiding note in his voice. "I understand you've been seeing some of our Jewish friends," he said, and winked.

I did not care. I had long since decided that everything I did would be in the open and that I could not consider myself locked up like a juror who must hear nothing, see nothing, know nothing except the facts and arguments presented in formal testimony. I looked upon myself—as most of my colleagues regarded themselves—as a member of a fact-finding commission and I was gratified that our procedure gave me freedom to hear whoever wanted to talk to me, or to seek facts where I thought I could find them.

I confess that one of my English associates managed this much more subtly. He asked me, in the presence of other members of the committee, if I would lunch with him at the House of Lords. I said yes. He called a cab and said distinctly, "House of Lords, please." But once inside, he told the driver, "Take us to Dorchester House." There he led me hurriedly down a long corridor and into a private dining room where he introduced me to a tall, lean, bemonocled Englishman who turned out to be Baron James de Rothschild, of the famous Jewish family which had been responsible for Britain's control of the Suez Canal. He now addressed the Baron as "Jimmy" and minced no words in expressing strong pro-Zionist sentiments. Baron Rothschild, who had dropped his title, was deeply concerned about Palestine. The early Rothschild philanthropic experiments in colonization in Palestine had not been too successful, he said, and after a long study he had concluded that the only program likely to succeed there was that of the Zionist Organization.

One afternoon, I returned to the offices which had been set up for us at 33 Grosvenor Square, near the American Embassy, to find George Wadsworth, our Minister to Lebanon, closeted with one of the American members of the committee. I was interested to know what an American diplomat, stationed at Beirut, was doing in London. He had come to us, it developed, as an emissary of the Arabs. The Arabs wished to testify before us—but *in camera*. I was against this. So were most of the committee. Until now, all witnesses had given evidence publicly, so that the opposition was able to hear what was said and have an opportunity to refute it. Wadsworth must have gained a rather lively impression of our reaction to his suggestion, for the following day a *note verbale* was delivered to us from the Royal Egyptian Embassy, announcing that five Arab spokesmen wished to appear before us—*publicly*.

Our hearings were held in the Royal Empire Society Building, in a large room with a horseshoelike gallery jammed with spectators. Here, for the first time, I saw several Palestinian soldiers of the Jewish Brigade, wearing the blue-and-white Star of David conspicuously on the shoulder patches of their British Army uniforms. Later I was to see this same emblem on the clothes of those who had been inmates of the Nazi concentration camps—a Star of David on the breast and back of each Jew.

47

The testimony to some degree repeated what we had heard in Washington. The Jewish representatives stated that they wished a Jewish state in which all persons, regardless of race or creed, had equal rights; they wanted an interim report issued at once recommending freedom and assistance for all displaced Jews to go to Palestine. The Arabs, in turn, were adamant against any further Jewish immigration into Palestine. But there was a new note here in London, the home of the empire. Whereas in Washington the British had felt somewhat on trial, here the witnesses refrained from bearding the lion in his own den. Our hearings were held, as it were, in a framework of sad rebuke.

Public interest in the hearings seemed intense, as evidenced by the overflow attendance of spectators and the press gallery, which included nearly fifty reporters representing newspapers all over the world. But though I glanced through the London newspapers daily, I rarely found more than two or three paragraphs referring to our hearings and frequently nothing at all. Newspapers in London were limited in size, but I could not understand why only a few lines were devoted to a full day's hearings at which internationally known figures testified on a subject of great importance to the British people.

Obviously, the importance of Palestine was recognized: for here on the very day that the Anglo-American Committee was ignored, I found a full column in the newspapers dealing with Jewish extremism in Jerusalem. Later I learned from a source high in government that it was customary for the British Foreign Office to advise the press on any matter which might affect the future of Britain. One of my British associates, quite unaware of this, I am certain, assured me that I had only to look in the newspapers for proof that Palestine was not of much interest to the British people. I gave thanks then, as I have many times since, for the free press of America. Our British friends might be shocked by the freedom with which reporters took us to task and commented upon our labors, but the truth was that the facts did appear in American newspapers and our people were the best informed in the world. The news columns of the American press were open on equal terms to any spokesman of a foreign power, and this was not true anywhere else on earth—including England.

Whatever the case, our audience unquestionably was interested. Time and again Sir John was forced to rap for order.

One of our first witnesses here was Nathan Jackson, who appeared on behalf of the Jewish Socialist Labour Party of Great Britain. Judge Hutcheson presented him with the basic question: "What do you mean by a Jewish state?" And with that habit of his of asking questions whose homespun simplicity invariably drew revealing replies he added seriously: "I couldn't justly say to an American that because I am of Scotch descent, 'I want a Scottish state in Texas.' Why do the Jews have to do that in Arabia when I can't do it in Texas?"

In answer, Jackson replied earnestly, "Gentlemen, nowhere has the Jew control of his own identity as a group —nowhere in the world. Other peoples have." Because Jews are a minority everywhere, he went on, they are "always dependent on the normal state of mind" of the people among whom they live. If, for one reason or another, this normal state did not obtain, the Jews were likely "to become the scapegoat of any attempt to sidetrack the attention of the masses from the real evils which beset them." He added that he felt his group had the right to ask the world, "especially after what our people have gone through, to allow us to concentrate our people, those who want it, in one place where we cannot only alleviate the plight of the individual but give the people a new status as an entity in the world."

What of the Arabs? Jackson quoted Sir Stafford Cripps: "There are wide dominions in which the Arabs can live in safety and happiness; not so the Jews. It would indeed be criminal to snatch from the Jewish race the last hope of having even a tiny territory that they may call their own."

Crick asked Professor Selig Brodetsky, President of the Board of Deputies of British Jews, "When excessive nationalism has made the world bankrupt, what is your justification for setting up another national status for people like the Jews? You will simply be compounding the position we are already in." "The essence of a Jewish state," replied Professor Brodetsky, "is this: wherever Jews are now, their position is determined by others. They wish to live in a country where the civilization, their status, and similar matters are determined by them. Our conception of a state is not that Jews should become a power, but that they should live freely, with their traditions, and not have a minority status."

Sooner or later, I knew, the issue of the British Labour Party's pledges on behalf of Jewish development of Palestine must come before our committee. In December, 1944, the Labour Party had adopted a Palestine plank reading, in part, "There is surely neither hope nor meaning in a Jewish National Home unless we are prepared to let the Jews, if they wish, enter this tiny land in such numbers as to become a majority. There was a strong case for this before the war, and there is an irresistible case for it now, after the unspeakable atrocities of the cold-blooded calculated German-Nazi plan to kill all the Jews of Europe." No promise could be more unequivocal. How would Labour M.P.s react to this pledge now? Part of the answer came with the appearance of Labourite Thomas Reid.

Reid was forthright. His party's pledges on Palestine had been highly overplayed, he told us. They were "hurried through" the Labour Party conferences. There was practically no discussion of them. He added, smiling, "I think the average member who attended these conferences had about as much knowledge of the Palestine problem as I have of the moon. These resolutions were put forward and accepted because nobody objected, as far as I can remember."

Crick, precise and formal, leaned forward. "Would you care, for the benefit of our American colleagues, in particular, to give us your view as to the weight which is to be attached to these declarations?" he asked. "The Labour Party is called upon to form His Majesty's government, and there might be some presumption that a declaration passed by the Party Conference could be expected, so to speak, to hold out a flag as to the direction in which the government might move when it assumed office. Have you any comment to make for our American friends on that prospect?"

Crick is the kindliest of men, and I am sure certainly had no thought of appearing patronizing; yet I could not keep from feeling uncomfortable at his emphasis on "our American friends." We in America knew the facts of political life. Political ethics could not be so far different in London and Washington. Whatever politicians might think in either country, pre-election pledges did count with the

51

people and were remembered by them; and we had definite attitudes toward parties which came into power and
promptly forgot the pledges which enabled them to do so.

"Would you agree," Crick continued, "that it is not
entirely without precedent that political parties, when
they are faced with the responsibility of government, do
sometimes qualify the policies they have expressed?"

"I am afraid it is worse than that," said Reid promptly.
"Sometimes political parties make promises which they do
not at all carry out. The Labour Party declarations, as
I said, did not enunciate a definite and complete policy.
I do not think the committee need pay an enormous
amount of attention to vague resolutions passed at Labour
Party conferences."

Since the British Labour Party was elected on the basis
of such resolutions, this struck me as unalloyed political
cynicism. McDonald, too, must have felt the same, for
he spoke up rather sharply:

"I'm a good deal troubled by these answers, Mr. Reid.
Being a rather naïve American, I had thought much about
the pronouncements of the Labour Party. I had supposed
that while they might not indicate a binding obligation,
they definitely indicated a party line. I suppose that is not
the line which you have suggested. Is that correct, Mr.
Reid?" Reid rubbed his nose. "You must not ask me, sir,"
he said. McDonald pursued, "I am only asking you the
line which any ordinary layman would deduce from the
Labour Party pronouncements on Palestine—is that line
similar to yours or the opposite?"

"If the line means the setting up of a Jewish state in
Palestine, then that line is opposed as a standard different
from mine, but I am not opposed to the Labour Party,"
Reid replied. "If you want to know the difference between

the resolutions passed by the Labour Conference and what His Majesty's present government is going to do, I am afraid you must go either to the Prime Minister or to Mr. Bevin, and not to me."

Lord Morrison cast oil on the troubled waters:

"You realize, I suppose, having attended the Labour Party Conference, that the resolutions passed at Labour Party conferences are not like those of the Medes and Persians? There is no compulsion upon any person to carry out every word and every syllable of every resolution that is passed."

Reid nodded. "No, we are a free party. I am at perfect liberty to express my views, even in the House."

I was studying the memorandum Reid had presented to the committee. One paragraph seemed to call for explanation. I read it to him:

"On pages eight and nine you state: 'The Arab states occupied some of the most important strategic positions in the world at least before the atomic bomb upset former world strategy. It behooves the practical man either to get their friendship, sealed in treaties, or to exterminate the lot, not a very paying proposition. Then Saudi Arabia has a lot of oil which the world needs. The practical man will conclude that the great warrior king, Ibn Saud, is worth cultivating.'

"Would you mind explaining that a little further?" I asked.

There were some chuckles from the gallery, and Reid reddened. "I am glad you gave me a chance of pointing out that I totally disapprove of the views of the narrow practical man, as stated here," he asserted emphatically. "I want to make it quite clear. I quoted the narrow practical man because I disagree with him."

"You don't think our decision should be made on the basis of oil and of friendship with Ibn Saud?" I asked.

"As I have stated in the memorandum," he said, "this committee should not bother their heads about the oil or the greatness of the position of Ibn Saud, but simply on the question of justice and legality."

It was interesting to read six months later, in *The New York Times*, an article by Dick Crossman asserting that Britain's decision on Palestine necessarily had to be one that protected her oil interests, because those oil interests were of primary importance to Britain, while to us and Russia the oil supplies of the Middle East were auxiliary only, since we had domestic oil supplies. Apparently, "justice and legality" were not the only determining factors.

I had no further questions to ask of Reid, but I could have wished, having a warm spot in my heart for the British Labour Party, that someone else had appeared as their spokesman. As I left this session of the hearings I came upon Harold Laski, the brilliant theoretician of British socialism. Laski and I had been in the same uncomfortable position not so long ago. He had spoken by telephone from London to the Madison Square Garden rally I had chairmaned. He had assailed alleged Vatican policy in Spain. I had had no advance knowledge of his remarks, but I felt, as an American, that he had the right to express his opinion. We both had been bitterly attacked. It was a pleasant surprise to see him, and we made plans to meet again at his home. But before we parted I checked with him on Reid's statement that the Palestine pledges were vague and hurried. Laski denied this emphatically. "Far from hurried," he said. "It was carefully studied for several years, I can tell you, and it represented the mature opinion of Labour Party members. I regard it as absolutely binding on the party." He pointed out that the Labour Party resolution was, after all, a repetition of resolutions passed for some thirty years by Labour Party conferences. The Labour Party had always been strongly pro-Zionist.

Why, indeed, had these pledges been treated with such disdain? Here, it seemed to me, we had the phenomenon of the British Labour Party moving toward socialism at home while practicing toryism abroad. For I found even the Conservatives ready to take the nationalization of the Bank of England, of the coal mines, and of transportation with good grace; but all parties seemed united in maintaining what certainly looked like traditional toryism in India, Burma, and Palestine. Perhaps one explanation was that the Labourites really hadn't expected to be elected; and once elected, unprepared for the touchy job, they thought they must first concentrate on the domestic scene. It was quite possible, as one friend told me, that when Bevin came into office he called in his advisers from the Middle East and asked them to analyze the situation there. These were the same men who had advised Churchill, and Chamberlain, and MacDonald. They had not changed their views, and none of them had been recalled from his post. A Labour government still had tory officials in the Middle East; was the tail wagging the dog?

The Labour Party's Palestine plank in December, 1944, had stated unequivocally: "Let the Arabs be encouraged to move out as the Jews move in. . . . The Arabs have many wide territories of their own: they should not seek to exclude the Jews from this small area of Palestine which is less than the size of Wales." No official Zionist spokesman anywhere had suggested anything as drastic as this. Yet now we heard a Labour Member of Commons assert that the Jews should not be permitted to move in at all, and that the practical man would "conclude that the great warrior king, Ibn Saud, is worth cultivating," because Saudi Arabia has a great quantity of oil which the world needs.

Apparently, fear weighed so heavily in some British thinking on this subject that even the expression of ideals was warped by it. How else could I explain the conflict between practice and principle, and the appalling indecision which the British were laying on the table before the world? How else explain this grasping and searching for every possible "out" to nullify the importance of the Labour Party pledges, this apparent relief when witnesses could be found either to dismiss them or to term them dangerous?

I had had no idea that the British were so frightened—not only for the stability of their empire, but also of the problems of administering it. Not only did the witnesses who appeared before us reflect this reluctance to face the troublesome task of empire management, but so did my British colleagues on the committee. The most insistent private question now beginning to run through our meetings, on their part, was, "Why should we be here? Why should we bear this burden?"

Among the Britons on the committee, it was my feeling that two—Dick Crossman and Major Manningham-Buller—had the sharpest understanding of what empire means. Either or both of them, I felt, might someday be prime minister. Yet they were two vastly different men. Crossman saw the empire in terms of today. He realized that, for Britain to survive, the social changes now taking place in the British Isles ultimately must extend to Britain's colonies. Although he could continue to nourish England on the substance of her millions of colonial subjects, he was capable, too, of understanding colonial grievances. I am sure he could plead their case better than they themselves. But he would sorrowfully conclude that first things come first. Manningham-Buller, the Conservative, would run the empire on the old line. Courageous, proper, certainly one whose word was to be relied upon, he felt an immediate affection for the Arabs. But he would want justice done to the Jews, and, as he saw it, he would do justice. However, neither Crossman nor Manningham-Buller, I was convinced, would continue for too long the essential weakness of British policy. Both knew that the British had never identified the governed with the governors and both knew that this is an inherent error.

Some American newspapers had pointed out that our British colleagues entered the Washington hearings feeling they had to defend the empire. As the testimony continued, this was remarked upon again in London, perhaps most bluntly by a London correspondent of the *New York Herald Tribune,* who wrote, in a widely quoted article, of the "intent, defensive attitude on the part of British members against any implications that anything ever goes wrong in the British Empire or that British justice ever miscarries."

It was Sir John, to whom the burden of empire proved so wearisome, who took most seriously any criticism of the British in Palestine. At one point, when a witness questioned an act by the British Administration there, Sir John stared at him and then inquired smoothly, "Why do you not realize that if an official actually did what you describe he would be removed by the British government at once?"

Some in the audience laughed.

On another occasion, Rabbi Kopul Rosen, a tall, dark-haired, embittered man who spoke for the British Federation of Synagogues, made an impassioned appeal to us. "I am taking the liberty of my cloth to preach to you," he said. He was not a politician, he said, not a statistician, and doubtless they could trip him up on the questions of economic facts. But he wanted to impress upon us the feeling of the Jews that elsewhere, as in Germany, tolerance might be transformed into persecution, hence their appeal to the committee, "If not in the name of simple humanity, then in the name of God, do not play politics with the remnant of the Jewish people."

This, it seemed to me, was an overflow of tragedy which could be heard compassionately whether or not it could be considered evidence.

Sir John, however, took umbrage again. It was apparent that he had the constant problem of remembering that the witnesses before him were not prisoners in the dock: that he was cochairman of a fact-finding body and not a court. "You said the committee might trip you up on this, that, and the other?"

"I did not mean it in that sense," the rabbi said. "I meant that I was ignorant."

"Allow me to finish, if you please," said Sir John. "Let this be clear. The committee is not here to trip anyone up. The committee is asking for the help of people to guide them aright, if that is possible; is that clear?"

He looked down at his notes. "One other matter," he went on. "You said, 'Do not play politics with the remnants of the Jewish people.'" He leaned forward, brandishing his spectacles at the rabbi. "You do not think, I hope, that this committee is out to play politics?"

"No, sir, I do not think so at all," replied Rabbi Rosen.

"You realize, I hope," went on Sir John icily, "that most of the members of this committee have no connection with politics, and that those who have are looking as best they can for help toward a just solution of this trouble?"

Perhaps the most noteworthy incident of this sort occurred between Sir John and Sir Simon Marks, who represented the Zionist Federation of Great Britain and Ireland.

Sir Simon, noted for his philanthropies in Palestine, pointed out that the 1939 White Paper closed Palestine to the Jews at the very moment of their greatest desperation, when they needed a refuge to escape from Hitler's massacres. In that sense, he charged, the White Paper had been responsible for the death of thousands of Jews who might today be alive in Palestine.

Palestine, he said, should be declared a Jewish state within the framework of the British Commonwealth of Nations. He quoted Lloyd George's World War diary: "It was contemplated that when the time arrived for according representative institutions to Palestine, if the Jews had meanwhile responded to the opportunity afforded them by the idea of a national home and had become a definite majority of the inhabitants, then Palestine would thus become a Jewish Commonwealth. . . . The notion that Jewish immigration would have to be artificially restricted in order to ensure that the Jews should be a permanent minority never entered into the head of anyone engaged in framing the policy."

Sir John said, "You are asking that Palestine should be declared forthwith to be a Jewish state, are you not?"

"Yes, sir," replied Sir Simon.

"If that meant trouble, it might involve another period of war, might not it?"

"With whom?" asked Sir Simon.

"Don't you know?" countered Sir John.

Sir Simon said doggedly, "Between whom?"

"Cannot you envisage trouble coming about?" demanded Sir John.

"Yes," said Sir Simon, "a period of war between whom?"

Sir John leaned back and looked over the heads of the audience.

"If you do not know or cannot think," he said acidly, "I shall leave it."

War between whom? Was Sir John suggesting that the establishment of a Jewish state would mean war between Great Britain and Russia? Or was it his point that the declaration of a Jewish state would unquestionably mean a Jewish-Arab war?

The most vehement attack we heard so far upon the Jews of Palestine was delivered by General Sir Edward Spears, who had been a stormy petrel in Middle East politics for some time. He had been defeated in 1945 as a Conservative M.P., and, I understood, had been associated with the Arab Office. In 1942, '43, and '44, he had been British Minister to Syria and the Lebanon, but was recalled after the French denounced him for intriguing behind the scenes to oust them from the Middle East.

He had nothing but evil to speak of the Jews. They were acting as *agents provocateurs* to goad the Arabs into rash action. The Zionists were spiritually Nazis. The Jews would not be loyal friends of Britain if they did achieve a Jewish state. In fact, during World War II Britain had to keep military forces in the Middle East against the possibility of a Jewish revolt against Great Britain. (This drew gasps from the audience, and Sir John had to rap for order.) And, concluded General Spears, in any event, the Jews returning to Palestine were not truly descendants of the Biblical Jews, but an admixture of various races and therefore had no historic right to Palestine.

Many of us questioned him on his more startling allegations. McDonald drew from him an admission that not all Zionists were Nazis—"just the extreme Zionists." Buxton asked if he knew the relative enlistments in the last war of the Arabs and the Jews of Palestine, adding, "My understanding was that per capita enlistments among the Jews in Palestine were a great deal heavier than the enlistments among the Arabs."

General Spears toyed with his spectacles and said he hadn't seen the figures.

Our sessions were broken by many opportunities to go behind the scenes in London. One occasion was a formal luncheon tendered us by Foreign Secretary Ernest Bevin. If I had hoped to have a few minutes with him, I was disappointed. It was my first opportunity to see Bevin in person—a large, powerfully built man, with heavy shell-rimmed spectacles and a way of holding his hands at his sides, fists clenched, as though he were impatiently on the verge of getting something done that had to be done. When he spoke, he spoke frankly. The British government, he told us, would accept our counsel: "We shall accept your recommendations," he declared.

When I charged publicly that Bevin had made this promise, the British Foreign Office stated that it had no record of it. There may be no record, for the press was excluded, but many members of the British Cabinet were there and heard his words.

Bevin added, in the course of his remarks that day, that racial states could no longer exist. This struck me as odd. The British had just set up the new kingdom of Trans-Jordan as a completely Arab state, in which Jews generally were not allowed. I knew of the huge subsidies paid to

King Ibn Saud and the smaller subsidies paid in Syria to eliminate the French with the help of the Arabs the British find so difficult to control.

While Bevin spoke, two of my British colleagues observed to us how difficult it was to deal with him because of his ego. "What we must do is convince Ernie that whatever comes out of this is really his idea," I was told. "Then he will get behind it." Another added, "Bevin is really in favor of the White Paper of 1939, in my opinion. He has always been opposed to the Labour Party's resolution supporting a Jewish state."

There was no question that Bevin was immensely popular. Yet, I know that he was feared, even by some of his own associates. I was told that his power over his fellow members in the Labour Party was almost absolute. One Labour M.P. confessed to me, "If Bevin wants to, he can break me."

I was discussing the quality of Britain's prime ministers one afternoon with Jan Masaryk, Foreign Minister of Czechoslovakia, when he told me this story of one of them.

"After Munich," he said, "Chamberlain called me to London. He told me about the Munich Pact and he said: 'I am sorry, but Czechoslovakia has to go.' " Then Masaryk added that Chamberlain went on to say, "Why don't you take over the presidency of the Skoda Works? It would pay you 100,000 pounds a year, tax-free." "I told him," said Masaryk, " 'Sir, my father raised me to be a diplomat. In the course of my education I learned to play the piano. Rather than take that position, I would prefer to play the piano in a house of assignation. I would be far more comfortable and have greater peace of soul.' "

Dmitri Manuilsky, Ukrainian Foreign Minister, with

whom I had had many an informative chat in San Francisco during the birth of the United Nations, was in London. I decided I would like to call on him at the Russian Embassy, and suggested to Harold Beeley, as our special Foreign Office factotum, that he accompany me.

Beeley looked over his spectacles at me, grinned, and said he thought it might be better if he didn't come along. But he did furnish a car which drove me to the Soviet Embassy. The moment I entered the huge building I sensed a different atmosphere. Guards at the door, who looked like what I assumed NKVD agents would look, observed me warily, but as soon as they learned that I was a friend of Manuilsky, the coolness was dispelled and they vanished into the background.

Manuilsky had been one of Lenin's closest collaborators, and at one time headed the dreaded Comintern. Stocky, with grizzled hair and mustache, looking slightly like a Hollywood idea of a gold-rush sheriff, he gave me the same impression of stolidity as Bevin, but touched with a definite Continental charm, at once ironic and sardonic.

I told him of our luncheon and he smiled. "The real difficulty about Mr. Bevin," he said, "is that he is conducting the foreign affairs of England as if he were trying to win a trade-union election, with all the other countries as so many contending labor leaders. I'm afraid, too, that he thinks the USSR is a revolutionary offshoot of the Transport Workers Union, and therefore he must fight it as he would any rebellious faction." He shook his head. "Since there are only two first-class powers in the world, the United States and Russia, Mr. Bevin makes it difficult for us by acting as if he were representing a first-class power."

We went on to talk about the Soviet Union's position on Palestine. Manuilsky was most careful in his choice of words. Ivan Maisky, former Soviet Ambassador to London, he said, visited Palestine in 1945, and wrote a glowing report to the Kremlin about the magnificent progress the Jews had achieved in Palestine. He, Manuilsky, in his own city of Kiev, had seen the sufferings of the Jews, he told me. He knew what they had gone through. He was proud that anti-Semitism was not tolerated in Russia. But he would be less than honest, he added, if he did not tell me also that there is a large Mohammedan population in the Soviet Union.

As for our committee—"Your country has made the situation rather difficult by not insisting that Russia be represented on your committee of inquiry. The fact that Russia is not represented can only lead to delay."

Then he added, "Great Britain, because of her activities in the Middle East, may make it impossible for us to accept the recommendation of your committee. She is using the Middle East as the military base of her operations. I believe that she will take her troops out of Egypt into Palestine, and then Palestine and Trans-Jordan will become Britain's arsenal in the Middle East."

He would do all in his power, he said, to help both in relation to Palestine and in opening the doors of the Soviet Union to such Jews as might want to find refuge and rehabilitation there.

"Does Moscow still believe that Zionists are the tools of British imperialism?" I asked. He smiled again. "They are not active tools of British imperialism, Mr. Crum, but Dr. Weizmann and his group have such confidence in the integrity of the British that Russia feels sometimes they are the unconscious tools of British imperialism."

A few days earlier, Beeley had assured me that the committee would not be permitted to go into Poland. Wilson, speaking on behalf of our State Department, had agreed. I mentioned this to Manuilsky. "Poland?" he asked in some surprise. "I shouldn't think you'd have any difficulty. In fact, I'm sure if you ask for permission, you will get it." Curiously enough, a day later, Leslie Rood, our American secretary, told us that he had just had word by telephone that the entire committee had free access to all of Poland.

One evening I met Dr. Chaim Weizmann, the outstanding Jewish leader of our time. He was not in good health. He had just been discharged from a hospital after a serious operation, but his handclasp was strong. It was astonishing to see how he resembled Lenin, a non-Jew. I was told that Lenin and he were in Switzerland at the same time years ago and were quite frequently mistaken for each other. Tall, broad-shouldered, with a black goatee, his dark eyes somber under a high-domed forehead, he struck me as a world-weary man, with an innate courtesy and an after-touch of bitterness in his words. Here, I felt, was a towering figure: a great man whose basic premise, his faith in Britain, was being pulled from under his feet. Because he had believed so implicitly that Britain would come through on its Palestine pledges, he now found himself in a well-nigh intolerable position but still had faith.

He had regretfully come to the conclusion, he said, that a partition of Palestine was the only solution. In the near future he hoped to see a democratic state with a Jewish majority in Palestine. The only way, though, he said, was by partition plus the immediate migration of 100,000 Jews into Palestine.

"I had a promise from Mr. Churchill," he said, "that if he were returned to office in the summer of 1945, he would immediately go forward with a generous partition plan. But——" He did not complete the sentence.

He told us that the idea of a "national home" came from Theodor Herzl, the founder of modern Zionism, and was a literal translation of a German phrase used by Herzl.

"We've had many difficulties with the words 'Jewish state,'" I observed. "Judge Hutcheson feels it suggests a narrow nationalism which he and, I think, many of us find abhorrent."

Weizmann nodded. "Yes," he said, "we are forever explaining that. Surely the world does not think that the Jewish people, who have suffered so much from narrow nationalism, would themselves succumb to it?

"What we have in mind is simply the machinery of government, through which we can get things done. Think of the Jordan Valley Authority. It is a splendid, a challenging project. It will help re-create the entire Middle East. Yet we cannot get that under way without government powers: we cannot do anything real without the machinery which enables us to do it. I am convinced," he said, "that we can come to an understanding with the Arabs if we have the machinery of government."

He told us something of the early history of Zionism. Much of the trouble in Palestine, he felt, stemmed from the fact that the Balfour Declaration coincided with the Bolshevist rise to power. Earlier, during Kerensky's brief regime, Russian Zionists raised 300,000,000 rubles to enable thousands of Russian Jews to emigrate to Palestine. Had the Bolshevists not come to power, Weizmann said, by the early 1920s there might have been a Jewish majority in Palestine. In 1917 there were only 600,000 Arabs in Palestine.

But the Communists then saw the Zionists as tools of

British imperialism. The USSR banned Zionism; the 300,-000,000 rubles were confiscated; and by halting all Russian Jewish emigration the Bolshevists cut off the principal source of Palestine's Jewish immigration. Despite this historical evidence to the contrary, some British subconsciously associate the Palestine state with Communism, Weizmann believes, and this identification has worked tragically against European Jewry.

He expected to testify before us, he said, but not in London. He would appear in Jerusalem.

Another figure who stepped out of history to appear before us was Viscount Samuel, first High Commissioner of Palestine. Like Weizmann, he is in his seventies. White-haired, soft-spoken, measuring his words, Lord Samuel was the only Jew to have been High Commissioner of Palestine. On the basis of his experience, would he tell us if he thought Arabs and Jews in Palestine could work together in peace?

Viscount Samuel folded his hands on the little table before him. "I think if you could get a political settlement at the top, things would shape very differently at the bottom. I do not think the bottom people wish to quarrel; at the top they do rather like it."

It was his idea that Palestine should be "cantonized," that there should be three communities, the Moslem Arabs, the Jews, and the Christian Arabs, each with representative institutions, with adequate revenues, and in charge of its educational and religious affairs. He joined with the other Jewish witnesses in urging that Jewish immigration into Palestine be reopened "on a large scale."

How did he explain "terrorism" in Palestine?

Palestine youth had become profoundly disturbed and horrified by what had been happening to the Jewish communities in Europe, he replied. "While we in this country feel it is something going on a very long way off, to these people it has been happening to their own relatives. Great numbers of them are new arrivals in Palestine. The great majority of the homes they have left have been the scenes of these atrocities; at the same time, they see all around them in Palestine homes readily offered to the survivors in Europe. They are profoundly indignant that these people are shut out and prevented forcibly from landing in the country. This they regard as contrary to international law, as declared in the Palestine Mandate approved by the League of Nations. Consequently, their feelings are intensely inflamed.

"These young people," he went on, "because they are mostly quite young, think the only thing to be done is to make trouble. I have been told by people in Palestine that they saw when the Arabs committed outrages—and there were many assassinations and much terrorism, and even an armed revolt in the years 1933 to 1936—the British government of that day enacted the White Paper of 1939. This said there was to be no more Jewish immigration after five years, except with the consent of the Arabs. I am told a certain section of the Jews said that when the Arabs made trouble, they got what they wanted. Now the Jews must make trouble. Then the two, it may be hoped, will cancel out, and a conclusion will be reached on the merits of the question."

The great majority of Palestine Jews strongly disapproved of terror, he asserted, and assassination had always been "an abomination" to the Jewish people. The Jewish authorities in Palestine had co-operated with the police "in tracking down those terrorists who committed hateful crimes, such as the assassination of Lord Moyne."

The Arabs were among our last witnesses in London. In the *note verbale,* the Embassy had told us that the Arab witnesses would be: Fares el Khoury, chief of the Syrian delegation to the United Nations; Sayid Ali Jawdat el Ayubi, chief of the Iraqi delegation to the UN; the Emir Feisal Ibn Abdul Aziz, chief of the Saudi Arabian delegation to the UN; Hamid Bey Frangie, chief of the Lebanese delegation to the UN; Dr. A. H. Badawi Pasha, chief of the Egyptian delegation to the UN. They appeared before us in a body.

I had first seen Prince Feisal, second son of the forty sons of Ibn Saud, at the United Nations Conference in San Francisco in 1945. At that time, the entire Saudi Arabian delegation swept in and out of hotels under the guidance of the Standard Oil Company of California. I remembered him as a tall, lean figure, with dark, glowing eyes, and a small black mustache and goatee. Now, colorful in white and brown flowing robes, with a white headdress and gold circlets, he moved in majestically and took his seat on a chair placed before us. His colleagues took chairs, two on either side of him. El Khoury acted as interpreter for the group.

Each spokesman sympathized with the Jewish plight. But, the Arabs agreed, they were not responsible for it. The world was not justified in forcing them to "pay" for the Jewish tragedy. They could not recognize Jewish rights in Palestine on the basis of the Balfour Declaration, because that document, in their eyes, was nothing more than a piece of British imperialism. Britain, they agreed, had helped free the Arabs from Ottoman rule; this, how-

ever, did not mean the British had a right to issue a
Balfour Declaration. They were adamant on the question
of allowing Jewish survivors to enter Palestine. Not
another Jew was to enter Palestine.

Suppose, they were told, all the other countries in the
world took their share of Jewish survivors: would Palestine take its share? The answer was no. "Palestine has
already taken more than its share."

Again, the question presented itself to me as it had
when Ambassador Phillips suggested we assure Ibn Saud
that we were his friends: by what right did the Foreign
Minister of Iraq rule on whether Jews could enter Palestine? Would the Palestine government be asked to rule
on the immigrant quota for Iraq?

El Khoury, the Syrian, told us: "Jews can't be assimilated with other people. They believe they are the chosen
people of God, a superior and isolated race. They have
been in continuous fights since the time of Abraham."
He warned that a Jewish state in Palestine would be
backed by all the Jews in the world and would thus become a vast imperialistic power threatening the security
of the entire Arab world. He turned to Judge Hutcheson:
"Why don't you give the Jews part of Texas?"

At one point the Prince raised a languid hand. El
Khoury paused and said, "His Highness wishes to make
a few observations." Prince Feisal spoke in Arabic, making
gentle gestures and somehow giving me the impression
of indifference, a sort of regal boredom toward the entire
hearing. "There has never in history been a misunder-
standing between the Arabs and the Jews," he said.
"There need not be one now if the Jews do not insist
upon going into Palestine."

We sought to determine the Arab attitude toward the

Lowdermilk plan for the irrigation of the Jordan Valley. Had they considered this as a step toward increasing Palestine's productivity and enabling the country to absorb a greater population? Would they oppose a measure which might be counted upon to lift economic standards in the Middle East?

El Khoury, speaking for the others, shook his head. "We will not oppose it, on condition that it is not done by the Zionists. If a Palestine Arab state is established, it would be fully qualified to undertake such a project. If Jewish immigration is involved, we will definitely reject such development, but we will not reject it if it is done for the Arabs."

As usual, much went on behind the scenes. Not until later was I to learn that two diplomats, one American, one British, were working industriously to create a bloc of Central and South American countries to fight against the incorporation of the terms of the mandate in any trusteeship agreement that might be contemplated for Palestine. This would mean that with adoption of a trusteeship, the Jewish National Home would be considered completed. This would legalize the White Paper. I do not speak of this intrigue as hearsay: I have seen a letter written to one of the South American groups approached on the matter. Nor was the Russian leitmotiv, which had been sounded in Washington, missing behind the scenes here. There had been repeated corridor talk of the Arabs turning to Russia if they felt that both Britain and the United States were deserting them. This had never been a convincing argument to me, and I felt it highly unlikely that feudal landed leaders would turn for assistance to a regime which stood for the breaking up of rich estates and abolition of a wealthy privileged class. I had dinner with an official of the British War Office, at the Oxford Cambridge Club. I put the question to him frankly about the so-called threat of an *entente cordiale* between the Arab political leaders and the Kremlin. He had had great experience in the war. His reply was, "Nonsense!"

Of course, he said, I must be familiar with the Arab record during the war. The Arabs had indeed caused great anxiety to His Majesty's government. He said the Arab leadership was generally for sale to the highest bidder, but added that he could scarcely imagine their selling out to the Kremlin, because even the Arab leadership recognized that that would mean its ultimate destruction.

Before we left London, McDonald and I paid a visit to Laski and had a long discussion on the enigma of British Labour Party policy, a discussion that had really begun the day Thomas Reid had testified. Laski was quite bitter. He expressed great indignation at certain Labour Party acts, both at home and abroad. It was no secret to him that in the United States millions of liberals of both parties, who had expected so much of British socialism, were baffled and discouraged.

"Yes," he said, "it is tragic. They feel we have let them down, and of course we have." But some Labour Party leaders, he observed, were "practical" men. They held a "long-range view." The problem of Palestine must be seen in that long perspective, according to them, Laski went on to explain. They had concluded that the party would need from fifteen to twenty years to entrench itself securely in power in the British Empire. Given general elections every five years, the Labour Party must therefore win three of four successive elections. But to win these elections—to continue in power so that they could put into effect the reforms they believed fundamental in England— they must have peace. Consequently, they could not afford to take any drastic measure on the international scene, any political decision, which might precipitate war. They dared not upset the applecart anywhere. India and Palestine, to be sure, were troublesome matters—but, essentially, only "police problems." Pour enough police into India and Palestine, and the situation would be held within bounds. "They see their task," Laski said, "as a serious one: to convince the English people that they are not out to destroy the Empire."

Policy in Palestine, therefore, must be as follows: do whatever necessary to cope with the situation from a police point of view. Do nothing politically irrevocable. Make no clear-cut political commitments. Muddle through.

If one accepted this analysis, Laski observed, it was possible to understand why men of good will, such as Bevin, Attlee, and their colleagues, could countenance shameful evasion and appear so callous to the Jewish plight.

At one of our final dinners before leaving England, I gathered that possibly what was in the mind of some of my British colleagues on the committee was this: let the Americans make whatever recommendations they wish, most probably that 100,000 Jews be enabled to enter Palestine. The reply would be, "Very well, that will require six divisions of soldiers. Will the American government provide three?" The Americans would say, "No," and the rejoinder then would be that under such circumstances Britain could hardly be expected to bear the burden alone of the consequences of a pro-Zionist policy.

Some of us were not unaware of this possibility and considered it a trap. Here both McDonald and I felt keenly our lack of a larger staff to which to turn, particularly since the British were so well served by Beeley and his colleagues.

The British had assigned their best Foreign Office men as experts to assist us; those provided us by our State Department were comparatively inexperienced, with the exception of Evan Wilson. He had been trained in State Department diplomacy, where, it appears to me, the most advisable thing for young career diplomats is to say nothing and thus displease no one. Wilson, as events turned out, discovered in Palestine that the State Department policy of playing off both ends against the middle was suicidal, and he sent a memorandum to the State Department from Jerusalem, urging it to follow a forthright policy.

McDonald felt we must have additional trained American aides at our side. He suggested that Professor Paul Hanna, of the University of Florida, recognized as one of the most objective and best-informed authorities on the Middle East, join our staff. This was agreed upon, and we immediately cabled for Hanna's services. He joined us later and proved to be one of the most valuable members of our staff.

In London Phillips met with Sir Harold MacMichael, former High Commissioner of Palestine. Sir Harold, he said, told him that we would find it difficult to travel about Palestine because it was an armed camp. Sir Harold narrowly escaped assassination in Palestine in 1944, when he was attacked by Jewish extremists. He was not sanguine about our mission.

The final problem now facing us was a technical one.

How were we twelve men to obtain in the brief time given us the most complete picture of the situation in Europe? We decided to divide into four subcommittees, and fan out across the continent, in a simultaneous investigation of the conditions of the Jews. We would reassemble in Vienna and pool our findings. We would determine there, on the basis of additional testimony, whether to issue an Interim Report.

Sir John, Judge Hutcheson, Frank Buxton, and Lord Morrison were assigned to Berlin. Aydelotte, Major Manningham-Buller, and Crick were to go to British Zone headquarters. McDonald and Phillips were to go to the French Zone, using Paris as their headquarters. Sir Frederick, Crossman, and I were to go into the American Zone of Germany, into Czechoslovakia, and into Austria. If possible, some of us would visit Poland and perhaps the Balkans.

We divided, and each group went on its own mission. At the last moment, Dick Crossman became ill: he was forced to remain in London. Sir Frederick and I went on to Paris, bound for Frankfort, Germany, headquarters of the United States Army in Germany. We would see for ourselves the condition of the displaced persons—those for whom President Truman had asked the chance to go to Palestine.

We would seek truth, so far as it was in our power to find it, on the troubled continent of Europe.

As we crossed the choppy Channel, I steadied myself in the small cabin I shared with Sir Frederick and tried to set down some of my thoughts on Britain and the British.

"Generalities are always suspect, yet I get a definite impression that my British colleagues in their relations toward the Americans on the committee are the representatives of an old actor who feels that his time on the stage is limited and is trying his best to caution the young understudy who is to take his place," I wrote.

"And yet I get the feeling that they think it isn't quite fair of God to have us Americans in a preferred position. They have done so well in running the world since the time of Queen Elizabeth—it must seem rather unjust to them. They don't like it, but with typical British courage they are prepared for the worst.

"I think they are genuinely afraid that the United States will become isolationist again. They are deeply hurt that we did not grant the British loan immediately. They desperately want Anglo-American co-operation. If things fall into our hands they are not too sure that we shall cope with problems with their finesse, their understanding. They fear Russian expansionism; they fear, dreadfully, that the United States may be the sole surviving free enterprise system in a world edging toward state control of business and industry.

"I cannot help feeling at once warm toward them—and perhaps a little sorry for them as well. And mixed with feeling sorry for them, I must admit, is a sense of apprehension about our own future. America does have a tremendous responsibility; shall we shoulder it? If we are now entering America's golden era, shall we come through half so successfully as the British?"

BOOK TWO

The Remnant of the Survivors

CHAPTER 4

Frankfort: "Nach Palästina!"

It is one thing to read in the newspaper the story of the deliberate murder of six million people; it is another to meet the survivors. What are you to say when a man like yourself carefully extracts a small snapshot, such as you might carry about, showing a pleasant-faced young woman with an infant in her arms and a little boy playing near by with a pail in the sand? "This is my wife and children," he says. And he adds, in the same tone of voice, "They killed the baby with a bayonet and she and the child were burned in the crematorium."

That man in his loneliness stands as a symbol of the remaining Jews of Europe.

It is difficult to grasp immediately how scientifically the Nazis went about destroying the Jewish race. They were not haphazard. Given 5000 Jews to destroy in a community of 10,000, for example, the Nazis saw to it wherever possible that family units were broken up. Their purpose was to kill life—and kill the desire for life in those temporarily spared, by making each survivor realize that he alone of his family was alive.

They segregated the intellectuals—the scientists, artists, writers, schoolteachers, scholars, political and civic figures.

These they killed off as soon as possible, to obviate the possibility of a leader rising to marshal the weak. They segregated the craftsmen—the tailors, shoemakers, carpenters, locksmiths—and allowed them to live temporarily because there was work for them. They segregated the young, able-bodied males and used them for slave labor. All who remained—the very young, the middle-aged and old, and the women—they destroyed.

Only rarely, therefore, did we come upon family groups among the survivors. One camp was specifically called to our attention because it did hold family groups. There were men with wives and, here and there, a brother or sister.

In Frankfort, the United States Army had taken over the huge I. G. Farben building as its headquarters. Waiting to welcome us were Federal Judge Simon H. Rifkind, of New York, then adviser on Jewish affairs to General McNarney, and Major Robert Straus, former New York City Alderman, who represented American Military Government in Frankfort. With them we called on Major Generals H. R. Bull and C. L. Adcock and discussed the work before us. AMG worked out an itinerary for us through typical camps in the American Zone of Germany and Austria. Earlier, Leslie Rood, secretary to the American section of the committee, had suggested that we avoid giving our findings to the press, on the ground that we might embarrass the military. I thought excluding the press was unwise and I took up the matter with the highest military authorities I could find: Generals Bull and Adcock.

"I agree completely," said General Bull, and General Adcock remarked, "I'm against hiding anything. The American people deserve to know about conditions in

Germany. The more facts they know, the easier it will be for the Army to do a good job."

That directive clarified, we began our tour, accompanied by Ruth Gruber, of the *New York Post,* and Gerold Frank, of the Overseas News Agency, who were to cover our entire investigation through Europe and the Middle East. Frank had accompanied us since Washington; Miss Gruber had joined us in London. Judge Rifkind and Major Straus accompanied us through Germany and Austria to Prague, together with Captain Lawrence Eno, of New York, Judge Rifkind's aide, Captain George Vida of Hackensack, N. J., a Jewish chaplain, and Lieutenant J. H. Zorek, both of whom served as interpreters, and a staff of secretaries. The best procedure, it was decided, was for us to interrogate the UNRRA and AMG officials in each camp or DP center; and later question representatives of the DPs elected by the DPs to speak to us.

In Frankfort, a patriarchal old gentleman was introduced to us by Judge Rifkind: "Gentlemen," he said, "this is Rabbi Leopold Neuhaus. I thought you might wish to speak to him as your first witness, for he is the only surviving German-Jewish rabbi in Germany. We have been able to find no other."

Rabbi Neuhaus nodded, and looked at us with resignation. He had been first arrested by the Nazis in 1938, when all the synagogues in Germany and in German-occupied territory were set afire.

Had he any explanation why he alone survived, I asked.

"Ah, yes," he said. He drew from his clothes a worn, tattered letter upon which the signature "von Hindenburg" was still visible. In World War I he had assisted the German Army in Prussia: this had come to the notice of Hindenburg, who had written him this warm letter of appreciation. Because he was able to show it to the Nazis, it had saved his life numerous times.

"What can you tell us about the wishes of the German Jews who survive?" I asked.

"The great majority wish to go to Palestine," he replied. "I think, however, you will find that some of the old people may remain here, because they are too old—they have but one wish—to die in peace."

Later in the day, Paul McCormack, representing the Inter-Governmental Committee for Refugees, told us that Jews now in Germany—both the surviving German Jews and east European Jews who had been brought to Germany by the Nazis—wanted to go only to Palestine.

"Give us a green light to move these people," he said, "and we could transport 100,000 to Palestine with little difficulty."

We found the Jewish DPs living in two kinds of quarters. Some lived in community centers in cities. In Stuttgart, for example, more than five hundred displaced persons, ninety per cent of them Polish Jews who had been in concentration camps, lived in one city block. They were relatively more fortunate than the great majority who live in rural camps or "assembly centers." Distribution of food was easier in cities than in rural areas, so that city DPs managed to have an almost adequate diet.

Housing facilities for the displaced persons were very bad: they lived in one- and two-family houses from which the Germans had been evicted, but in which every room had been converted into a bedroom holding from four to five people. Even the kitchens were bedrooms, for meals were prepared in central mess halls. As a result, from twenty to thirty Jews were forced to live in a house which once held one German family of six or seven persons.

We began to understand why Jewish DPs could tell us, "It is better to be a conquered German than a liberated Jew."

We found few Jewish children left alive in Europe. In a camp such as Landsberg, with about 5000 Jewish displaced persons, there were one hundred children between the ages of six and fourteen. There were another hundred children under one year of age, born after liberation. There was not one Jewish child between the ages of one and six. In the cities, there were even fewer. We spoke with several of the native Jews of Stuttgart: German Jews whose families had been in Stuttgart for centuries, and were thoroughly German in culture, in world outlook, in loyalty. Before Hitler, there were 4000 Jews in Stuttgart. Today less than two hundred are alive. A spokesman for them said:

"We have no children among us. This situation you will find in all Jewish communities still existing in Germany. Nor do we have any old people. The young people will emigrate; the older among us, who are too weary to go anywhere, will die. In one or two generations there will be no more Jewish communities left in Germany."

I asked him if there was still anti-Semitism in Stuttgart.

He smiled wryly. "I can only tell you that I have myself heard Germans pass by our *Kultusgemeinde* [Jewish Community Center] and say aloud, 'It is a shame they did not burn all the Jews.' "

He had been born in Stuttgart of a family that had lived there for eight generations, he said. "I was in a concentration camp. I returned here to look for my people. I learned that my mother was taken away in a transport in 1941 and shot in 1942. My brother who lived in Hanover and the remainder of the family were taken to Warsaw.

They died of starvation. My sister was taken from Berlin to somewhere in Poland and never heard from again. My brother-in-law killed my sister and himself." He paused. "Surely you do not expect me to put any further faith in the German people? That is why it is my reluctant conclusion that there is no place for the Jews any more in this land. Some few, I know, will stay: but the rest, the young, those who have their lives before them, must go."

"Do you find that the Germans exhibit any sense of guilt or shame?" I asked.

"A very few," he said. "We recognize them. They were the 'decent' people before 1933. Now they are embarrassed when we meet them. But the majority do not feel guilt or shame: they feel regret that they lost the war. The stories of the concentration camps they think were propaganda. And if they themselves took no part in these 'alleged' atrocities, why should they be blamed, they ask. They feel the war is over, the slate is wiped clean, and we all begin new again."

Although officially all discrimination has been banned, Jews applying for jobs frequently find clerks listing them as "non-Aryan." The habits of more than a decade are difficult to break.

"We receive ration cards like the Germans and stand in the same queues," he said. "Often when we reach our turn, the merchant has no more rationed items to sell— but when we pass on, we see that he has managed to find that item for a non-Jew behind us."

Zeilsheim, near Frankfort, was the first displaced-persons camp we visited. We were taken to a central building, a one-story wooden structure. With a view to

helping our inquiry, UNRRA officials had taken cross-
section polls of the DPs in various areas in the American
Zone. Two questions were asked: "Do you wish to remain
in Europe? If not, where do you want to go?"

In Zeilsheim we were given the result of a poll of 18,311
DPs in the area. Of the 18,311, thirteen said they wished
to remain in Europe. Of the 18,298 who said they wished
to leave, 17,712 said they wished to go to Palestine.

We did not accept these figures without exhaustive
questioning of our own. Seated in the little office, with
our stenographers taking down verbatim transcripts, we
asked: Why was Palestine so predominantly the first
choice? Had any pressures been brought to influence these
men and women? Did they realize immigration into Palestine was not a simple matter? Were they aware of the
troubled political situation in the Middle East? Were they
aware of the Arabs?

The faint sound of marching feet came to our ears. We
looked out the window. Men and women were marching,
three and four abreast, toward us. They were DPs. Some
wore the striped uniforms they had been forced to wear in
the concentration camps. They lined up at attention outside the window facing us. They carried a Jewish flag and
banner reading, "Open the Gates of Palestine!" It began
to rain. We turned back to our questions. For the whole
of the following hour, while we sat inside and asked our
innumerable questions, the men and women stood outside
at attention, heads up, silent, the rain beating down on
them. The voices droned on inside the little room. Outside, the people waited.

Sir Frederick and I were both impressed by this, but
Sir Frederick was troubled. He had not forgotten General
Spears' charges of a militaristic, Nazilike nationalism

against the Jews in Palestine. Here were Jewish DPs marching in military fashion and lining up before us in traditional military formation.

"Are these people Zionists?" Sir Frederick asked an UNRRA official.

"It is impossible to organize this camp along any line without accepting that fact," was the reply. "If you organize a boys' club to read, to talk, to debate, to conduct dances, at the second meeting it turns out to be reading Zionist books, debating Zionist problems, and dancing the *Hora*."

"Does this mean that the Zionists are running the camp?" Sir Frederick asked.

"No, sir. The people are Zionists. Without any outside influence they have developed into Zionists. It is part of their lives. It is in the background they brought with them from their past lives in Poland. They grew up with it, and now that they are alive after the concentration camps, it is tremendously strengthened. The only way they can survive is to live as Jews in Palestine."

Sir Frederick was insistent; the picture of Zionist Fascism drawn for him was very much alive in his mind. "Isn't it the case that the Zionist element suppresses any minority feeling? All you say seems to support that argument—they're just as the Nazis were." The director of the camp was equally positive that any inmate was *"absolutely* free to express his views without harm to himself." Here was neither Fascist regimentation nor Zionist propagandizing, he asserted. Sir Frederick appeared unconvinced. "It strikes me as dreadful that there seems to be no way to make these people realize the limitations of Palestine. There is such bitter disappointment ahead for some of them."

Sir Frederick, who has a warm spot in his heart for children, and is a kindly man, was particularly disturbed when a group of children broke out in a Hebrew song, singing it with a chantlike precision which sounded almost martial. It was entitled, *Hatikvah,* meaning "Hope," and we were told it was the anthem of the Zionist movement and had become the Jewish national anthem wherever Jewish national sentiment was alive.

"You see what I mean," Sir Frederick said to me quietly. "That is nationalism implanted even in the hearts of the very young, after the Nazi fashion."

I disagreed completely. "Would you feel the same way if you saw a group of British youngsters singing *God Save the King?*"

Sir Frederick smiled. "You know that's ridiculous."

But we had additional questions to ask. Off to one side sat a little man in a heavy red sweater. He and I engaged in the following political catechism:

QUESTION: Why do you wish a Jewish state?

ANSWER: What kind of question is that? We are Jews. The Americans have America. The English have England. The French have France. We want a Jewish state. Palestine is the only state in which we can order our own existence. If you tell me that we are not Jews, but Germans or Poles or Austrians, I give you the testimony of six million dead.

QUESTION: You speak of Palestine. You realize there are Arabs in Palestine and you must get along with them?

ANSWER: If outsiders will not disturb us, we will get along with the Arabs in and out of Palestine.

QUESTION: You know some Arabs are hostile?

ANSWER: I do not know that the average Arabs are hostile to us. Perhaps their political leaders say so, but we who go to Palestine are aware of the situation. We are all working people and we believe that working people cannot have enmity against other working people.

QUESTION: Ibn Saud says he will not permit the Jews into Palestine.

ANSWER: We heard this, but we didn't know who told him to say so.

QUESTION: Do you think it is democratic to impose a new majority on an Arab majority already there?

ANSWER: The Arabs have possessed this land for centuries. They have let it become desert. It has no value for them, but at the moment it is being blown up into a political problem.

QUESTION: Who blew it up?

ANSWER: Excuse me, but I think the Colonial Office is responsible.

QUESTION: You know that under the Balfour Declaration Britain is required to protect the rights of the Arabs as well as the Jews?

ANSWER: The Jews have observed this, but unfortunately Britain has not.

QUESTION: You know that experts testified that Palestine is unable to absorb more than 100,000 people annually?

ANSWER: History has shown that experts can be wrong. For instance, experts said in this camp only two thousand people can live, but there are four thousand here now. Every problem can be approached from two directions. One is the academic direction and the other is the direction of the idea. The second way prevails and can prove the experts wrong.

QUESTION: Suppose the Arabs declare war?

ANSWER: If they are not talked into it they will not do so.

QUESTION: But if they should, who would you have maintain order? Britain? America?

ANSWER: Haven't we Jews proved to the world that we also have good soldiers? Haven't we given the world great statesmen? We can handle the situation if we are not disturbed from the outside.

An eighteen-year-old girl was asked: "Are you interested in going to the United States?"

Answer: "Yes, if that means I shall reach Palestine sooner."

This was the story, told over and over again, in camp after camp. This was the explanation for the great mass movement of Jews across Europe. Organized? Inspired? I felt, of course, it was organized, but organized by the desire to live and not to die.

In each camp we were greeted by the same silent demonstration of the DPs.

When we were ready to leave, we found ourselves surrounded by the inmates, pleading, tipping their hats, and making little speeches in which they tried to express themselves. A man would plant himself before me, tears streaming down his face, and say, "What have I done? Why am I here? When will you let me go? What crime have I committed?"

In one camp, we were about to leave when a boy—I learned later he was thirteen, but he looked nine or ten—pulled at my coat. "Mr. America, Mr. America," he said, "when are you going to let us out of here?"

I patted him on the shoulder. "You must have patience, son," I said.

"Patience!" he exclaimed. "How can you talk to us of patience? After six years of this war, after all our parents have been burned in the gas ovens, you talk to us of patience!"

All I could think of to say to him was: "I can only tell you to have faith. It's the genius of your people that they have always had faith."

"Faith?" the boy shouted. "Faith! In whom? In the British, who have been promising for twenty-six years that we can go home to Palestine? In the Americans, who have been following the British? We want a home!" There simply was no comforting answer for such desperation.

In one poll, I was told, the DPs were asked to put down a second choice if Palestine was unavailable, and hundreds wrote "Crematorium." In many camps I was told that Jewish women had deliberately suffered abortions rather than bear a child on German soil.

Time and again witnesses told us, one way or another: "Yes, of course, Hitler and the Nazis sought to exterminate us. Hitler made the plans: but it was the peoples of Europe, regardless of nationality, who were our executioners. Hitler wanted us exterminated in Poland, but it was the Poles who executed us; Hitler wanted us exterminated in Rumania, but it was the Rumanians who executed us; and so it was in Slovakia, in Hungary, in Bulgaria, in Austria—everywhere."

They did not trust the people about them. They distrusted the world; they distrusted humanity and they distrusted the promises of humanity.

"We know massacres of the Jews did not stop because of a change of heart," one woman told us. "The Nazis stopped killing us because the war ended and they had no more power to kill us. The same hatred, the same murder, still lives in their hearts. They have not changed, and we cannot live among them."

If we granted this—and said, "But why Palestine? Five million Jews live happily and in dignity in the United States. Great numbers of Jews live happily and in dignity in England and other countries of the British Empire. Why not the United States or Great Britain? Why insist upon Palestine?" the answer was, in one way or another: "Yes, we know Jews live happily in many lands. But they lived happily in Germany, too. We do not say that what took place in Germany will take place in the United States or in Great Britain. But we do say that we are too weary to go further. We have suffered too much to take another chance. The end of our road is Palestine—a Jewish land with Jewish people who are simply Jews and nothing else. We are too tired to go to any country where, some-day, someone may say, 'Jew, get out. Go to Palestine!' "

I remember the clarity with which one witness put it. He was in charge of vocational re-education at one of the camps. He explained that only the Zionist goal could make the DPs work. They had done such inhumanly hard labor for the Nazis that their attitude to work could become positive again only when they were inspired by a great ideal. "I, myself," he said, "would never have wanted to do a day's work again in my life if I were not imbued with the ideal of Palestine."

One of the visitors observed that it was disturbing to think that Jews wished to leave Europe so completely and to build so separatist an existence.

The witness thought a moment and said, "I want to make only one remark. Up to the time the Nazis segregated us all in a ghetto, I had not been a Zionist. In the ghetto I said to myself: 'I have sinned. I have sinned by thinking wrong thoughts.' "

"But," the questioner argued, "the Jews can't isolate themselves in Palestine. The world must be united if we are to have peace."

"When we will have a nation in Palestine of two, three, or four million Jews, then the Jews in America and in the other countries will have also peace because then the world will know that there is a Jewish nation somewhere in the world."

UNRRA here had polled 3629 DPs. Not one wished to remain in Germany. Nine wished to go to the United States, one to Australia, and 3619 to Palestine.

CHAPTER 5

Munich: "We Beat Our Breasts"

FROM FRANKFORT TO ZEILSHEIM, from Zeilsheim to Stuttgart, from Stuttgart to Leipheim, from Leipheim to
Munich, the same tragic story unfolded. As we proceeded
through Germany, one name, however, the name of a
Jewish physician, was repeated to us time and again. It
was that of Dr. Zalman Grinberg, chairman of the Central
Committee of Liberated Jews, in Munich. In Frankfort,
Chaplain Vida had spoken of him as an extraordinary
person. In Stuttgart the faces of UNRRA officials lit up
when his name was mentioned. And as his story grew in
the telling, it was evident that he had become almost a
legend among the Jewish survivors of the concentration
camps.

He had been born in Lithuania, and received his medical degree in Switzerland. In 1939, he returned to Lithuania and there married. The war came, and, with it, the
Russian armies. Dr. Grinberg became a surgeon on the
staff of a Russian military hospital. Then the fortunes of
war changed: the Germans marched into Lithuania, and
the Russians were pushed back. Dr. Grinberg and his wife,
who was about to have a baby, were caught in a mael-
strom. The child, a boy, was born. When it was one

month old, they found themselves interned in the ghetto of Kovno, Lithuania.

The Nazis habitually seized all infants and asphyxiated them as soon as possible. The Grinbergs were frantic. Dr. Grinberg managed to smuggle the child out of the ghetto to a non-Jewish friend. He removed a valuable gold wrist watch he had brought from Switzerland. "Here—this is the only thing of value I can give you," he said. "Keep my son, take care of him for me. If God is willing, somehow I shall get in touch with you."

But the Nazis made no move to molest the Jewish children. Nearly four months passed, and Jewish women still nursed their infants and still slept with them by their side. Mrs. Grinberg pleaded with her husband to bring the child back to her. Dr. Grinberg managed to smuggle the baby back inside the ghetto. Two days later, the Nazis suddenly began rounding up all Jewish children for transportation to the gas chambers. Grinberg determined on a desperate plan. He waited until nearly midnight. Then he gave the child a hypodermic injection of a sleeping drug almost sufficient to kill it.

He wrapped the child, now virtually unconscious, in blankets and stole with it to a remote corner of the ghetto. Near by was a pile of empty barrels. He dug a pit, placed one of the barrels in it, then tenderly lowered the child into the barrel. With a scalpel he whittled two holes in the barrel lid, detached the rubber tubes of his stethoscope, and inserted them through the lid. Then he replaced the lid on the barrel, and arranged the earth over it carefully so that perhaps half an inch of the tubes protruded, assuring the child sufficient air.

During the next two days, the Nazis went through the ghetto, house by house, and seized all Jewish children.

They were never seen again. On the second night, after the baby had been under the earth for nearly forty-eight hours, Dr. Grinberg slipped out, found the living tomb he had made for his infant son, and brought the child, still breathing, back with him. Mrs. Grinberg nursed it. Dr. Grinberg gave the child a second injection that night, lest it wake and cry out; somehow, too, he managed to slip the sleeping child out to his friend once again.

Months later, Dr. Grinberg and his wife were removed to Danzig. There he was put to work in a German hospital. His wife was sent away. For nearly three years Dr. Grinberg, alone, went about his work in the hospital. In 1944 he was transferred to the concentration camp at Dachau. In 1945, with the Allied forces becoming triumphant, the Nazis packed several hundred Jewish inmates of the camp into freight cars, and the journey to the crematoria began. Dr. Grinberg was among them. While still miles from their destination, American planes suddenly appeared in the skies and strafed the train. The German military leaped for cover, warning the Jews they would be shot if they attempted to escape. But at Grinberg's signal, they poured out of the cars and fled into a near-by woods. When the planes departed, the Germans ordered them back to the cars: the Jews refused; the Germans set up machine guns and methodically strafed the woods, killing all but perhaps forty Jews. The train went on with the Germans, leaving the Jews alone with their dead.

Dr. Grinberg, who was one of those unhurt, gave first aid to the living. Then he organized all who could walk into a unit and marched with them for a day and a half, until they reached a German village.

Walking at the head of his tattered group, Dr. Grinberg strode into the village and asked the first man he met to take him immediately to the office of the town burgo-master. The villager looked at this man—hatless, his face encrusted with blood and dust, his clothes ragged—and was about to pass him by.

"I said, 'Take me to your burgomaster!' " Dr. Grinberg repeated, and there was something in his voice that made the other tip his hat, mutter, *"Jawohl, mein Herr,"* and lead him into the burgomaster's office.

The burgomaster was seated behind his desk and did not rise.

"Good day," said Dr. Grinberg. "I am medical repre-sentative of the International Red Cross. I have people with me who need medicine, food, and shelter. I request you to turn over to me all necessary facilities at once."

The burgomaster, a stocky, middle-aged man, glanced up at Dr. Grinberg. "I am sorry," he said indifferently; "I have no facilities," and turned back to his papers.

Dr. Grinberg advanced one step toward him. "The Americans are twenty-four hours behind me," he said. "I assure you that if you do not give me what I demand, you will be hanging by the neck five minutes after they arrive."

The burgomaster, taken aback, stared at the thin little man with the gaunt face and burning eyes, and at that mo-ment there was a commotion outside. A German motor-cyclist roared through the village with a sign reading, "The Americans are coming. Take cover."

The burgomaster rose behind his desk and bowed. *"Bitte, sitzen sie, Herr Doktor,"* he said courteously, indi-cating a chair. At that moment Dr. Grinberg knew he was a free man.

The Americans did not arrive for nearly four days, but Dr. Grinberg maintained his authority in the village by sheer force of personality. After the war he founded St.

Ottelein Hospital, near Munich, and manned it completely with physicians and nurses who were former concentration-camp inmates. It is today one of the finest in Europe.

Six months after the war's end, he received a telephone call from a town less than a hundred miles from Munich. "So I find you at last," said a voice—and he recognized it as the voice of the Lithuanian non-Jew to whom he had entrusted his child nearly five years before. "Are you not interested to know how well your son is doing? He is in excellent health and with me now." When the Russians pushed back the Germans, Dr. Grinberg's friend had traveled with the Russians, identifying the child as his own. Three weeks before Sir Frederick and I arrived in Germany, the director of a Berlin hospital had sent a message to Dr. Grinberg, reading in effect, "We have in Ward 3 a woman of about thirty years of age whose name is Grinberg. She tells us her husband was a physician. Is she possibly your wife?"

It was Mrs. Grinberg.

The Grinbergs were one of the rare instances I encountered of a Jewish family left intact in Europe.

Sir Frederick and I met Dr. Grinberg—a slight, little man, looking much older than his thirty-four years, with clear dark eyes and simplicity of manner—at the headquarters of the Central Committee of Liberated Jews in Munich.

What was it that he wished to tell us, we asked.

"I could speak to you of the way of suffering of the Jew," he began. "For us the major stations of this way were the ghetto of Kovno and the concentration camp at Dachau. We could sit here all night and the time would

97

not suffice to tell about everything. It is a story of bestiality and brutality, combined with miracles, that no one could understand who has not experienced it.

"The miracle is that I am still here sitting before you today and I can talk to you. But what I want to describe if possible is the state of mind of the average Jew in the average settlement today.

"When we were in the concentration camps, we had ample time to think. Thinking was the one privilege the Nazis could not rob from us. We had time to draw a balance sheet of our individual lives and the balance sheet of our lives as a nation. We thought again and again: what could we have done to avoid falling under the Nazi steam roller? What could we have done even before the war?

"Nearly all of us might have been able, though with difficulties, to emigrate to Palestine. I tell you we beat our breasts with our fists every day in the concentration camps and we asked ourselves in the ghettos, 'Why didn't I go to the land of Israel? I could have avoided all this.' Thus, every man for himself, and every man for his family. In the ghetto and in the concentration camps, all differences between Zionists and non-Zionists, assimilationists and non-assimilationists, cosmopolitans and Communists, disappeared completely. Each one of us regretted that he had not gone to Palestine. We stood before a law which looked upon us as an entity and our only guilt was that we were Jews. All our sacrifices of the last six years were the result of this single accusation: we were Jews.

"We never dreamed we would be free, we who were in the concentration camps. Millions of Jews had already found death in the gas chambers; why should we be the exception? We knew the Nazis were methodical and efficient. Some of us tried to imagine how it would be if by

some miracle we would become free. We imagined the
entire world would join to help us, to comfort us, to con-
sole us, and to help us reach our goal. We thought, surely,
when the Nazis are gone, when the barbed wire disappears,
immediately behind that we—the *Sh'erith Hap'letah* [the
remnant of the survivors]—shall find waiting for us the
land of Israel.

"Now, months after liberation, we have come to realize,
with such agony of spirit and soul as I cannot describe to
you, that the world has built an even higher barbed-wire
fence around Palestine. They do not want to let us enter
into that land."

He had talked steadily, and no one had interrupted him.
Now he paused, and I asked: "Whom do you mean by
'they,' Dr. Grinberg?"

"Mankind and humanity," he replied. "If one nation
prevents our going in, the others look on and do nothing."

"You know we are here at the suggestion and order of
President Truman and the British government to try and
find ways and means of accomplishing the objective," I
pointed out.

"We have lost six years," he said. "We cannot wait. Let
me come back to the state of mind of the average Jewish
man in the displaced-persons camps. It is based on three
factors: a bitter, terrible yesterday, an impossible today,
and an undetermined tomorrow."

He could not understand, he said, why it was that "after
we have been dying for six years as Jews, the world doesn't
want to let us live as Jews." And he went on: "To me, personally, fate was kind in saving the life of a four-and-a-half-
year-old son. Now I must consider in what language and in
which way I shall bring up my son. I am thinking about
the language in which my father, my grandfather, and

my ancestors prayed, and about the contents of their prayers. These prayers were national prayers. We Jews have a national religion, or, rather, perhaps we are a religious nation. The unhealthy thing in our past was that in spite of the fact that we had a national religion, we had no home of our own, and that is the basis of our tragedy.

"My eyes, they have seen children and old people murdered, gassed, strangled: my eyes when they look upon my child alive today force me to a higher resolution that this child must grow up in the country to which my ancestors desired to go and speak the language in which they prayed.

"This is not only so with me, but with all the Jews in all the settlements and camps."

The Jewish displaced persons, he said, came out of the concentration camps strong in the determination to go to Palestine.

"You must understand the psychological factors," he said. "The Nazi SS education of work was something that took from the Jew the love to work—because work meant death. Twelve hours of work a day under malnutrition meant death. Therefore, as an example, we have to re-educate our people to love work. And this job of re-education can happen only in Palestine, where two factors exist absolutely indispensable for such re-education: one is the love and comfort of our people; the other is the strength of conviction, the discipline of work. May I repeat: the two factors are, first, the love and comfort of our people; secondly, the Jewish population of Palestine has the moral quality to re-educate our people in making them feel that they are working for themselves, for their families, for the future." He paused again. "Gentlemen," he said, "for us here, Palestine is not too far. All our thoughts and all our sentiments are continually in Palestine. Whether they let us or not—the 'they' I spoke of before—we shall go, and we shall be in Palestine."

There was a pause again.

Sir Frederick, more deeply moved than I had ever seen him, rose.

"I am emotionally exhausted," he confessed. "I beg you, Dr. Grinberg and gentlemen, to believe in the good intentions of our governments. We do not intend to delay: we do not intend to retard the justice which you deserve. We shall give you that to which you are entitled as soon as certain preliminary steps are taken."

Our day-by-day investigation continued. In Munich we found newly arrived infiltrees from Poland who were temporarily sheltered as persecuted displaced persons. They came with stories of vicious anti-Semitism among the people of Poland. Here was a woman whose brother-in-law had been killed a few weeks before: she herself still carried a bullet in her hand. UNRRA workers told us of calls from one town or another, near by, reporting a train just arrived from Poland with four hundred or six hundred Jews, half dead, who had been on it for periods ranging from six to ten weeks.

The story varied in detail. One after another who had returned from Poland told of being the only survivor of a family group of twenty or thirty; of having returned to a home town where once there were thousands of Jews and now only a handful—ten or twenty—remained. "I came to my town and found none of my people there. Not a single Jew left. I visited the mass grave where they were all buried. I stayed two days and then I fled. There is nothing left for me now but to go to our own soil in the land of Israel."

In Landsberg camp, Judge Griengaus, formerly a magistrate in Memel, reported to us the unfriendly attitude of some of the American military police to the Jewish displaced persons. Men and women were arrested and held incommunicado without the knowledge of their camp officials. They were imprisoned on suspicion and sentenced without a right to counsel. In the trains, American MPs had said, "All Germans to the right; all Jews to the left." Only Jews were searched. There were cases when American military police stopped people on the street and asked, "Are you a Jew? Get off the street and walk in the gutter." This treatment by the Allies was almost unendurable to the Jews. It made for complete disillusionment. This sense of not only physical but spiritual exclusion made them feel that the entire world, Nazi and non-Nazi, had turned against them.

I felt then, and I said so to the representative of the Jewish newspaper, *Our Way,* in Munich, though I asked him not to print it: "If the movement of Jewish people from Poland to Germany is not organized, I wish to God it were organized and legalized soon."

It would be unfair to suggest that Sir Frederick and I experienced no encouraging moments in the displaced-persons camps of Germany. Repeatedly we were heartened by the morale of these men and women. One thing seemed certain: morale was highest where doubts about the future were least. Throughout Germany, wherever we found DPs on farms preparing for communal *Kibbutz* life in Palestine, the men and women were remarkably buoyant.

Not far from Munich we found what had once been the model farm of the late Julius Streicher, arch Jew-baiter. It was now an agricultural training center for *Kibbutz* life in Palestine. Organized under a British UNRRA worker, here were twenty-four teen-age boys and girls overwhelmingly confident that they would reach Palestine, and who worked as if this was a temporary stopping-off place on the way to Palestine.

In the main house, prominently displayed, hung two portraits. One was of Dr. Weizmann, the other of Theodor Herzl. "Hitler's photograph once hung there," a strapping youth said to me. "As those photographs have changed, so we are changing, becoming new human beings." They filled us with production and crop statistics, but their conversation inevitably returned to the same theme: "If we can do this here, what will we not be able to do with the good earth of Palestine?"

Before we left, they broke into the *Hora,* the Hebrew folk dance. I do not know how Sir Frederick felt watching them; I knew that here, perhaps the only time in Germany, I lost some of my heaviness of spirit.

Two girls, laughing, came to Sir Frederick and pulled him into the group. "I say, look here," he began to protest, but before we knew it, he was in the circle, stamping vigorously first to the right and then to the left.

As we visited camp after camp, certain facts became unmistakable. These Jewish DPs had been deprived of two great needs, and from a psychiatric point of view, they could not be made normal again until these were satisfied. First was the need of family, of intimates upon whom they could lavish love and from whom they could receive love. Second was the need for purpose in their lives. There was nothing to work for, no goal. In the camps there was nothing to build for the future, for the Jews expected no future in Germany. There was no incentive for thrift because German money had no value outside Germany. Palestine, alone, seemed able to satisfy both these fundamental hungers.

I determined I would fight for an Interim Report calling for an immediate cleaning out of the DP camps. If we were not to issue one, I decided I would present the case to the American people through the press. The facts should be revealed. I would get them out at the first possible chance.

Though the physical devastation of war was shockingly evident in the cities of Germany, even greater, I felt, was the spiritual devastation among the people. War had settled nothing. The people of Germany whom we saw and with whom we talked were sullenly unfriendly or obsequiously servile: their acquiescence to our authority was only outward. There was no doubt that Nazi cells flourished. The martial spirit was not dimmed. The war had been lost through error. In "the next war," many hastened to tell me, Germany would not make the basic mistake of antagonizing the Jews of the world.

But there were other German spokesmen who revived one's hopes for the future. Munich was the home of Michael Cardinal Faulhaber. He had been a monumental figure during the war, standing up so resolutely against the Nazis that in the early days they had made an abortive attempt on his life. I called upon him in his ancient palace, which still showed the marks of Nazi efforts to burn it.

He confirmed the presence of strong anti-Semitism in the hearts of many Germans, but he had faith that the Jews could still live in Germany. He was outspoken in his contempt for anti-Semitism and his repugnance for Nazism. I told him frankly that what had distressed me so deeply during the war was that Nazi excesses were greater in Catholic Bavaria than anywhere else in Germany.

"Persecution of Catholics and persecution of Jews are one and the same thing," he declared. "You know the attitude of the Holy Father—that all Catholics are spiritually Semites and that anti-Semitism is really the most despicable form of anti-Catholicism." Anti-Semitism itself he regarded as a curse against humanity, for the Christian religion itself was founded on the Old Testament, which was a product of the Jewish spirit. Therefore, anti-Semitism "was completely an act of Antichrist."

He insisted, he said, that a pastoral letter be read from every Catholic pulpit in Germany, denouncing anti-Semitism as anti-Christian and anti-Catholic. "As Cardinal, I shall do everything in my power to convince the Catholics of Bavaria that they must eradicate from their hearts any remnants of this evil scourge of anti-Semitism."

A Germany without Jews, he went on, was unthinkable. "We must have Jews in Germany," he said. "Jews have the same right to live in Germany as I, having been born in Germany, have a right to live here. They likewise have a right to live in peace here."

He had hoped, he said, to see Germany's great Jewish doctors return, and he expressed his astonishment that, as far as he could determine, only one German Jewish physician had come back. It was apparent that His Eminence did not know that the reason they had not returned was because they had virtually all been murdered; he had no idea of the tragic extent of the mass murder of European Jewry.

The Cardinal's faith that Jews could again live in Germany was not shared by the U. S. military authorities. Our military frankly feared for Jewish lives in Germany if our armies were withdrawn.

The attitude of the aged German porter who took my

bags at the hotel in Nuremberg also would have helped the Cardinal to understand Jewish fears. Who were the American gentlemen, he wanted to know. I said we were part of a committee investigating the condition of Jews in Germany.

The old man, who had been all amiability and obsequiousness, turned red with almost maniacal rage. He spat out, "They all should be killed! We want none of them!"

At Fahrenwald camp, near Munich, we heard a story which I felt symbolized in its individual tragedy the entire tragedy of the Jewish people of Europe. Four witnesses sat before us. Three spoke of politics, of the two-thousand-year-old dream of Zionism, of the need of the Jewish people for a homeland. They were impassioned, eloquent, and moving. Then the fourth and youngest—Littman Boroshek, a blond, husky youth—began. He spoke in short simple sentences, each sentence translated by Judge Rifkind. "I shall not speak of politics," the boy said, "or of other questions. I shall only relate a few personal facts and tell you that there are thousands more like me and that my story is the story of my entire generation as Jews. I was born in Brest-Litovsk. I went to general school and then high school—not a government school, because they would not admit me. I went to the University of Vilna in 1939 to study chemistry. The non-Jews beat me." He pointed to scars on his lip.

"We Jews were forced to sit on separate benches in the university. I managed to finish my studies, but I was unable to obtain any position." He paused, and holding out his hands, palms up, he said slowly, "I am twenty-eight years old and I have never eaten bread that I have earned with my own hands." He pointed to his shirt. "This shirt I wear was given to me by the Red Cross." He pointed to the ragged coat he wore. "This coat I wear came from the partisans; this sweater, from my sisters in Palestine, who knit it for me. My uncle in the United States sent me a dollar bill, and I bought these boots you see on me. During the war," he went on, "I was in the ghetto. Later I joined the partisans. I was called 'The Jew.' When we were victorious, all was well. When we were defeated, the Jews were blamed. When we went into a village, if I was not recognized as a Jew, everything was all right. If I was recognized as a Jew, the non-Jews reported me to the authorities, and I had to flee. When I was with the partisans, non-Jewish partisans were called partisans. Jewish partisans were called Jews.

"When the war ended I returned to the town in which I had lived. There were seven thousand Jews there when I left. Now two small children remained." He pulled out a tattered photograph from his clothes. "This is all that remains of my family. One went to war. He was taken prisoner and killed by the Germans. All the rest were slaughtered by the Poles. I do not even know their grave. I have a photograph of a meadow supposedly their grave. Here is the photograph of my mother and my father, both killed by the SS. They were told, 'You are enemies of Hitler.' This photograph here," showing another photograph, "is a photograph of my school class. All who went to Palestine—ten—survived. They are alive. All who remained in Poland—thirty-three—are dead.

"My uncle in the United States wrote me a letter saying, 'I can send you some money.' My sisters in Palestine wrote me, 'Come to us.'

"This is my story, and it is the story of thousands and thousands more."

CHAPTER 6

Nuremberg: "Arabs! Rise and Kill!"

IN MUNICH we had learned the point of view of Joseph
Aumer, Minister for Jewish Affairs of the Bavarian government. Mr. Aumer's sole duty, it appeared, was to persuade
Jews to remain in Bavaria. Dapper, punctilious, and
proper, himself a half Jew, he called upon us at our hotel.
The sum of his observations on the Jewish problem was
this: Hitler had made one great mistake: the persecution
of the Jews. Hitler himself had pointed out, Aumer said
soberly, that the Jews controlled international banking.
By the same token, therefore, the German Jews controlled
Germany's economic future. A Germany without Jews
would be an economic vacuum, for if Jews did not handle
Germany's economic affairs, the international bankers
would have no confidence in German economy. "We shall
not receive aid from the international banking fraternity,
nor shall we have any foreign trade to speak of," he said
earnestly. "Germany must have a Jewish community so
that it can become a substantial world power again."

It was an unusual lesson in unusual economics. It depressed me deeply to hear this man repeating the most
odious of Hitler doctrines, reminiscent of the *Protocols
of the Elders of Zion*. "All the testimony given us so far

by the Jews themselves, Mr. Aumer, is that they do not
wish to remain in Germany," I observed.

"Ah, yes," he replied, "but now we need them."

A few weeks later, I learned, Herr Aumer had been discharged from his post.

Sir Frederick and I visited the war trials while we were
in Nuremberg, and I spent some time talking to the American investigators who were reconstructing the Nazi conspiracy, for the prosecution, from the massive archives
which the Allies had unearthed.

I remembered Edgar Ansel Mowrer's scoop in London
when he printed the text of an affidavit that incriminated
the ex-Mufti in the mass murder of the Jews. I understood
that there was a large file on the Mufti in the archives of
the Allied War Crimes Commission and I spoke to Judge
Rifkind about it.

"I imagine you'll have a job digging it up," he said. The
best procedure, he thought, was for me to talk with Mr.
Justice Jackson. I visited Jackson the next day. I mentioned the Mowrer affidavit to him. He replied that he was
familiar with it, but he did not believe that was sufficient
evidence to deal with the matter. I could see that the subject was unpleasant to him, so I dropped it.

There were others much interested in seeing that the
Mufti's story was told. An Army intelligence officer, at
three o'clock one afternoon, made it possible for me to
enter a room and sit down at a table upon which was a
thick file of documents.

I opened the first and began to read.

The record of the ex-Mufti's intrigues was fantastic.
This file showed clearly that he had climaxed a record of
Fascism, anti-British intrigues, and anti-Semitism by help-

ing spearhead the extermination of European Jewry. I had my hands on a German document signed by an agent of the Mufti scarcely twenty-four hours before Germany surrendered. In this the Mufti, in consideration of monies in gold paid up to that date, agreed to set up a new Pan-Islamic Empire and "to fight against the common enemy." If this was true, the Mufti had been paid by the dead hand of Hitler to carry on Hitler's work where Hitler left off. I saw another document—a deposition of Dr. Rudolph Kasztner, a Hungarian Jew, who conducted negotiations with the Nazis in an attempt to ransom Hungarian Jews. Many of these dealings were with Adolf Eichmann, the Gestapo specialist in Jewish affairs, who had been the confidant of the Mufti. During his negotiations Dr. Kasztner spoke frequently with one Dieter von Wisliczeny. Von Wisliczeny was at this moment held in a cell in Nuremberg as a war criminal and an important witness. "The Grand Mufti," he said, "has repeatedly suggested to the Nazi authorities—including Hitler, von Ribbentrop, and Himmler—the extermination of European Jewry." The Mufti told Wisliczeny that he "considered this a comfortable solution to the Palestine problem." And Nazi records show that, accompanied by Eichmann, the Grand Mufti, incognito, visited the gas chambers of Auschwitz, where hundreds of thousands of Jews were exterminated. Hitler had instructed that in any ransoming of concentration-camp inmates, no Jews were to be included because an agreement had been reached with the Mufti that all Jews be exterminated. I also learned that the Hitler-Mufti agreement included relegation of Ibn Saud to secondary importance by making the Mufti the supreme head of a new Pan Islam. This became clear as I read on. It was the Mufti who insisted to the Nazi leaders that no matter what deals were made, no matter what monies were paid for the ransom of the Jews by Jews, no Jews should be permitted to go to Palestine. Negotiations were under way at that time for the ransom of the Jewish community of Bratislava. These negotiations broke down because the Mufti refused to countenance their being ransomed and as a result the entire community was liquidated.

It became evident that Nazi policy in relation to the Jews could be divided into three phases. Until 1940, the general policy was to settle the Jewish question by forced expulsion of them, coupled with extortion. From 1940 until 1942, the Nazi plan was to concentrate them in ghettos in Poland and in occupied eastern territories.

In 1941 the Mufti fled to Germany for refuge. He immediately set to work with all his influence to agitate against ghettoization of the Jews and for a final solution: extermination. The result was the third stage of Nazi policy: the planned destruction of the Jewish race.

There was proof of this in these documents before me. A letter from the Mufti to Foreign Minister von Ribbentrop, on July 25, 1944, complained of German clemency toward the Jews:

"Your Excellency: I have previously called the attention of your Excellency to the constant attempts of the Jews to emigrate from Europe in order to reach Palestine, and asked your Excellency to undertake the necessary steps so as to prevent the Jews from emigrating."

Other letters of the Mufti showed that he encouraged the deportation of European Jews to Polish extermination camps. On June 5, 1943, he protested to the Prime Minister of Bulgaria against a plan by the Bulgarian government allowing emigration of four thousand Jewish children. These children, he argued, presented "a degree of danger to Bulgaria whether they be kept in Bulgaria or be permitted to depart from that country." Instead, he said, they should be sent to a place in which they would be "under stringent control—as, for instance, Poland." The Mufti's protest was successful. No children's transport left Bulgaria after July, 1943.

A few weeks later he dispatched a similar letter to the foreign minister of Rumania, concerning eighteen hundred Jewish children. This time he again suggested Poland, pointing out they would be under what he called "active supervision," a euphemism for the gas chambers.

On the same date he wrote again to the Bulgarian foreign minister, concerning a proposed transport from Hungary of nine hundred children and one hundred adults. Again he pointed out that surveillance in Poland was the appropriate course.

A few days later he wrote to the Italian foreign minister on the same subject. This time he urged the Italians to take necessary measures, with the governments of Bulgaria, Hungary, and Rumania, to prevent the escape of Jews.

On July 27, 1944, the Mufti wrote to Heinrich Himmler. Von Ribbentrop and Himmler were too lenient toward the Jews, he declared, because, though he had protested to both of them on July 5, 1944, some Jews had been permitted to depart from Germany. "If such practices continue," the Mufti wrote, they will certainly be "incomprehensible to Arabs and Moslems and provoke a feeling of disappointment in them," and he warned that such practices might also encourage the Balkan states to permit Jewish emigration.

On November 3, 1943, the Mufti broadcast from Berlin, in one of his numerous exhortations to the Arabs: "The Treaty of Versailles was a disaster for the Germans as well as the Arabs. But the Germans know how to get rid of the Jews. That which brings us close to the Germans and sets us up in their camp is that up to today the Germans never harmed any Moslem, and are fighting our common enemy who persecuted the Arabs and the Moslems."

This "common enemy," of course, was Britain. He went on to say, "But most of all they have definitely solved the Jewish problem. These ties, and especially the last one, the common war against Jews, make of our friendship with Germany not a provisional friendship dependent upon conditions but a permanent and lasting one based on mutual interests."

At the beginning of the war the estimated number of Jews in the world was seventeen million. Even in 1944 we had no knowledge of the extent of Jewish massacres. The Mufti had. In a broadcast from Berlin on September 20, 1944, he asked the Arab world the rhetorical question, "Is it not in your power to repulse the Jews whose number is not more than eleven million?"

By this time, six million Jews had in fact been murdered. What was the source of the Mufti's information? He could have learned it only from Adolf Eichmann.

I had done enough reading for my purpose. I was to learn more about this notorious figure in Palestine.

Before we left Nuremberg, Army authorities invited us to a private showing of German and American motion-picture films, taken during and after the concentration-camp period. I saw the unexpurgated films of the actual mass murders, of bodies piled like cordwood to feed the crematorium fires: pictures that the Germans had carefully preserved, perhaps with the thought that well-documented files might legalize massacre. I became so ill at the sight that I was unable to remain throughout the entire showing. I could no longer look upon these scenes of victims dying, of victims dead, of piles of dead bodies being pushed by German bulldozers into huge pits dug into the ground. It was the more unforgettable to me since I had just come from the people themselves—the men and women who, but for the sudden end of the war, would have been buried like these; men and women who had endured such horrors as these.

As Sir Frederick and I walked back to the hotel, we were accosted by a German boy about fourteen, begging for a cigarette. Sir Frederick said, "We must take care of these young German people. What will their future be?"

We drove on to Prague.

CHAPTER 7

Prague: Even in Czechoslovakia

Our motor convoy, flying the American flag, literally stopped traffic in Prague. Crowds jammed about our cars as we came to a halt before the Hotel Ambassador. We were besieged with demands for American cigarettes and American candy. The crowds stared at the American uniforms of our drivers and accompanying officers. As for ourselves, we were behind the "iron curtain" and we looked about with interest as great as theirs.

Prague seemed the least affected by the war of all the cities we had seen so far in central Europe. The city was drab, but shops were open and nowhere did your eye meet the vast masses of ruined buildings and huge mounds of rubble which characterized the cities of Germany.

An American captain greeted us in the hotel lobby. Sir Frederick, Judge Rifkind, and I were invited to be the guests of Ambassador Laurence Steinhardt at the American Embassy, a rococo building which was once the Paček Palace. A Czech official told me that the government almost fell because Steinhardt moved into the palace. He explained that the Soviet Embassy had hoped to take over the building and that the government, forced to choose, nearly resigned in its dilemma.

Our hearings in Prague were conducted in one of the

large rooms of the embassy, with witnesses seated at a long table. Near by sat Ambassador Steinhardt, frequently interpolating explanations when the occasion arose. Even here in Czechoslovakia, where the government had already passed laws condemning anti-Semitism, we found the same plea—"Let us go to Palestine!" The situation of the Jews in Prague and surrounding Czech areas was not too serious. But real panic, we were told, was felt by the Jews who lived in traditionally anti-Semitic Slovakia. There had been recurring anti-Semitic incidents, and only a few months before, Jews had been killed in a full-dress pogrom in Velke Topolčany. Our witnesses said that sixty per cent of the Slovak Jews hoped to leave Slovakia and that the general feeling of most Jews was that they could put little trust in promises of minority rights.

Sir Frederick and I paid our respects to President Eduard Beneš, calling upon him in the old palace of the Czech kings where he lives and has his office. The parquet floors, elaborate crystal chandeliers, and enormous white-and-gilt porcelain stoves, relics of a past long vanished, contrasted sharply with the sparse and simple modern furnishings in Beneš' office.

The man often described as the wisest statesman in central Europe, the guiding spirit behind the prewar Little Entente, struck me as a sad man who carried on his shoulders the burden of this fine small country which had for so long been a democratic island in a sea of totalitarianism. Certainly, I felt, if any one man could be said to be the embodiment of his people, Eduard Beneš was the embodiment of the spirit of Tomáš Garrigue Masaryk, its founder.

He explained the policy of the Czech government in relation to Jews; he abhorred anti-Semitism.

"I regard every attempt to incite anti-Semitism in

Czechoslovakia as a Fascist plot to undermine our government," he declared. "I am determined to defend the reputation of Czechoslovakia against these new efforts to cause dissension."

He admitted that the government had been having difficulty with the Slovaks, who were infested with anti-Semitism. He called our attention to the formal position of his government, which was made public on October 2, 1945, after the Velke Topolčany pogroms. Later Ambassador Steinhardt gave us a copy of the government communiqué.

However, Czech Jews told us that the perpetrators of pogroms in Slovakia had not been brought to trial. They were in jail, but no charges had been lodged against them. They had not been punished. "It is this," witnesses told us, "that encourages the anti-Semites. They feel the government frowns, but does not take any clear action to punish."

Beneš was concerned about other aspects of the Jewish problem. An unintentional hardship, it appears, was inflicted on Czech Jews. "We took a census early in 1930 in which many assimilated Jews had registered as German or Hungarian, according to their mother tongues, considering themselves ethnologically German or Hungarian, not Jewish," Beneš explained. "The result is that they have to be deported either to Germany as Germans or to Hungary as Hungarians, unless they can prove they participated in the underground partisan movement against the Nazis or fought actively against them."

Beneš supports Zionism. He told us that Jews who wish to go to Palestine should be permitted to do so. Those who do not go "should be assimilated completely with the people of the country in which they wish to live, or otherwise live in that country as citizens of a foreign state."

He asked us if we had seen any antidemocratic evidences in Czechoslovakia. I said yes. I had been surprised, I said, to see persons in the street wearing arm bands identifying them as Germans and to be told that these men and women were scheduled to be sent back to Germany. Some whom I had met told me they were being humiliated because they were Germans.

Beneš thought for a moment.

"Perhaps our greatest mistake prior to the war," he said slowly, "was that we were too democratic. We do not intend to make that mistake again."

Ambassador Steinhardt, at dinner that night, spoke warmly of the Czechs. I knew that Steinhardt's name had been inscribed in the *Golden Book* in Jerusalem because of his magnificent and humanitarian work while our Ambassador to Turkey during the war. He had greatly assisted Ira Hirschmann, special envoy of President Roosevelt's Refugee Board, in bringing Jewish displaced persons out of the Axis-dominated Balkan states and was responsible for saving hundreds of lives. Steinhardt told me of some of the extraordinary dealings between Cretsianu, the Rumanian, and Hirschmann, and how he had been obliged to go over the heads of both the British and the Russians and, with Hirschmann, make secret arrangements with *Haganah* and British Intelligence to get these people out. He explained with eloquence to Sir Frederick why it was to Britain's own interest to open the doors of Palestine to the Jews.

In Prague we met a spokesman for Slovakian Jewry. He testified briefly. Sixty per cent of the Jews of Slovakia—about 16,000 to 20,000 persons—wished to leave the country as soon as possible. Of these, ninety per cent were determined to go to Palestine. Most had been Zionists of long standing: what had happened in the last decade had only confirmed them in their conviction that Jewish "homelessness" was responsible in great part for the Jewish tragedy.

"You must understand that many here are disillusioned with the democracies," he said. "I can tell you that in 1942, we here in Slovakia were the first to notify London about what was taking place in Auschwitz. But London did not wish to believe that Jews were being deported to Auschwitz and burned to death. When the Hungarians continued to deport Jews there, we sent a plea to London: we sent along a map showing the railroad on which the trains took Jews to Auschwitz, and all other necessary information, and begged the British military authorities to bomb these railroads. But it was decided not to bomb them because the military situation didn't warrant it. We asked, too, for Sebenev to be bombed, where millions of Jews perished in huge gas chambers. But Sebenev was not bombed either."

CHAPTER 8

Vienna: "They Should All Have Been Burned"

OUR CAVALCADE set out the next morning for Vienna. We came within sight of the Czech-Austrian border at midday and found a Soviet Army captain waiting for us there. He would accompany us, he said smilingly, into Austria and see to it that our journey was expedited. But a little farther on, still in Czech territory, we were halted by the Czech police. We were less than fifteen feet from the frontier. Despite our papers and our vehement protests—in which the Russian captain took as indignant a part as we—our entire party was placed under arrest. We must remain in a tiny border guardhouse until cleared by Prague.

Our party—Sir Frederick, Judge Rifkind, Major Straus, Captain Eno, Lieutenant Zorek, Chaplain Vida, two correspondents, the Russian captain, and I, together with half a dozen American GI drivers and our six military staff cars—was halted for nearly six hours.

By telephone I attempted to reach Ambassador Steinhardt, the Czech Minister for Foreign Affairs, the Minister of War, and the Minister of the Interior. I lodged stiff protests all along the line. Then we waited for action, seated there with Czech soldiers keeping their rifles trained on us.

The Czech police were polite but firm. Our papers were

in order, our credentials were of the highest: but all this seemed only to prove how dangerous we must be. Word finally came through for our release. Still suspicious, they reluctantly permitted us to cross the border.

Later we received an apology which explained that only a few days ago an American military raiding party had entered Czechoslovakia and stolen a number of top-secret documents believed wanted at the Nuremberg trials. The Czech authorities had issued an order to all border posts to seize any American military group attempting to leave the country.

Sir Frederick and I arrived in Vienna several hours before the remainder of the committee, who were gathering from different parts of Europe. The plight of the displaced persons was on my mind, and I prepared myself to make the strongest possible plea to my colleagues for an Interim Report. Yet I knew that without an aroused American public opinion, I should have great difficulty prevailing upon the committee to issue one. Despite the efforts being made to keep secret all evidence heard by the committee, I was convinced the American people were entitled to know the facts.

At three o'clock that afternoon, I took it upon myself to hold a press conference with foreign correspondents. I told them as frankly as I could what Sir Frederick and I had found in the camps of Germany. I added nothing and subtracted nothing. Our over-all conclusion, I said, was that the camps had to be cleaned out. The displaced persons must be permitted to go where they wanted to go, and if that was Palestine, so be it. If they did not get out, I said, they would become utterly demoralized.

"If these settlements are not cleaned out, sooner or later we will have either a wave of mass suicides or they will fight their way to Palestine," I said: they might not only kill themselves, but kill the Germans about them to boot.

There was a limit, I was convinced, to what these men and women could endure, how long they could take this frustration, this constant denial of the most elementary needs of a human being. Sir Frederick spoke briefly to reporters later. He told them that nearly one hundred per cent of the Jews we had seen wished to go only to Palestine.

By nightfall, the remainder of the committee had arrived, including Crossman, who had been ill in London. We assembled in Judge Hutcheson's sitting room in the Hotel Bristol to exchange notes.

Dr. McDonald and Ambassador Phillips summarized the hearings they had held in Paris. Among the witnesses before them had been Edmond Fleg, the French writer, and Guy de Rothschild, son of Baron Edmond, who had joined de Gaulle's staff in London after a dramatic escape from France.

"Rothschild told us he had been in Palestine recently," McDonald told us. "He said there must be a Jewish state, particularly for the Jews in Palestine and for European Jews who wanted to go to Palestine. For these two categories, he asserted, the Jewish nation was a fact. Obviously, such men and women could no longer feel allegiance to any other nation. He said they wanted two things: the right of immigration into Palestine and the recognition of their independence." McDonald added that he and Phillips, curious to learn the attitude toward Zionism of this famous Jewish family so thoroughly assimilated in so many countries of the world, had asked the question of Guy de Rothschild. He had replied that all the younger members had become Zionists. This included not only himself, but Lord Rothschild in England, a sister-in-law there, and two sons of Baron Robert de Rothschild, who had been prisoners of war in Germany and in 1940–41 had had a pretty bad time of it at the hands of their French fellow prisoners.

Both McDonald and Phillips had been deeply touched by Fleg's testimony. Two of his sons had been killed by the Nazis, and his personal grief underwrote the eloquence of his words as he spoke of the desperate need for a Jewish homeland. The Jewish section of the French Maquis also sent a representative to testify, and he took a strong pro-Palestine line.

After the report on France, we heard from Buxton, of *The Boston Herald,* Major Manningham-Buller, and Wilfrid Crick, who had visited Poland and the American Zone of Austria. As had been our experience, in Austria they were met by demonstrations of the DPs. In Bad Gastein the men and women were badly crowded, but their quarters were clean and they were rather decently ministered to. "Watching them dance the *Hora* for us," Buxton told me, "with the dancers moving in concentric circles and singing, I thought that I was watching an exercise of religious devotion rather than a pastime designed to lift the spirit. I felt that here were thousands of men and women, all victims of anti-Semitism, still fearful that later persecutions might take place in Austria, and all of them with little to do but idle and wait and pray for delivery and admission to Palestine."

He said that he was disappointed by the small proportion of DPs who had expressed preference for the United States rather than Palestine. He disagreed with one of his colleagues who asserted that this pro-Palestine attitude was the result of artful indoctrination by Zionist agents. "The feeling we found was too deep, too passionate, too wide-spread to be accounted for in that manner," Buxton said.

Their committee also investigated the "underground railway" to Palestine. Buxton's reaction was much the same as mine: that the individuals and groups composing this underground railway—which he said might better be described as an elevated railway since the treks were carried out openly—and those lending aid to homeless, penniless, terrorized, wandering Jews, "deserved praise for their fraternal ministrations." Buxton, who acted as chairman of the three-man subcommittee, wrote in his report to us, "If the Underground Railway were not operating, authorized governmental and other agencies, Jewish and non-Jewish, would be under the necessity of establishing one."

The desire to reach Palestine, he said, had become a passion among the Jews, and he doubted whether it could be checked by official steps of any kind—whether "a disappearance of Zionist propaganda, the elimination of the Jewish Agency in Palestine, or any other measure would have any effect."

In Poland, the committee spent five memorable days, principally in Lodz and Warsaw. They interviewed individuals from ambassadors and prelates down to shivering men and women and children who were selling goods in an open-air street market in a snowstorm. They found everywhere among the Jews the same burning determination to get to Palestine. "Constantly we inquired of these people," Buxton reported, "if they were aware of the opposition to Jewish immigration, that Jews and Arabs had been in open and covert conflict, and that life in Palestine might be hazardous. Their answers were usually impatient and vehement. Yes, they knew these things, but whatever was involved they would rather die in Palestine than live in Poland."

Dr. Emil Sommerstein, chairman of the Central Jewish Committee, told them that most Polish Jews were making frantic efforts to leave the country because they feared for their lives. They learned that of nearly a million Jewish children under the age of fourteen who had lived in Poland in 1939, today scarcely 5000 were alive. "We were told that there are less than a hundred Jewish families intact in Poland," Buxton related, "and that of the country's thousands of synagogues, only one, in Cracow, remains standing."

The committee concluded after investigation that while the government of Poland was not anti-Semitic and was making vigorous efforts to reduce anti-Semitism in Poland, the people were so imbued with it that laws were futile, and anti-Jewish outbreaks continued. Anti-Semitism was so deeply rooted in Poland that it appeared doubtful whether it could be eradicated in the next decade or two. In Lodz, for example, the manager of a textile plant told the committee he employed few Jewish workers because other employees objected to "taking orders from Jews." Apparently, the non-Jews did not complain openly about working side by side with Jews in nonexecutive jobs, but promotion of Jews was so bitterly resented that the management dared not reward even the most skillful and deserving of them with elevation to better positions.

Major Manningham-Buller returned obsessed by the idea of Communism: a Polish minister had assured him that the presence of Jews in the cabinet of a Soviet-inspired Polish government led to anti-Semitism because this seemed to support the old Nazi charge that Jews were Communists. Buxton, on the other hand, told me it seemed clear that one of the roots of Polish anti-Semitism was economic: the Poles resented the Jews who had trickled back into the country because they knew that, sooner or later, they must return Jewish property.

The committee was most deeply affected when they went through the ruins of the Warsaw ghetto, and stood on the banks of the huge pits still flecked with the bleached fragments of human bones, the only remains of Jews who had been shot. Some of the committee members wept as they stood there, encompassing as it were in a single glance this incredible burden of human suffering. Later, Jews marched in a demonstration before the committee's hotel, carrying banners, "Open the Gates of Palestine." A delegation called upon them and appealed to them to recommend lifting the ban on immigration into Palestine.

Perhaps the most moving story brought back from Poland was this. When the committee came into one of its hotel rooms in Warsaw, they found a small box on a table. At first they did not realize that it was an urn. A note was attached to it, reading, "This urn contains the ashes of a Jew burned to death at Maidenek. For God's sake, let the living go!"

There was a bitter epilogue to this. One member of the subcommittee, reading the note, observed, "Isn't it terrible!" But a second member looked at it, and said, "Yes, what bounders these people are!"

It was the height of bad taste, he felt.

Judge Hutcheson, Sir John Singleton, and Lord Morrison had visited the British Zone of Germany. The Judge had been impressed by the reaction of the Jews in the big Honne camp at the site of Bergen Belsen, where there are 10,000 Jews among 20,000 residents. "We found a feeling not of hope, but of Palestine," he said. He had been cha-

grined, he added, to learn that Jewish DPs were not interested in emigrating to the United States. *"Wir wollen
nach Palästina"*—"We want to go to Palestine"—that was
the statement he had heard everywhere.

Thus, here in Vienna, it was clear that all twelve of us
on the committee, having spread across Europe and come
together again, had found everywhere much the same picture. Our subcommittees had come to much the same conclusions: the existence of anti-Semitism as a potent factor
that had to be recognized; the desire to go to Palestine so
strong among the Jewish displaced persons that little less
than death could destroy it; the overwhelming wish of the
military to clean out the camps not only for the sake of
the displaced persons, but to help normalize life in Europe
itself.

It was at this point that news of my press conference
came out. Judge Hutcheson was disturbed; some of the
British were annoyed. Again it was evident that some of us
had far different views on the subject of the press and its
value. Buxton, the one professional newspaperman among
us, kept his peace, but managed quietly to goad me on to
make as many statements as I could, to keep reporters
informed.

"Bart," he said, "this is the time for indiscretion in
utterance."

However, in the interests of unity, the committee decided that night that hereafter only the two cochairmen
were authorized to speak to reporters on behalf of the
committee.

To make this clear and, I am afraid, to take the curse
off my interview, Sir John and Judge Hutcheson held a
press conference of their own the following day. Both British and American reporters then stationed in Vienna were

invited. I was among those present. Here I was rebuked by Sir John—the rebuke was implicit rather than stated—for having spoken to the press. Sir John went so far as to place a hand warningly upon my arm as I was about to reply to a reporter's question relating to a statement of fact I had made the day before.

I felt no qualms of conscience for having spoken to the press as freely as I had. Neither then nor later did I feel myself bound to secrecy, so far as the press was concerned, about what the committee saw, heard, and did. I felt that since only Sir Frederick and I had seen the major part of the problem of the displaced persons, it had been up to me as the American member of the subcommittee to tell the story.

The discussion of all this led to the question of the Interim Report. This had been a subject of conflict in the committee from the very beginning, but now, in Vienna, it brought about the most acrimonious debate among us so far. Our terms of reference authorized us to take interim action. Every expert on the record—military, UNRRA, JDC—agreed that the Jewish plight was so serious that not even the military could answer for the consequences. Sir Frederick and I now felt clearly the deep gap between those who had seen the displaced-persons camps and those who had seen only part of the picture. Crossman, who of course was familiar with the situation in Germany as a result of his work in psychological warfare, supported Sir Frederick and me.

The British generally refused to go along with our demand for an Interim Report recommending that the camps be emptied, on the ground that the Arabs would take this as a political move and charge that we had prejudged the case. Both Manningham-Buller and Sir John were prepared to vote for an Interim Report—one that would criticize the American policy which permitted the movement of Polish Jews into the American Zone. They wanted us to urge the American government to follow the British policy—namely, close all borders at once. But this was tantamount to bottling up within Poland Jews who were in peril of their lives.

"I won't take the responsibility if these people continue to move," declared Manningham-Buller. He added that, should the unlimited influx of refugees lead to grave results, he wanted "to be able to say in the House that it was against my advice." I pointed out that American policy was to keep the borders open, and that policy had been established by General Eisenhower. Anyone fleeing in fear of his life should be permitted to enter the American Zone. Judge Hutcheson said that he would not sign the unfair kind of report suggested by Manningham-Buller.

I agreed. Buxton followed suit. So did the other Americans. I felt so deeply that I asserted that I would resign if an affirmative report were not forthcoming. The following day I received a telephone call from Judge Hutcheson. He said, "I am going to ask you as a good American not to insist upon an Interim Report. You must take my word for it that the reasons behind this are good. I can tell you no more."

I learned later that word had come from the White House, asking that no Interim Report be made; instead, that short-term recommendations be made when we filed our final report. What deep maneuverings were behind this I do not know.

Weeks later, in Palestine, I received a confidential cable from the White House, expressing hope I would not resign and adding that the President was following our labors and had confidence in us.

In Vienna I learned for the first time that the British Foreign Office cabled daily to Beeley, giving him a summary of American press comment relating to what we were doing, with special emphasis upon what appeared in the New York and Washington newspapers.

I think I felt more disheartened during our three weeks in Vienna than at any other point during our proceedings. Not only was I so discouraged by the decision not to issue an Interim Report, but we were everywhere presented with such evidences of anti-Semitism that it seemed hopeless to continue. Here in this city, where once there had been 135,000 Jews, there were today less than 4000, but anti-Semitism, instead of decreasing, had grown. We found it powerful in high quarters and in low. For twelve years Hitler had used all the techniques an evil and cynical mind could invent to inculcate hatred, suspicion, contempt, and fear against the Jews everywhere in the world.

A shocking expression of this occurred when Crossman and I had cocktails with one of the British officers in charge of the displaced persons and prisoners of war in the British Zone of Austria. A red-faced, militant figure, he was not hesitant about discussing the problems of the thousands of displaced Jews with whose care he was charged.

"It is too bad the war didn't last another two or three months," he said, toying with his glass. "They'd all have been done away with by then. We'd have had no problem."

Crossman and I stared at him.

"Frankly, I'm an anti-Semite," he said. "I honestly hate the Jew bastards. I wish they'd all been burned to death."

I'm afraid I gasped a little at this, and he turned his ruddy face to me. He leaned forward and tapped me on the knee. "Ah-ah," he said chidingly. "I wager you have some of them as your clients, eh?"

This, perhaps, was an extreme case. But I had another experience in Vienna when, with other members, I heard His Excellency, Monsignor Francis Kamprath, Auxiliary Bishop of Vienna, second only to Cardinal Innitzer, and Father Braun, head of the Austrian Catholic Charity Organization. I was present at the beginning, but as the meeting went on, I felt, as a Catholic, such shame at their interpretation of Christianity that I excused myself and left.

Chaplain George Vida acted as interpreter.

Judge Hutcheson asked the two churchmen what they thought was the extent and nature of the Jewish problem in Austria. The two priests made their position clear.

"We have no official opinion, but personally we feel this: we do not hate the Jews, we hate only the Jewish spirit," they said. "We believe that the best solution to the Jewish problem would be to change this Jewish spirit into a Christian spirit. The Jews should become Christians."

Judge Hutcheson asked what they understood by "the Jewish spirit." They had used the German word *Judengeist*. They proceeded to make two accusations. First, the Jewish community had collaborated with the Nazis during the war and discriminated against baptized Jews in favor of Jews of Jewish faith. When asked to submit lists to the Gestapo of Jews to be sent to extermination camps, they preferred to give the names of Jews who had professed Catholicism or Protestantism.

Chaplain Vida told me that, unable to contain himself

at this charge, he interrupted to point out that in the statistics submitted by the Catholic Charity Organization, of 152,000 Jewish people in Vienna in 1942, who professed the Jewish faith, today only 4000 are alive. On the other hand, of 8000 Catholic Jews in Vienna at the beginning of the war, 7200 were still alive. His observation was ignored.

Their second accusation was that the Joint Distribution Committee provided packages of food and clothing only to Jews who professed the Jewish faith, discriminating against Catholic Jews. This, they asserted, increased anti-Semitism and was responsible for a growing hatred against "the Jewish spirit."

Judge Hutcheson asked, "Has anti-Semitism in Vienna increased, decreased, or remained constant since liberation?"

"During the war and in the time of the Nazis there was a great deal of mistaken racial anti-Semitism," came the reply. "Today all anti-Semitism in Austria is religious anti-Semitism. That is justified."

Judge Hutcheson asked as to their present opinion on the question of whether Jews should remain in Austria or leave. "It doesn't make any difference to us," was the reply. "We do not wish to advise them. If they choose to remain, we shall not drive them out. We do not intend to go that far."

Our two chairmen later apologized to Chaplain Vida for his ordeal in translating "such anti-Semitic" remarks.

The testimony of these Catholic dignitaries distressed me deeply. Here were two men, I thought, servants of the Church, who certainly as Catholics knew that the Holy See had in effect placed the Jews under the moral protection of the Papacy as early as 1758, and also that anti-Semitism had been condemned by the Church as "a sin of peculiarly anti-Christian viciousness." Yet such was the strength of nationalism that these two men could indulge in such slanderous and evil beliefs.

But this constant injection of anti-Semitism made me ponder the question anew. Here we were, twelve non-Jews, immersing ourselves in a problem in which our own basic attitudes must inevitably come into question. I brought it up with Dick Crossman.

"I have never attempted to ignore that question," he said. "I have always felt that every non-Jew had a virus of anti-Semitism in his veins and that in time of moral stress—when his moral resistance, as it were, is broken down—that virus can break out into the disease itself. I don't think even we, on this committee, are completely immune, for we all have prejudices of one kind or another—we British, the prejudices of the gentile and the Englishman, and you, the prejudices of a gentile and an American. This anti-Semitism, either conscious or subconscious," he said, "I think is our real problem."

I tried to examine myself. I had had Catholic instruction. As a boy in school, I had heard the ancient, terrible charge: Jews had killed Christ. When I attended the University of California Jews were not generally admitted to non-Jewish fraternities, nor were they generally admitted to certain clubs in San Francisco.

My early conditioning, I decided, had been to some extent anti-Semitic. Somewhere along the line I began to realize that my schooling had been wrong. Perhaps the first strong point of view I had ever heard on the other side was advanced by an exiled English Roman Catholic priest, Monsignor Capel. He had been attached to the Papal Court in Rome, but was silenced for a number of years because of alleged liberal leanings. Later he was allowed once again to speak. When I was in my teens, he began to preach in the Cathedral in Sacramento and he enjoined us to remember that every Catholic is spiritually a Semite.

Wendell Willkie had always held that any racial or religious prejudices were symptomatic of a sickness affecting civilization itself and that any nation which practiced anti-Semitism suffered from an internal weakness which led to self-destruction.

This was my conviction as well.

Chaplain Vida told me that he had offered his resignation as interpreter because certain members of our committee had insisted to him that Jews had no right to segregate themselves in any kind of organization, unless it was purely religious, that they had no right to any activity except purely religious activities, and that such organizations as the Joint Distribution Committee would always provoke anti-Semitism.

The Chaplain pointed out to me that these members of the committee were saying, in effect, that while Jews could be segregated for persecution and murder, Jews must not take joint action as Jews in their own defense and for their own survival. If this was the understanding of the problem by the very men appointed to judge it, as a rabbi he felt he must offer his resignation. But the resignation was not accepted.

Chaplain Vida gave me a number of notes he had taken during the trip. I placed them in the drawer of my desk in our committee office. Two days later they had disappeared. One of my British colleagues approached me later and said: "Bart, I happened to see quite a few papers and documents on your desk last night. I hope you don't mind if

I put them away. I do think we must be careful not to leave any of our confidential material about where it can be read by unauthorized persons."

I said nothing. I did not mention the notes, lest it mean disclosing whose they were, which would have greatly embarrassed the Chaplain.

While we were lunching one day with General Mark Clark, American Commander in Austria, at his villa on Vienna's outskirts, several hundred Jews came from the Rothschild Hospital, where they were billeted, to march in protest before our hotels and to present us with a resolution.

Several American newspaper correspondents later told me what had occurred. The marchers carried banners reading, "Open the Gates of Palestine" and "Are Not 6,000,000 Dead Enough?"

When they discovered that the committee was not in the city, they proceeded to the Jewish Community House and there slowly disbanded.

An elderly Viennese gentleman, soberly dressed, with discreet black hat, muffler, and gloves, looked on curiously. He turned to an American newspaper correspondent who stood near him and asked, "What is this? Who are these people?" The reporter said, "This is a demonstration. These people are Jews and they wish to go to Palestine."

The old gentleman drew himself up indignantly. "Well, let them!" he snapped. "Did they not cause all this?" And he gestured with his arm—a wide, all-embracing sweep, taking in all of ruined Vienna—the roofless buildings, the rubble, the misery, the devastation.

I could well understand why Viennese Jews were so deadly afraid of this all-pervading Austrian anti-Semitism.

They believed that they were fighting for their lives when they fought to get out of the country. "The Austrian government preaches democracy for external consumption, but the fate of the Jews depends upon the executives in the government," a Viennese Jew told us. "Practically no Jewish property has been restored. Only a few days ago a friend recognized in the Department of Police nine men who had belonged to a Nazi extermination squad in Poland which murdered twelve thousand Jews. These murderers are wearing police uniforms, moving among the population. Do you wonder we cannot bear to stay here?"

Another, representing the Jewish Community Organization, which feeds nearly half of the Jews in Vienna, testified that anonymous letters came almost daily, warning them, "Hitler's task will be finished when the last Jew has been liquidated."

Our committee did not obtain the necessary permission from the authorities in Hungary and Rumania to enter those countries. Although we were given no reason, it was generally assumed that this resulted from the fact that the Soviet Union had not been consulted. I remembered Manuilsky's observation on this subject. However, in Vienna we heard Dr. Ernest Marton, Rumanian delegate to the International Red Cross, who presented, I thought, a masterful analysis of two major problems before us—the movement of Jews across the borders and postwar anti-Semitism.

"It is inevitable that the Jewish people are in a great mass movement," he explained. "They return from the concentration camps only to begin a feverish search for their lost relatives. They travel to all parts of their country—and find nothing. Everyone has been killed. When they become convinced of this, a great crisis enters their lives.

Either they commit suicide or they flee. They cannot remain in places where once they were happy, but where now they can see in the faces of every neighbor the murderer of their families."

Analyzing anti-Semitism, which, he declared, was stronger today than at the height of Hitler's power, Dr. Marton listed as the first reason for this the anti-Semitic education that began in kindergarten. "The results of that education will continue for another generation or two.

"Second," he said, "we are hated because we returned from the dead. They thought of us as dead. They buried us. They were quite satisfied that there were no more Jews and no more Jewish problem. Our return was a painful surprise to them. They look upon us as ghosts, and no one loves ghosts. Even the politically liberal were unpleasantly surprised, because while they had sympathy for us, at the same time they recognized the advantages of our absence, because with our absence the Jewish problem was solved. Now we are returning, and, though in small numbers, with us return anti-Semitism and the entire overwhelming Jewish problem.

"Third, a large part of the population feels personally cheated by our return because they must give back the Jewish property they have taken. The Nazis saw to it that Jewish property was as widely distributed as possible so that the majority of Austrian people would have a stake in Nazism. Fourth, there is a collective feeling of guilt among these people, which makes them resent us. And fifth, the Jews who returned from the camps are nervous and distraught. They are difficult to live with."

"The Communist Party is reputedly anti-Zionist," Crossman observed. "Do you have anything to say about this?"

Dr. Marton replied that there was no official Soviet statement on Palestine, but it was his opinion that the Communists resented Zionism because they felt it siphoned off abilities among the Jews which might otherwise help to build the new social order.

"Because the economic and social grouping of the Jewish people in Europe is more unhealthy than ever before," Dr. Marton went on, "the percentage of Jews in nonproductive work is increasing. The returned men and women cannot return to economic life. They need an environment that can substitute for their loss of families and that will give them productive work. That is possible only in Palestine."

The picture was made still clearer for us at our lunch with General Clark. Long and lean, carrying out a delicate assignment at this juncture of French, British, Russian, and American interests, he was doing an effective job with a small force, and insisting upon the maintenance of American ideals and policy in the face of many great difficulties.

General Clark emphasized to us that the American policy was to keep the borders open at all costs. "We want to give the Jews trying to get out of Poland a chance to save their lives." This policy, originated by General Eisenhower, and strongly backed by President Truman, was carried out with great difficulty, I gathered, because of transportation troubles, absence of adequate food supplies, and opposition from British sources.

The British in Austria sought to compel the Jews to rehabilitate themselves in Poland. The British position was based on Bevin's assumption that it would mean Hitler had won the war if the Jews left Europe.

The military point of view on the camps and the desire of the American military to clear them out was most clearly put to us by Brigadier General Ralph H. Tate, General Clark's Chief of Staff.

"Gentlemen," he said tersely, "I wish you Godspeed in your labors. We need your help. For God's sake, help us! We are at the end of our rope."

We were guests of General Sir Richard McCreery, British commander in Austria, at his Schönbrunn Castle headquarters. I thought it instructive when one of my British colleagues on the committee, a Labourite, observed that he would like to see Otto living in Schönbrunn, which should again be a royal residence for the Hapsburgs. He confided that the British Foreign Office would like to see not only Otto on the throne of Austria, but also Juan back in Spain and Umberto in Italy, all ruling as constitutional monarchs on the British plan, thereby re-creating royalty in Europe. This from the British Labour Party!

Crossman and I were assigned to investigate the DP camps in the British Zone of Austria. We left late one night, accompanied by Dick's secretary, Miss Elizabeth White. In one town there was a wait until the British military escort recognized us. "We didn't expect Crossman, Crum, and Miss White! We thought the people coming were Rabbi Grossman, Rabbi Cohen, and Fräulein Weiss," an embarrassed British captain told me.

The same case of mistaken identity occurred when Judge Hutcheson and Sir John called upon Chancellor Figl and were greeted as "the distinguished representatives of Anglo-American Jewry." It was a shock to Sir John, who thought his Aryan cast of countenance unmistakable.

The camps in the British Zone of Austria were the most depressing I had seen. The inmates were in bad physical condition and living under far sterner military discipline than in the American Zone. The camp commander, a British officer, told us that the DPs would do no work around the camp. They were extremely hostile both to Crossman and to me. Living only a few miles from the Italian border, which was closed to them, they had been made almost desperate by their long detention. They were bitter, unwilling to talk of anything except Palestine.

One boy, about sixteen, turned on us almost savagely.

"Why did you come here to ask us questions, questions! Am I on trial? What have I done to the world to lose my parents and my entire family? What have I done except to be born a Jew?"

He seemed ready to break into tears.

"Don't ask me questions," he said bitterly; "ask the world!"

We drove on to Bari, where a plane waited to take us to Cairo. We had to cross the Austrian-Italian border at Udine, where the British had established an extremely effective patrol system, so thorough that we had difficulty getting across, although we were driving in a British military car.

We were put up in Bari at a hotel reserved for the British military. I sought to question some of the servants, some of whom were Jewish refugees, but their replies were noncommittal. Later I learned that they had been warned by British officials to make no complaint of any kind to any members of the Anglo-American Committee.

The fact was that many of the Jews who managed to get over the border and into Bari sailed surreptitiously for Palestine. I sympathized with those who managed to do this, for it was evident—to anyone who wanted to hear, to anyone who wanted to see—that no Jew, facing the bitter realities of his position, would dream of remaining in central and eastern Europe.

BOOK THREE

Arms and Intrigue

CHAPTER 9

Egypt: "Our Problem Is Britain"

IF MY EXPECTATION of Cairo was a city peopled with the Hollywood approximation of the romantic Arab sheik, luxurious and elegant in flowing robes, I was sadly mistaken. The glamorous preview of the Middle East given me in San Francisco in 1945 when the United Nations delegation of Arab princes blocked traffic as they glided in and out of the St. Francis Hotel was, I learned quickly enough, a far cry from the real thing. Actually, I was not able to see Cairo itself until nearly two days after the entire committee had reassembled. For, according to arrangements made by Beeley, we were taken to the Mena House, in the shadow of the Pyramids, some twelve miles from the city proper, and here we held our sessions in the same chamber in which Roosevelt, Churchill, and Chiang Kai-shek had met.

There were a large number of Egyptian police guards, colorful in their huge shakos, posted at the hotel. Every effort was made to impress us with the danger, the explosiveness, of the political situation. Here was the first foreshadowing of the situation in Palestine, and it was an atmosphere in which we felt not only guarded, but watched. The chief of the Egyptian police, a gigantic man, wearing a red fez, frowned when I suggested going into town. Antiforeign feeling was intense, he warned me. For many days, all American and British military forces were not permitted in town because the sight of a foreign uniform was sufficient to start angry murmuring among the crowd. The police official made it clear that this xenophobia had no relation to the Jews: privately, he said that the Egyptians wanted Great Britain out of Egypt, and this ferment had grown since the war's end, with demands that British troops leave. It would be far safer, he said, for me to remain at the Mena House.

But finally I went into Cairo. It was a revelation—and a long step forward in my education. Here, for the first time, I saw the Middle East stripped of the travel writer's star dust: I began to feel its tempo, to begin, in limited measure, to understand the world of Islam. Here the contrasts and the conflicts were most obvious.

The Mena House, with its cool, elegant rooms, its sunken swimming pool, its terraces, and its gardens, was no more characteristic of the real Egypt than was the Arab delegation in San Francisco. Here in this hot, sun-baked city I saw the street Arab in his native habitat and native dress—incredible numbers, wearing their long, single-piece, nightgownlike robes, representing a degree of poverty and a level of subsistence I had seen nowhere in the Western world. I walked through the market area, through the narrow, malodorous streets, wandered through the Mouski, the bazaar section, with its tiny crisscrossing alleys and byways, and out into the main thoroughfares of the city. Arab boys pulled at my elbow, whispered in my ear; street salesmen importuned me to buy everything from canes to questionable pictures; dragomans and guides clutched me by the arm and would not be shaken off: and everywhere streets, alleys, and cubbyholes swarmed with humanity. I took an ancient horse-drawn fiacre and was carried with a steady clatter of hoofs down cobblestoned streets. I saw Arabs sprawled sleeping in doorways and in the shadow of buildings, and Arab women crouched with their young, munching bread undisturbed while flies clustered in seething masses on the abscessed eyes of their infants, and I was sickened. I dismissed my fiacre and continued to walk and explore. I came upon the ornate Shepheard's Hotel, in whose high-pillared lobby Levantine intrigue had flourished for more than a century. I climbed the few steps leading to its terrace facing the street, took a wicker chair at one of the tables, and ordered Turkish coffee. About me sat the upper-class Cairenes, languidly brushing away the flies with horsehair switches; with their Western clothes, their red fezzes, their air of well-fed imperviousness, it was impossible not to sense their remoteness from the squalor about them. What, indeed, had these richly dressed men to do with the crouched women I had seen, with the scrawny, hurrying figures who filled the dirty streets of Cairo? I realized truly, as Wendell Willkie had pointed out, that what we know as the middle class in the United States and England scarcely exists in the Middle East. Here were the few wealthy, and the many poor, and scarcely anything between. Of Egypt's more than 17,000,000 people, 16,000,000 were peasants or fellahin: twentieth-century serfs whose poverty was taken for granted.

I do not know how Cairo affects others who see it for the first time. I found much of it noisy, intolerable, and oppressive, a city whose human degradation I could not put out of my mind, and in which I could not free myself from the impression that disease stalked me as I walked. We had been warned to eat nowhere but at the Mena

147

House and to drink no water but that served us at the hotel.

This was my introduction to the Middle East.

We had heard the Arab case presented in Washington and London; now we heard it more definitively here in Cairo, seat of the Arab League. The Arab spokesmen, headed by Azzam Pasha, the dynamic secretary-general of the League, came to the Mena House, where our conference room was jammed with witnesses and newspapermen. Some attempts were made by representatives of Egyptian student movements to see us, but apparently they were warned off by the Egyptian security.

I managed, however, to see several young Arabs, who spoke in behalf of the Wafdist or Egyptian Nationalist Party. One of their number saw me by entering the hotel in the company of three reporters and was not disturbed.

His name was Tewfik, and later I had an opportunity to hear what others like him had to say. He spoke French and English fluently and was most intelligent. His father was very rich, he said, with complete matter-of-factness, and owned half a dozen villages. We discussed Egypt's 80,000 Jews. He said a few, principally merchants, were quite wealthy and as Egyptian as any Egyptians. The great majority, however, were frightfully poor. Perhaps 20,000 of them in Cairo alone lived in poverty undistinguishable from that of the Arabs in the Mouski section. I gathered that he was impatient with me for bringing our discussion around to the Jews. The important thing, he said, was to get rid of the British. Insofar as the wealthy Jews were identified as part of the British "invasion," the Jews suffered.

"You see, there are other questions which interest us

more deeply than the Jewish question," he said. "Our freedom, and the Sudan, for example. We count Britain as our problem. We want her out of Egypt completely.

"The war is over, and there is no longer any military justification for British troops here. And she has exploited us long enough. Egypt is awakening. We young, educated Egyptians realize that the future of Egypt depends upon us. We want a greater Egypt, with the Sudan as an integral part of our country." Egypt's future, he and his friends explained to me, depended on the Sudan. "Egypt is fertile only a few miles on either side of the Nile and in the delta at the mouth of the Nile. The rest of Egypt is desert," Tewfik told me. "The Sudan is fertile; it has water: with it, Egypt becomes a power." He said that Britain and Egypt jointly ruled the Sudan as a condominium, but that ever since the assassination by Egyptians in 1924 of a British official, Sir Lee Stack, Sirdar (that is, commander of the army), the condominium rule had existed only on paper. Britain, he said, ruled the Sudan, and British concessionaires exploited it. "Our program," he said, "is clear. We want Egypt for the Egyptians and not for the British, nor for the French, nor—and I hope you will excuse my words, because I do not mean them offensively—nor for the Americans."

It was my impression, after speaking with Tewfik and the young intellectuals he represented, that they were unsure of themselves. During the war, they did not know whether to be pro-Nazi or pro-Ally. Democracy, as a term, confused them. In a land in which eighty-five per cent of the population is illiterate, in which a tiny group representing perhaps five per cent possesses nearly ninety-five per cent of the country's riches and rules with complete cynicism so far as responsibility to the people is concerned, democracy, with its emphasis upon power in the hands of the masses, is a frightening concept. I felt that Tewfik and his colleagues sought a return of the pre-Ferdinand-and-Isabella Arab culture, but expressed in modern terms. I felt that they recognized that if they were to pull Egypt from the morass in which she had lain for so many centuries, they must do away with the alliance between the five per cent who rule and the British economic concessionaires. Tewfik was aware of the tremendous problem involved in such a revolutionary program. His father belonged to that tiny, land-rich, ruling group. No common intellectual meeting ground existed between father and son. The son struggled to orient these dangerous, challenging thoughts and to see himself and his country in the perspective of his time.

Our discussion moved in circuitous paths, but it came back again to the cry of young Egypt: "We want a greater Egypt with the Sudan a part of Egypt. We want Egypt for the Egyptians, not for the British, nor the French, nor for anyone else."

This was worth considering. Here in Cairo was an indication from the Egyptians themselves that perhaps it was not the Jew that was the source of all evil in the eyes of the Arab world, but rather the Western world that was suspect. Azzam Pasha's words before the committee tended to bear this out, I thought. He did not object to Jews, as Jews, returning to Palestine; he objected, he said, to the fact that they returned to Palestine as Westerners in disguise.

"He has returned a Russified Jew, a Polish Jew, a German Jew, an English Jew," he said. "He has turned back with a totally different conception of things: he has turned back a Westerner and not an Easterner." The Jew returned without "the intention to be an Easterner." "Our old cousin" was coming back "with imperialistic ideas, with reactionary or revolutionary ideas of all sorts. . . ."

This was the basic theme of the Cairo hearings, for only the Arabs testified. Dr. Mohammed Fadel Jamali, director-general for the Iraqi Ministry of Foreign Affairs, prefaced his remarks by telling us that the Iraqi government saw no need "for any commissions to study the question of Palestine." He invited us to "come to Baghdad and see our Jewish population there and listen to their point of view."

Palestine, he suggested to us, actually belongs to Iraq because the coastline of Palestine "represents the seaport of Iraq." This was, I felt, the Polish Corridor approach to the Palestine problem and one which up to now we had not been called upon to consider. He bade us consider that "our petroleum pipe lines run from Iraq to Haifa." He concluded that Palestine was in essence the heart of the Arab world.

Here, for the first time, the name of the former Mufti appeared in our testimony. Hassan el Banna, described to us as a rabble-rouser and leader of the fanatical Moslem Brotherhood, demanded that the Mufti appear before us. The Brotherhood was characterized as a Fascist religious organization whose members are sworn to fight for Islam against the infidel West. A dark-bearded, heavy-set figure with glowing eyes, speaking Arabic in a spate of harsh gutturals, el Banna insisted that the Koran mentioned Christians and Moslems favorably, but had nothing good to say about the Jews, and that the religious bonds between the Jews and Palestine meant nothing because these bonds "were diametrically opposed by the Koran and Moslem practices."

151

As the roll call of witnesses continued, it was evident that their antipathy was toward Westernism: that was the encroachment they fought. Was this not perhaps the basic tragedy of the Middle East? Westernism meant higher standards of living; it meant reduction in infant mortality, in disease, in poverty; it meant opening the door to some measure of freedom and happiness to the forgotten men and women of this area of the world. It was this, precisely, to which our witnesses objected. Most tragic of all, as long as they remained representatives of a feudal aristocracy which draws its power from its privileged position, supported by the toil of the Arab masses, they had to object. I felt that even on the highest intellectual levels here there was no confidence in democratic processes, and, I am afraid, little understanding of them.

Walking about Cairo later, immersing myself in its fluid, nervous life, I thought much about this. I felt there could be no real conflict between the deepest aspirations of the Jew, as expressed in Palestine, and those of the Arab peoples. The Jewish ideal based upon the philosophy of the European West seeks a way of life in which man achieves dignity and a measure of fulfillment of his deepest needs. Westernism is not an evil. The common man of Egypt was pleading for help. A chance for a decent life as free as possible from squalor, disease, corruption, exploitation; the "life, liberty, and the pursuit of happiness," which we hold as the inalienable rights of every man—surely these Western ideals are not evils.

If the Arab leaders were truly concerned with the poverty and disease which condemns their people to constant misery, would not their first concern be to feed their populations, to eradicate illiteracy, and to raise the standard of living by developing the great latent resources of their lands? Syria and Iraq were half empty. Iraq had only a fraction of its cultivable land worked. It seemed to me it would be the mark of wisdom for the Arab leaders to devote themselves to such causes—which would give them genuine power—and at the same time welcome the Jews for the economic good they would bring and the "know-how" they would furnish.

At no time, however, did the witnesses in Cairo speak in terms of the masses and their improvement. One felt their ever-present sense of fatalism. A child born crippled limps through life; a child made blind by trachoma is a victim of Allah's will, not man's. And who was to say that Allah chose wrongly in singling out this child?

In this gateway to the Middle East, I realized I had plunged back through the centuries to an almost unbelievable way of life. I did not blame the Arabs for it: they were the products of a cruel physical environment where nature sapped strength and vitality. They were the products of a political and social environment which only compounded their helplessness. For four centuries under Turkish rule they had been subject to every pressure of ignorance. Human welfare had no part in the Ottoman Empire. It was truly pointed out to us that as far as the Middle East was concerned, the French and American Revolutions might never have taken place. The doctrine of human rights and personal liberty—the concept that man had dignity as a human being and the latent power to lift himself from the mire of animal existence—had not penetrated the citadels of Islamic authoritarianism. Why had this entire area, only one day by plane from London and two from New York, simply dropped out of existence as far as modern man was concerned?

There was little help to be had on this question from

our witnesses. There appeared to be no effort by them to view the problem in its wider phases. Palestine, they insisted, was a poor land, would always be a poor land, and was already congested. In any event, they did not wish to have skyscrapers in Palestine. Some of those who testified came from countries 1000 miles from Palestine, but they did not hesitate to assert their right to determine the future of Palestine. "We Arabs don't want to live as Americans live in New York or Chicago," said Dr. Jamali, in whose native Iraq, I learned, man's average life span is thirty years, ninety-five per cent of the population cannot read or write, and one out of every two children born dies before the age of five. His Eminence Saied Ahmed Morad el Bakri, Grand Chief of the Sufi sects, imposing in his spotless white turban, refused to discuss the subject. "We reject uncompromisingly all Zionist demands in Palestine made on historic, geographical, legal, national, and humanitarian grounds," he declared. He declined to answer questions or expand upon his stand. Mohammed Zaki Aly Pasha, of the Young Men's Arab Association, informed us that the Jews were working a hardship on the Arabs in Palestine because "the Jews of Palestine are young men and women and the Arabs are old people, so that the reproduction of the Zionist party will be greater than that of the Arab party." Maître Habib Bourkeiba, who introduced himself as "leader of the anti-French ultranationalist party," of Tunisia, speaking in behalf "of the Tunisians, the Algerians, the Moroccans, and the Cyrenaicans," suggested, "Keep the persecuted Jews of Europe where they are now and induce those who persecute them to perhaps reform and change themselves."

If there was any real desire on the part of the Arab leaders to come to grips with our problem, I could not discover it. They evaded the question. Their basic interest seemed to be the preservation of the *status quo*. I remembered Wendell Willkie's observation that he had found the wealthy landowners "largely uninterested in any political movement except as it affected the perpetuation of their own status." In that desire, I concluded reluctantly, they were joined by the British Colonial Office and its staff throughout the Middle East.

In Washington, Einstein had pointed out that the English had two interests: raw materials for industry, and oil. Large landowners, he said, found themselves in a precarious situation because "they fear they will be gotten rid of. The British are always in a passive alliance with those land-possessing owners." People who are ruled, he pointed out, will accept rule as long as they are depressed by illiteracy and poverty and know no better; but as soon as they realize that serfdom is not preordained, they begin to resist the bondage placed upon them by "those land-possessing owners." Neither rulers nor landlords wish this, for it means the end of their privileged status: thus the "passive alliance" cited by Einstein.

When the Arab leaders were pressed on specific matters, as, for example, by Crick, our economist, as to why they were boycotting Zionist goods, and how they would distinguish between "pure assistance and capital and tainted assistance and capital" (they had declared that they wanted no help from "imperialist, Bolshevist, or Zionist sources"), four began to speak at once and, after disputing with one another, rose in a body and refused to answer any further questions.

In Cairo I reread those parts of *One World* dealing with the Middle East. "The great mass of the people, outside of the roaming tribes, are impoverished, own no property, are hideously ruled by the practices of ancient priestcraft, and are living in conditions of squalor." Because Wendell Willkie had written that truth, evident to anyone who has eyes to see, I found his memory not always popular with the Arab leaders. But the younger intellectuals remembered him with fondness and respect; he had been courageous enough to lift the curtain and show the Middle East as it was.

He had written of the undercurrents he had found among these students, among the newspapermen and the rising generation of Arab intelligentsia, such as the young Arabs who had visited me. "The veil, the fez, the sickness, the filth, the lack of education, modern industrial development, the arbitrariness of government," he wrote, "all commingled in their minds to represent a past imposed upon them by a combination in their own society and the self-interest of foreign domination." And it became plain to me that the Arab leaders, aware of this growing ferment among the new generation, had been wily enough to attempt to identify Zionism in the minds of this seeking generation as the "foreign domination" which would exploit them and keep them submerged—whereas actually Zionism was probably the only force within sight which would help to release them. This was the crime against the Jewish people, compounded by the Arab leaders and the British Colonial Office: this was the "passive alliance" —now no longer so passive—which Einstein had so unerringly pointed out.

Cairo was the only capital in which no Jews appeared to testify before us. I looked into this matter and was told that the Sunday preceding our arrival in Cairo, King Farouk had summoned the Chief Rabbi of Egypt and Cattawi Pasha, one of the wealthiest Jews, to an audience.

The King saw each separately. He had long conversations with each, ranging over many subjects, but at no time did His Majesty speak of Palestine or of our committee. Both the Chief Rabbi and Cattawi Pasha understood this to mean that the King preferred them not to appear before us, a fact to be deduced from His Majesty's silence on the subject.

One reason for this, I was informed, was the probability that if they testified they could not avoid discussing the mob attacks on Jews in Cairo and Alexandria which had occurred only a few months before. This might prove most embarrassing to His Majesty, and certainly to the Arab claim that Oriental Jews had no need of a Jewish state to protect them because they were sufficiently protected by Arab democracy.

I learned also that Cattawi Pasha and Cairo Zionists had agreed that if one would not appear, neither would the other. The American Legation, however, arranged a cocktail party for several members of the committee. Cattawi was present and he used the occasion to deliver an attack on the Zionists. I was told that Cattawi represented a small anti-Zionist group among Egyptian Jewry; if I wished to understand how the Jewish masses felt in Cairo, I must remember that when the two Palestinian youths who assassinated Lord Moyne were hanged, a twenty-four-hour self-imposed fast was observed in the poor Jewish quarters.

Cattawi's point of view was that Jews in the Arab states would be endangered if Jews achieved their political aspirations in Palestine. The Egyptian Zionists argued that an anti-Zionist solution by us would prove disastrous for Oriental Jews, because it would prove to the Arabs that the Jews were weak and had no support. In the Moslem world, the weak invariably suffer at the hands of the strong. My reaction was that whatever the ultimate solution, Britain must guarantee that the position of these Jewish communities would be safeguarded.

Before our departure we held an *in camera* session with the British High Command, Middle East. One of the officers revealed to us a "Jewish conspiracy" which, he said, unfortunately included the use of U. S. Army planes. As he understood it, an American plane had flown to Palestine at the request of General Eisenhower: the purpose was to lay the foundation for the air transport of Jewish DPs to Palestine!

This story was finally straightened out, and I thought it an amusing illustration of how far wrong a person can become if he begins looking under the bed. What had happened was that Judge Rifkind and his assistant, Captain Eno, had flown from Palestine in a U. S. military plane furnished by General Eisenhower, but only to determine the truth of claims made by the Jewish Agency that it was prepared to find food, housing, and employment for 100,000 new immigrants.

We left that night by train for Palestine and Jerusalem, six hundred miles away.

CHAPTER 10

Palestine

DURING THE TRAIN'S interminable pauses in Egypt, I had had my fill of its desert scenes—the mud hovels; the faceless children, for so they appeared, wrapped up in the same nondescript robes as their parents; the slow, painful, miserable existence. But once in Palestine, the tempo and color of life changed sharply. Things seemed to quicken, to become more alive; children suddenly were no longer tiny bundles of rags, but youngsters, wearing shorts, with sturdy arms and legs and open smiling faces and bright eyes—alert and human again. The Egyptians shielded themselves as much as they could from the sun; the Jews, as though reveling in it after the drab ghetto years, seemed unable to soak in enough of it. After the vast expanse of desert and mud flats, it was a treat to see man's order upon the earth again: green fields, regularly plowed, brown trees, and green foliage. That was my first impression of the Holy Land.

The train which brought us from Cairo labors for sixteen hours to cover the six hundred miles between Cairo and Jerusalem. But in that sixteen hours, it spans two worlds. We boarded the train at dusk, and from my compartment window I could see the garish lights of Cairo, the flickering yellow, blue, and red neon lights which endlessly dazzle one's eyes. With morning our train made its first stop in Palestine, at Gaza. Here, amid the Philistines, the blinded Samson had pulled the Temple down about his shoulders. I looked about me curiously. The day was clear, the sun warm. The country looked much as the country between San Francisco and Los Angeles. The Arabs in the countryside seemed better dressed than in Egypt; their headdress was different and neater; and the Arab women, instead of being covered with black robes, wore bright peasant blouses with colorful embroidered designs. But many still had their upper lips tattooed blue. For the first time, too, I became conscious of the British military. Barracks built of corrugated iron stood near the station, and hundreds of Tommies were about.

From Gaza to Jerusalem the train chugged slowly, climbing from the shores of the Mediterranean to the Holy City on the hills 2500 feet above sea level. Again the terrain reminded me of California—the quick change from the sea to the mountains, from fruitful rolling hill country to the stony, ravaged Judean hills.

Looking at a map, I noted that on the first part of our trip through Palestine our train had taken us through a "Zone B." Under the White Paper of 1939, this is an arbitrarily mapped-off portion of Palestine where Palestine Arabs are permitted to sell land only to other Palestine Arabs.

When, finally, we arrived about noon in Jerusalem, we found armed guards everywhere. Curious spectators were kept at a distance as we got into waiting limousines and were driven with armed escort to the King David Hotel, which was to be our residence in Palestine. It was immediately apparent that Jerusalem, at least, was an armed camp, for barbed wire in great coils was everywhere, tanks could be seen at various intersections, special pill boxes had been put above the entrance of the hotel, and on the roofs and on the lawn of the imposing YMCA building across the street, soldiers manning machine guns surveyed all avenues of approach.

Nevertheless, I saw Jews and Arabs strolling along the streets together, and Jewish and Arab shops side by side. Apparently impervious to this armored menace, mothers were calmly wheeling their babies in modern white perambulators.

After Cairo, Jerusalem surprised me with its modernity, until I learned there were in reality two Jerusalems— ancient Jerusalem, the old walled city, perhaps a mile square of history, and modern Jerusalem, which surrounds it. Modern Jerusalem, with majestic buildings built of rugged blocks of buff-tinted stone, lay basking rose and golden in the sun.

If the atmosphere of intrigue and surveillance had been evident in London and Cairo, here it literally shouted at one. Our first morning in Jerusalem, we were informed by the British that they had tapped our telephones so that all our conversations were overheard. By this method they hoped to uncover any terrorists seeking to reach us surreptitiously. Agents of the Criminal Investigation Department of the Palestine Police—the CID, or British FBI— were assigned to each of us. We were warned not to venture outside the hotel without our bodyguard. These young men spent most of their time in the lobby, scrutinizing incoming and outgoing visitors and making detailed reports on everyone we saw. I determined at once that the only sensible course was for me to see everyone openly and not attempt any secret rendezvous. When we toured Palestine, later, we were preceded by armored cars and sometimes by tanks searching out land mines. Our rooms were spacious, and the entire second floor of the hotel was given over to us. The British Military Headquarters for Palestine occupied the entire third and fourth floors. A twenty-four-hour armed guard, with a submachine gun on the table before him, commanded both elevator and stair entrances. All visitors had to register with him, giving their names, the purposes of their visit, and whom they saw. They were checked in and out by time.

All this was, in a way, exciting. But, as I soon learned, at that time it was quite superfluous. We were not in danger. No one had reason to harm us: we had not yet arrived at our conclusion. And the voice of the Jewish underground, the *Kol Israel*, made several broadcasts assuring us that the committee members were perfectly safe and that no incidents of extremism would take place while the committee was in Palestine. That word was kept.

Nevertheless, British and Palestine government officials took us to one side and warned us that we were in constant danger. Their protective precautions soon became annoying, but the very absurdity of their measures made any protest seem equally absurd. Even our stenographers and typists were escorted to dinners and tea in armed cars, with a CID agent seated protectively beside them. Newspaper correspondents assigned to the hearings were obliged to call for a new press card each morning at the Palestine Government Information Office, lest—as it was explained to them—they be kidnaped at night, their press card stolen and used the following morning by a terrorist to gain entrance to the hearings, where, presumably, he would assassinate one of us. Everyone entering the hearings was searched for weapons; women's handbags were opened, and guards stood at the windows to prevent the curious from peering inside.

The press, I know, was both annoyed and amused by these tactics, and on one occasion took revenge. A photographer appeared with both arms laden with equipment, and his pockets bulging.

"What's in your pockets?" the guard demanded.

"Flash bulbs," the photographer said.

The guard thrust his hands into the bulging pocket and brought them out dripping with rotten eggs.

As for us on the committee, if these measures were designed to impress us with the British view that the Jewish resistance was an unreasoning gangster movement dedicated to blind violence for violence's sake, I am afraid they did not succeed. We could have been murdered a score of times with the greatest of ease, had there been the slightest desire to do so. Proof of this has since been evinced by the tragic bombing of the King David Hotel. Had the extremists wished to act then against us, they would have done so, and I am sure that all the cloak-and-dagger precautions would have been of little avail. Nonetheless, every effort was made to impress upon us that we had come to a land on the brink of civil war between Jew and Arab: to convince us that the tenseness lay between Arab and Jew rather than between Jew and British; that Jewish nationalism was rampant and the Arabs in immediate danger of having their collective throat cut.

After two days in Jerusalem I felt like a character in a Hollywood mystery film. We maintained offices in the near-by YMCA, but the lobby, bar, and dining room of the King David Hotel became our unofficial headquarters. Here we found ourselves in the center of an extraordinary social-political ferment. Every special pleader in the Middle East was on hand, and here Levantine intrigue flourished unashamed. Jews and Arabs, Syrians and Lebanese, Assyrians and Armenians, American oil men and British agents, correspondents from Moscow, Sydney, and New York—all rubbed elbows at the King David bar, where, appropriately enough, a Swiss bartender presided. Every influence was brought to bear upon us. In the course of one afternoon, seated at a table in the bar, I found myself drinking cocktails with an Arab journalist and member of one of the best-known Arab families, who proceeded to tell me of the deep hostility between the Nashashibi family in Palestine and the Husseinis, of whom the former Mufti is head. He would depart and his place would be taken by Harry Beilin, the Jewish Agency liaison officer, who would relate another yet unpublished story of bravery behind Nazi lines by *Haganah* parachuters recruited by the British. Beilin would leave, and I would find myself tête-à-tête with a toothy French correspondent whose secret explanation for anti-Semitism was that all Jews were circumcised and all Christians were not. I spoke with Arabs of every political persuasion ranging from Fascist-clerical to Communist, and with Jews of every political color ranging from Revisionists—those who insisted on a Jewish state in all Palestine, on both sides of the Jordan River, including Trans-Jordan as well—to Bi-Nationalists, who wanted both Jews and Arabs to have equal political control of a binational Palestine.

I was delighted to renew acquaintances again with John Savage and John B. Hays, the American engineers who had prepared the material for us on the Jordan Valley Authority and whom we had heard in Washington. Savage had designed the Grand Coulee and Boulder Dams and had a remarkable grasp of the engineering possibilities in Palestine. It was instructive to meet Katie Antonius, widow of George Antonius, author of *The Arab Awakening*, who had been the outstanding interpreter of Islam to the Western world. I lunched with Mrs. Antonius in the residence of the Mufti, where she was then living—at that time he was still in France—and learned that she had two great obsessions: Communism and Zionism. Germany, she felt, had been wronged. She did not conceal her sympathy with the German cause. It was obvious that she, like so many other intellectuals of the Middle East, had little faith in the democratic processes. Easterners had been brought up to distrust the masses and they had no faith in the common man. The Mufti, she said, was misunderstood and would yet prove himself a great leader. When I met her, she was busy grooming Albert Hourani, a brilliant young Syrian who later testified before us, to succeed her husband as an Arab spokesman. Hourani had been born in Manchester, England, and educated at Oxford, where, by an interesting coincidence, he had once been a student of Dick Crossman.

I met Gershon Agronsky, editor of *The Palestine Post*, one of the best four-page English-language dailies in the world. A one-time Philadelphia newspaperman who had fought in the Jewish Legion which helped General Allenby liberate Palestine from the Turks, Agronsky not only was a fount of information, but opened his newspaper files to me for as much research as I wished to do on the Palestine question. I found that he had a deep sense of his responsibility and insisted that all sides of political controversy be presented in his newspaper. Although an ardent Zionist himself, he gave full coverage to the Arab position. In my opinion, *The Palestine Post* furnished an example which the British press, both in London and in Cairo, might well have taken. It maintained objectivity even when the *Post* was banned in Syria and Lebanon as a "Zionist product"; and this despite the fact that, though the British proclaimed there was no outgoing censorship in Palestine, Agronsky was forced to submit every story and editorial to the government censor for approval before publication.

At his book-lined home in Jerusalem, presided over by Mrs. Agronsky, who had been born in Baltimore, I met the leading figures of the Jewish community. To Agronsky's "Friday Nights" came members of the Palestine Orchestra, described by Toscanini as one of the great symphony orchestras of the world; scientists and scholars from the Hebrew University and Hadassah Hospital; actors of the Habima, the internationally known Hebrew theater of Tel Aviv; composers and poets, British military leaders and visiting novelists. It was an intellectual and social crossroads of the world. Whether in New York, or San Francisco, or Jerusalem, the problems of existence, the goals of living, the aspirations of men, were the same. Surely, I felt, some way must be found to preserve and strengthen this civilized corner of the world, and to accomplish this with justice for everyone concerned.

Our hearings were held in the lecture hall of Jerusalem's magnificent YMCA, one of the show places of modern Palestine. Complete to classrooms, music rooms, library, cafeteria, tearoom, gymnasium, swimming pool, and boasting a modern campanile and tower observation gallery from which one saw all Jerusalem, it had been built at a cost exceeding $1,000,000. The money had been donated by an American who considered this an investment in interreligious faith. He had hoped this center of Christianity in the birthplace of Christianity would serve to bring together Christian, Moslem, and Jew. It was saddening for me to learn that this institution had, instead, become a center of Arab nationalism and that Jews were rarely to be found there.

Before we began, we discussed again the problem of how to cover the greatest area of investigation in the time allotted to us. The need to complete our work in 120 days was ever present in our minds. It was decided that in order to obtain a more comprehensive understanding of the situation in and about Palestine, we would break up our hearings in Jerusalem by a week of subcommittee investigations. Sir John, Manningham-Buller, and Buxton would pay a four-day visit to Iraq and Saudi Arabia, holding hearings in Baghdad and Riyadh; at the same time Judge Hutcheson, Lord Morrison, and Dr. McDonald would visit Syria and Lebanon and hold hearings in Damascus and Beirut. We six who remained would make as exhaustive a study of Palestine, by visiting and traveling about the country, as time would permit.

This settled, we opened our Jerusalem hearings in the lecture hall while British soldiers with tommy guns guarded the entrances and exits, and the streets outside were patrolled by armed tanks.

CHAPTER 11

Jerusalem: "Gentlemen, We Warned You!"

DR. CHAIM WEIZMANN was our first witness, speaking as President of both the Jewish Agency for Palestine and the World Zionist Organization. All morning was devoted to hearing the aged leader of World Zionism tell his story. As he spoke, seated a few feet to the left behind him sat Jaamal Effendi Husseini, nephew of the ex-Mufti, who had only recently returned to Palestine after having been interned during the war because of anti-British activities in Iraq, and Auni Bey Abdul Hadi, a prominent Palestine Arab leader. Dr. Weizmann spoke in a low voice, slowly, once more pleading an ancient cause before the bar of history. It was an impressive occasion, and I am sure that all of us were aware of its importance. Newsreel cameras ground, and outside the tanks and police patrols toured the streets. We sat about a huge, semicircular mahogany table, the same, I learned, that had been used by the Peel Royal Commission which had preceded us in an exhaustive study of this problem in 1938. I wondered what must be going through Dr. Weizmann's mind as he sat before us. Seven years before he had sat before this very same table, pleading the same cause. Only the faces before him are changed. These are twelve new men he sees before him, twelve strangers who have come only lately upon this

168

problem with which his entire life has been concerned. Before, when he spoke, arguing the case for his people, there were more than seven million Jews alive in Europe. Now, as he spoke, there were little more than one million surviving. His bitterest prophecies had come true.

He spoke of world Jewry. He spoke of anti-Semitism. He sat in his chair, leaning forward a little, his notes before him:

"Why is there anti-Semitism?" he asked. "One of its fundamental causes is that the Jews exist. The growth of anti-Semitism is proportionate to the number of Jews per square kilometer. We carry the germs of anti-Semitism in our knapsack on our backs.

"Here is a people who have lost all the attributes of a nation, but still have maintained their existence as a ghost nation, stalking the arena of history—maintained it for thousands of years. It is our belief in a mystical force, our conviction of a return to the land of Israel, which has kept us alive."

He spoke of the tragedy that was Europe.

"We warned you, gentlemen," he said. "We warned you. We told you that the first flames that licked at the synagogues of Berlin would set fire in time to all the world." He pounded his fist soundlessly on the table. "My brain reels when I think of the six million Jews who were killed off in such a short time, and nothing has been done to prevent a repetition. . . . We are an ancient people. We have contributed to the world. We have suffered. We have a right to live—a right to survive under normal conditions. We are as good as anyone else, and as bad as anyone else.

"I stand before young Jews today as a leader who failed to achieve anything by peaceful means. Despite all promises by British and American statesmen and leaders, despite the fact that the new British government is committed up to its neck to the Jewish people, Jews are able to enter Palestine only as illegal immigrants and have no freedom of movement in the land."

He paused. "I ask you to follow the course of least injustice in determining the fate of Palestine. European Jewry cannot be expected to resettle on soil drenched with Jewish blood. Their only hope for survival lies in the creation of a Jewish state in Palestine. The leaky boats in which our refugees come to Palestine are their *Mayflowers*, the *Mayflowers* of a whole generation."

The Jews did not want the trappings of statehood, he went on. "We want to be able to exploit all possibilities of development of this country to the utmost advantage of all inhabitants. This can be done only if we have state powers. Then the present population of Palestine can be doubled and even trebled without displacing a single one of the present inhabitants.

"In the future Jewish state Arabs would have complete freedom of culture and language. The Jews have no desire to dominate the Arabs. At best, the Jewish state will be an island in an Arab sea."

On the other hand, he observed, while he did not want to charge the Arabs with illiterate anti-Semitism, in view of what the Arab leaders said in the heat of polemic, and the pogroms in Baghdad, Tripoli, and Cairo, Jews without a state might become hostages of the Arab majority, as they were once hostages of the Nazis in Europe.

He said that he wanted peace with the Arabs. "I stand ready at any time, any day, any moment, to meet with them and discuss the future of the country," he declared.

Judge Hutcheson toyed with a pencil. The question which had echoed in Washington and in London sounded in Jerusalem. "Dr. Weizmann, can you explain to me how the establishment of a Jewish state would eliminate anti-Semitism?"

"Sir," said Dr. Weizmann, "we appear to the gentiles to be a peculiar people, suspended between heaven and earth. We must explain ourselves, and every person who does that is condemned in advance." By having a Jewish state, Jews could be settled in a country where they would lead a normal life and where they would make their contribution to the common stock.

"Are you suggesting that Europe as a home for Jews is really finished?" Crossman asked.

Dr. Weizmann slowly nodded.

"Don't you think that means that although Hitler lost the military war he won the ideological war?"

"Hitler may have lost the war," Dr. Weizmann said, "but as far as the Jews are concerned, he won a complete victory."

"But if the Jews left Europe, would it not be an admission that democracy is through in Europe?"

"It would be an admission that Europeans are sick, and it will take a long time to get rid of the sickness," Weizmann said. "The presence of Jews in Europe today might exaggerate the sickness."

The question before us, I thought, as Dr. Weizmann, his testimony finished, rose and bowed to us, each in turn, and left the stand, touched not only upon international politics: it touched upon international morality, upon the meaning of democracy—and, even more fundamentally, on the meaning and scope of Christianity.

There was a recess. The doors opened, and the reporters rushed out to file their stories. They had not been able to leave the room during the entire morning, for the guards refused to open the doors under any conditions. Outside, the YMCA veranda was crowded with spectators. The bright sun dazzled our eyes as we hurried across St. Julian's Way and into the King David Hotel for lunch. And because this was Palestine, even the dining room was a political center and members of the committee took the opportunity to dine with leaders of the community—British, Jewish, and Arab. There was a constant, ceaseless, and uninhibited exchange of opinion.

The next Jewish witness who appeared was David Ben Gurion, chairman of the Executive of the Jewish Agency. Stockily built, with a halo of white hair, a determined jaw set as in stone, with piercing blue eyes under heavy white shaggy brows, he was an extremely forceful personality. Deeply respected as a pioneer who came to work on the soil of Palestine, Ben Gurion arrived there as a youth of seventeen from his native Poland. Later, he served in World War I under General Allenby in the 40th Battalion of the Royal Fusiliers, a part of the Jewish Legion, which was composed of units of American, British, and Palestinian Jewish volunteers, and which helped liberate Palestine from the Turks. He has remained in Palestine since.

As so many others before him had been asked, he was asked to give us his interpretation of the words "Jewish state."

"We mean simply Jewish independence," he said. "And when we say 'Jewish independence,' we mean Jewish soil, labor, agriculture, industry. We mean Jewish language, schools, culture. We mean Jewish safety and security—complete independence as for any other free people. We need a Jewish state in order to make the Jewish National Home a reality."

To those who said that the Jews had only a "mystical attachment to Zion, and not to this physical Zion," Ben Gurion said, "You have seen here 600,000 living human beings who have been brought here by the love of Zion. They are attached to the living Zion, although it has for them a great and deep spiritual significance as well."

Manningham-Buller wanted to know what assurance an Arab minority in a Jewish state would have that it would not be oppressed by the Jewish majority.

It would not be a real minority, Ben Gurion replied, because the Arabs "would have in the neighboring Arab states such support that they could not be oppressed, even were one to grant that the Jews wished to oppress them. They would be surrounded by Arabs and even have a preferred position. That could never be the case with a Jewish minority."

Again, he said, the question here was a matter of justice—the greater justice.

At the conclusion of his long presentation, Crossman said:

"I take it, Mr. Ben Gurion, that you belong to the left wing or revolutionary philosophy of Zionism."

Ben Gurion observed, "Sir, everything depends upon how you define revolutionary philosophy."

Crossman nodded. "Well, do you feel that a position has now been reached where, when a human being comes to absolute despair, he takes to violence? Is it your feeling now that that point has been reached?"

Ben Gurion smiled. "Now I am afraid I know your definition of revolutionary is violence. I am against violence."

173

Crossman pursued this question, finally restating it: "Do you feel that the point has now been reached where the free human being owing to the weakness of the Administration has the right and the need to take up arms?"

"I cannot answer that," said Ben Gurion. "It depends upon what you will do: whether this policy, which was condemned by the moral conscience of the civilized world, will continue. I hope it will not. I know something about the British people. I know something about the movement which brought the present government to power in Great Britain, and I cannot conceive that this policy will continue. That is my hope."

Jaamal Husseini appeared first for the Arab case. He had listened carefully to what Dr. Weizmann and Ben Gurion had said, now silent, now whispering to Auni Bey beside him, now smiling, now shaking his head in disagreement.

Now, as the two Arab leaders appeared before us, the room was more heavily guarded than usual. The press was put through an even more rigid search for bombs and weapons. We knew something of these two men—two of the principal Arab leaders in the Middle East. From information furnished us, we knew that both were representatives of the self-designated Arab Higher Committee. Neither possessed authority from the masses of the Palestine Arabs, and, as it was pointed out later, the young Arab intellectuals I had met at the King David were conspicuously absent.

Because of my prior knowledge of the Mufti's activities in Germany, I was, of course, particularly interested in meeting his nephew. Jaamal had been in open rebellion against the British authorities during the war. At one time he had a price on his head.

Making it clear that he recognized neither the Balfour Declaration nor the League of Nations Mandate for Palestine by which Great Britain became trustee for Palestine, Jaamal declared that we had no right to arbitrate or decide any questions "relating to the Arabs' natural rights in their own country." These rights could not be argued, he said.

"Moreover," he went on, "we find ourselves in this inquiry deprived of the presence of our first leader, the Grand Mufti, for whom we can accept no substitute."

I had not quite expected to see the Mufti's name injected so soon. When Hassan el Banna in Cairo publicly supported the Mufti, it was excused on the ground that el Banna was irresponsible. I was rather surprised that Jaamal and the Arab Higher Committee chose to stand publicly in support of one of Hitler's arch-collaborators.

He pictured the Arab world in contrast to bickering, heterogeneous Europe as a mighty expanse extending from the Atlas Mountains to the Nile, from the Nile to the Euphrates and the Tigris and the confines of Persia, and from the borders of Turkey to the Indian Ocean. "One nation, one people, who speak one single language, who have a historic background and who have one future, one aspiration, one aim in the world—such are the Arabs."

The British had made conflicting promises to both Arabs and Jews, he asserted, and the promises to the Arabs of Palestine had not been carried out. He cited four basic demands by the Arabs of Palestine: recognition of the right to complete independence; abandonment of the attempt to establish a Jewish National Home; abrogation of the British Mandate for Palestine; immediate ending of all Jewish immigration and of sales of land.

Sir John asked him:

"Is it your wish that the British forces and police should be withdrawn from Palestine forthwith?"

Jaamal nodded.

"Have you considered what would happen the day following?" asked Sir John. "Quite clearly, bloodshed."

Jaamal demurred. "I don't think so," he said. "If these pampered children, these spoilt children of the British government, the Zionists, know for once that they are no more to be pampered and spoilt, then we will be friends probably."

If, however, the British troops were withdrawn, and there were a war . . ., pursued Sir John.

"Well, let it be, I say," exclaimed Jaamal. "It has happened all over the world that people have solved their difficulties by their fists."

"So you want us away and you want the British Army and the British police away and to leave you and the Jews together?"

"That is the best policy," said Jaamal. "If they can do it."

"Then you would not allow any more immigration?" asked Sir John.

Jaamal agreed.

"What would you do about those who are in already?"

"Well, sir," said Jaamal, "supposing you withdrew just now, I suppose that at least thirty per cent of the Jews who have been brought into Palestine under the impression that they were going to build a Jewish state here will leave of their own free choice."

During this exchange, the audience was a study of pantomime, the Arabs nodding in agreement, the Jews vigorously indicating their disagreement with Jaamal's analysis.

"Suppose you are wrong," said Sir John. "Suppose there should be bloodshed. What would the world say if the British government failed in its duty under the mandate and left the Jews and the Arabs to fight it out?"

Jaamal replied, "If the people of the world were reasonable they would say, 'Here the British government and the American government have created a problem which they cannot solve,' and finding that the two parties are willing to solve it by force because there is no other solution, why not?"

"You don't think the trouble might extend further afield?"

"No," said Jaamal. "The Jews of this country will not be fighting, but they then, with a good heart, will extend a hand to the Arabs, and the Arabs will stretch their hands, no, their arms, and embrace them. That is what you will see."

Since Jaamal had introduced the name of the Mufti, I decided to go into the subject. I asked Jaamal: "Is the Grand Mufti regarded as the present leader of the Arab Higher Committee?"

He replied that the Mufti was "potentially" the leader of the Arab Higher Committee; he added that if the Arabs were to give the Arab Higher Committee a mandate, it would become the provisional government of an Arab state. In other words, if Palestine were established as an Arab state, the Mufti might well become head of it.

"What, under your concept of an Arab state, would be the position of the Jews here now?" I asked.

"The Jews will have the same privileges and the same rights as the Arabs, and they will live with the Arabs in Palestine as the Jews in Iraq or in Egypt are now living."

"Do they have the same privileges and position in all

other Arab countries as they have, say, in the United States?"

"Oh, yes, they do, sir," said Jaamal. "In all democratic Arab countries they have. We can't say, for instance, that Yemen is a democratic country, but we can say that Egypt and Mesopotamia and Syria and Lebanon are democratic countries and the Jews are living there on the same basis as all other inhabitants."

"What guarantees would the Arab state you envisage give to the Jews by way of protection?"

"They have all sorts of guarantees in the constitution," Jaamal said.

"They had them, did they not, in many other constitutions in Europe?" I asked.

Jaamal spread his hands. "That is the most that we can give. What did you give the Jews in America excepting to say in your constitution that all Americans are on the same level in the eyes of the law?"

"We think we practice what we preach," I said.

"We have before the Balfour Declaration exactly practiced what we preached," rejoined Jaamal.

Crossman proceeded to question him.

"I take it that you are a supporter of the principles of democracy, and I take it that you equally dislike Fascism and dictatorships and all that that pertains to," he observed. "Now, you say the Arabs find themselves deprived of the presence of their leader, the Grand Mufti. I take it that means that you on the Arab Higher Committee would rate the Grand Mufti the outstanding man of the Palestinian Arabs in their democratic philosophy?"

"Yes, sir," said Jaamal firmly.

"Has your committee's confidence in the Grand Mufti

either strengthened or weakened during the last five years?" asked Crossman.

Jaamal said, "I think it has remained the same."

"You feel that during the last five years the Grand Mufti's whole policy and activity have been a struggle for democracy?"

There was suppressed laughter, and Sir John rapped for order.

"Well, sir," said Jaamal, "the mandatory government chased him from one place to another, until he had no place to go to except Germany."

"You feel that all he did during the war was not collaboration with the Germans?" demanded Crossman.

"Well, sir," said Jaamal, "you know that when you're in the hands of the Germans during the war you can't act totally according to your wish."

"Some people did and died for it," said Crossman.

The Mufti only wanted the interests of the Arabs served, Jaamal explained, and thought that if Germany won, Germany would serve the Arabs' interests. Generally, he admitted, the Arabs were "spiritually neutral in the war." He added, "Anyway, the Mufti didn't work for the victory of the Germans. He was only seeking to get something out of them in case they were victorious."

This led to a colloquy between Crossman and Jaamal. If, as between the Axis and the democracies, the Arabs were spiritually neutral, did they expect to be treated as well by the victors, since, at the moment of need, they gave no assistance?

Jaamal smiled again.

Ah, well, he said, he had read somewhere that this was a "Jewish war," anyway.

"Where did you read that?" Crossman demanded.

"I understand it was written on walls of subways in London and places like that," said Jaamal.

Gerald L. K. Smith in a fez, I reflected. But I realized it went deeper than that: this man Jaamal was no petty rabble-rouser; he was one of the Arabs' most influential political leaders.

Jaamal gave way to Auni Abdul Hadi, who had been private secretary to King Feisal. Auni introduced a new subject. He suggested that the Emir Feisal, who had signed an agreement with Weizmann of sympathy for Zionist aims, did not really know what he was signing because the agreement was not in Arabic. Colonel T. E. Lawrence—Lawrence of Arabia—had acted as interpreter at the time.

I asked, "Are you suggesting that Colonel Lawrence deliberately muddled Feisal?"

Abdul Hadi nodded. "Certainly. I know it. When Feisal and Weizmann discussed the matter of Palestine there was no other Arab person present at all. Lawrence was careful not to allow any Arab to be at that meeting."

Since this was the historic meeting in which Feisal, speaking for the Arabs, said in effect that if the Arabs were given their big Arab state, they would not begrudge the Jews their tiny Jewish state, Abdul Hadi was saying to us that Lawrence of Arabia, one of the greatest friends the Arab peoples ever had, had tricked Feisal deliberately and with foreknowledge. And that, presumably, Weizmann, too, was in on this plot.

Abdul Hadi was not pressed too hard on this point. It was incredible that Feisal should be ignorant of what was in the statement, because he had initialed an Arab translation, and added a postscript in his own hand saying that he could not be held to his promise if certain conditions were not carried out.

The committee possessed a copy of a photograph showing the Mufti reviewing a group of Moslem storm troopers whom he had recruited in Yugoslavia for the Nazi army. When Abdul Hadi also brought up the subject of the Mufti, Crossman produced it and tossed it across the table to him. A spirited exchange took place between them. Significantly enough, the official transcript of the hearings here reads as follows:

"(At this point, the witness dispensed with the services of the interpreter, and unfortunately the reporter could not make a continuous record.)" To make matters even more absurd, however, the very next sentence in the record is a compliment from Sir John to Abdul Hadi on his command of English: "Mr. Justice Singleton: Thank you, sir, I would like to say this to you: I believe if you had addressed us in English, the language in which you have answered questions latterly, you would have saved yourself a good deal of time."

But if the professional court reporter could not take down the testimony, newspaper reporters seated several rows back had no difficulty. They heard Crossman ask Abdul Hadi, "What have you to say about this photograph?"

He looked at it. "It could be forged," he said.

"Oh, no," said Crossman. "It is a reproduction of the first page of the *Wiener Illustrierte Zeitung*. It appeared in Vienna when the Mufti was in Germany."

Abdul Hadi hesitated, and finally said, "The Mufti was only trying to make a deal in case Germany won the war."

After we adjourned, the committee met privately. Crossman and I were taken to task for having questioned the two Arab leaders on the subject of the Mufti. I defended

Dick, and one of his colleagues observed, "In our country we consider a man innocent until he is proven guilty."

Sir John, who was one of the subcommittee of three which was to visit Saudi Arabia, added coldly, "You know, such questioning will make it most embarrassing for us when we see Ibn Saud. You should have thought of that."

CHAPTER 12

"Mr. Effendi, Do Not Believe All You Hear"

WHEREVER POSSIBLE between and after hearings I spoke with the younger Arabs—Palestine counterparts of my friend Tewfik in Cairo. Educated at the American University in Cairo and in Beirut, and some at Oxford, most were extremely wealthy. Though they stemmed from the effendi stratum of Arab society, as did the young intellectuals in Egypt, it was my feeling that, given a free hand, they would become socially progressive. They made it clear, however, that in Palestine the political scene was dominated by the Mufti through Jaamal Husseini.

The younger Arabs appeared strongly influenced by Mrs. Antonius, yet I was perplexed to discover that despite her antagonism toward the Jews, several of her protégés believed that the key to the Palestine problem was not in keeping the Jews out, but in urging them to enter and build the cornerstone of a new Greater Syria, roughly corresponding to the old Greater Syria. This, it was explained to me, would utilize Jewish brains and Jewish capital. But there was little they could do about it because the Mufti, as well as the older effendis and cadis, maintained that the Zionists were in league with the British. They preached that it was impossible to get rid of the British unless they got rid of the Zionists. This they translated into keeping the Jews out.

Unquestionably, definite fear and hatred of the Mufti existed among the Arab opposition families in Palestine. They expected his return to the Middle East, but doubted if he would come immediately to Palestine because of the danger he faced as a result of the blood feuds still raging between many of the leading Arab families and the Husseinis.

I explored this subject with a member of the Nashashibi family who called on me at the King David Hotel. Seated in the luxurious lounge of the hotel, listening to the tea-time chamber music, he told me that his cousin, Fakhri Nashashibi, a second-ranking member of his clan, had been killed in Baghdad in 1941 by the Mufti's men.

"We have never avenged his blood," he said. "Sooner or later we shall catch up with the Mufti."

I told him of the Mufti's record, as I had come upon it in Nuremberg. I said I was convinced of his guilt as a war criminal. I hoped sooner or later to see him tried, I assured him. "You will wait a long time," he said soberly. "I have lived in Palestine all my life. My family has been here for generations. We know the ways of the British in such matters. You will see—the Mufti will be allowed to escape from Paris, then he will turn up in Saudi Arabia or some near-by Arab state and presently come back to power again." He gave me the background of the long-standing feud between the two families and explained how strenuously his family had been seeking to rid Palestine of the Husseinis' deathlike grip.

When the British conquered the Turks they succeeded to the right of the Sultan of Turkey to name the Mufti of

Jerusalem. Sir Herbert Samuel, the newly appointed High Commissioner, looked about for a proper appointee. Haj Amin el Husseini at this time was a fugitive from justice in Trans-Jordan, having fled there after the British government sentenced him to prison for ten years for organizing anti-Jewish riots in Jerusalem. According to civil procedure he was fourth in line for the muftiship of Jerusalem. At that moment the feud between the Husseinis and Nashashibis had simmered down: the Mayor of Jerusalem was Ragheb Nashashibi, chief of the Nashashibi clan; Haj Amin asked him to use his influence to get him appointed to the post. Mayor Nashashibi acquiesced. At the same time, Sir Ronald Storrs, Governor of Jerusalem, then one of Sir Herbert's Oriental advisers and always a stanch supporter of the Arab cause, placed his support behind Haj Amin. Perhaps Viscount Samuel believed it would be a master stroke for him, a Jew, to appoint this troublesome young Arab to a position of responsibility. Perhaps he thought such responsibility might temper Haj Amin's intransigence. In any event, he appointed him Mufti of Jerusalem.

"It was the old story of appeasement," Nashashibi told me now, "and like all appeasement, it proved a major error. As soon as Haj Amin came to power, he was more intransigent than ever. He purged the Arab leadership of every Arab who threatened his domination, and I do not exaggerate when I say the Mufti's gangs simply eliminated by murder hundreds of his political opponents." The Mufti, he added, was publicly charged with "direct responsibility" for the murder of twenty-eight men, all distinguished Palestine Arab leaders, in an affidavit entitled "Voice from the Arab Tombs of Palestine," published in

Cairo on January 2, 1939, by a Sheik Ali Yassin, who had escaped to Egypt from Palestine. "The Mufti is a great problem for us, as you can see," he added.

As to the question which brought the committee to Palestine—Nashashibi's solution, which I heard with some surprise, was partition. His reasons were these: first, the Jews could have an independent democratic state with a Jewish majority; second, the Arabs could have a large Arab state comprising Trans-Jordan and the Arab-populated part of Palestine, all under King Abdullah of Trans-Jordan; and third, the British would be eliminated, which, he said, was what both Jews and Arabs wanted.

"From a dynastic point of view we Nashashibis would like to see that solution," he said. "Abdullah has no love for the Mufti, and if Abdullah were to reign over a greater Trans-Jordan, he would put the Mufti in his proper place. Our family fortunes would prosper, because we have always enjoyed excellent relations with the Hashimite dynasty, to which Abdullah belongs."

He added: "Of course, these things cannot be said in public. If you should quote me specifically——" He brought the edge of his hand, fingers outstretched, against his neck in a vivid chopping motion. *"Hélas!* I would be finished."

Later I reported his prediction on the Mufti to Manningham-Buller. "I am afraid someone has been pulling your leg, old fellow," he said good-humoredly. "I don't think the Mufti will ever be allowed back in the Middle East."

Another Arab of influence with whom I discussed Middle East politics was Yussef D., a Middle Eastern personage whom I cannot otherwise identify. One day I received a note from him in French, in a sort of spidery handwriting, telling me that he had learned that I had been a friend of Wendell Willkie, that he, too, was staying at the King David, and that he would like to see me. I invited Beeley to accompany me, but for one reason or another, he was unable to come along. Mr. D. greeted me in French rather than in Middle Eastern fashion and began our discussion by saying that he thought of Willkie as his *grand ami*—a man who had really understood that all men were brothers.

He told me that the Arab world, even at the top, was far from unwilling to co-operate with the Jews. The entire Middle East needed the intelligence, ingenuity, and productive capacity they represented. Coming from an Arab dignitary this rather startled me, although I knew from conversations with Weizmann and with other Jewish leaders, and from my own examination here, that the relationship between the Arabs and the Jews—save when someone else was looking—was good.

Mr. D. cited the vast unsettled and undeveloped areas in the Arab world. "You must not forget that the Middle East was the cradle of civilization and in Roman times the granary of the world. It once held many millions of people and boasted great civilizations." I asked him what he thought the needs were. First, he said, was education. For centuries the Arab peoples had had no opportunity for education. He took me to one of the windows of his suite and pointed to the distant hills which were being reforested by Jewish settlers.

"Whether the present Arab leadership likes it or not," he said, "we must realize that what the Jews are doing in Palestine must be done for all of the Middle East, if we are to take our rightful place in the community of nations." Again I must have expressed some surprise at these conciliatory words, for he remarked, "You should not think what I say strange. I was a friend of Wendell Will-kie." He drew a wallet from his pocket and showed me snapshots taken of him and Wendell together. "I believe with Mr. Willkie in one world," he went on. "I believe in peace with our neighbors. When I look at the Middle East, I think of it in terms of a great customs union, a great trading area. Therein lies our hope."

But what of Arab nationalism, I asked. What of such men as Ibn Saud and Farouk? He replied, "Here we all know that when Ibn Saud dies, his kingdom will pass away and there will be trouble among his many sons."

Our conversation veered to democracy. "Our people unfortunately are not ready for democracy as you know it," he said. "We have a parliament, but no real freedom. We have the forms of democracy, but not the substance. Take, for example, Lebanon. It is a republic. It has a parliament. But out of the fifty-five members of that parliament, not one represents the farmers, the artisans, or the workers. They are all wealthy landowners, lawyers, or merchants. That is why I say we have the forms of democracy, but not the substance. We can get the substance of democracy only by raising the living standard of all of our people, by education and by developing the land. This is why I believe in all irrigation and electric-power projects in this area."

I knew that Dr. Aydelotte was interested in the idea of re-creating the old Greater Syria as an economic rather than a political unit, and I asked Mr. D. how he thought this could be achieved. He shrugged his shoulders and said, "We can never do these things as long as it is to the interest of outside powers to keep us apart."

He lit a cigarette and thought somberly for a moment. "I say to you honestly, Mr. Crum, I am sick at heart. I have seen my own people telling your committee lies. You must not believe what they say to you in public—they say what they feel they must say for public consumption, but I assure you many of them are neither as recalcitrant nor as belligerent as they appear!

"If they were sure that Britain and America wished the Jews and Arabs to get together, we would. But they are not convinced, these Arab leaders: they wish to maintain their position of power, and they know that depends upon keeping to the Colonial Office line."

I interrupted, "You mean the witnesses who appeared before us?" He said, "Yes, you must not believe what most of them say to you in public."

Topside Arab leadership, he said, was extremely cynical about Western civilization. They used democratic catch phrases because they thought it pleased the Western world. In his opinion real democracy could come to the Middle East only through economic development of the whole area in co-operation with the Jewish community in Palestine. Medical needs were all-important, he added. Disease was appalling among his people. "They desperately need education so they will understand that the modern world offers them a better way of life."

"Do you think the Arab people will accept education?" I asked.

"It will not be easy at the start," he replied. "Some of them at the top will not like it and will not co-operate. But the real contribution the West can give is to make education available at the lowest level." He concluded by emphasizing again that the fundamental Arab error was in not sitting down with the Jews. Unfortunately, he said, the Jews, too, were guilty of this error and sometimes fell into the trap of thinking of the Arabs as their enemies.

There was no question that this man heads a school of thought in some Arab countries which has not been able to speak out. At this date I still do not feel free to reveal his name.

I tried to see as much of Palestine as I could, and the necessary facilities were given me. One afternoon I came into the King David lobby to find a tall, dark Arab youth, about twenty-four, waiting for me. "Mr. Crum?" he asked, and put out his hand. "My name is Michael. I am to be your chauffeur. I am a Christian, sir. I am named after a saint. I have a wife and a coming baby. I live in Bethlehem, and I have a hard time, sir, to make a living." He grinned. "At your service, sir."

A little overwhelmed, I shook hands with him. This was the beginning of a most pleasant friendship with Michael, who took his Christianity more seriously than many a Western Christian I knew.

Michael was perhaps the nearest approximation that I could find of the literate Arab man on the street in Palestine. He had gone to school. He could read and write Arabic and was able to speak English and some Hebrew in addition.

He could have obtained a government post, but said that it paid too badly and that he preferred to drive a taxicab. I pressed him on political questions. He was reluctant to reply specifically, protesting, "Of these things I should not speak, sir. I am a common man."

"Michael, I want to know what the common man thinks," I said. "In America if our government does not do what the common man wants, we say it is a bad government and we kick it out."

Michael said apologetically he did not wish to be involved in such matters, but that some of the Arab Christians—perhaps one in five Palestinian Arabs was a Christian—felt that the presence of the Jews in Palestine helped safeguard them. The Christians had been persecuted by the Moslems long before the Jews, he said.

"Then, Michael, what is the truth about trouble between you and the Jews?"

Michael spread his hands. "Sir, I am interested in making enough money for my wife and my baby that is coming. I hope I shall have a son. I wish him to go to school and learn many things, and perhaps learn how to go away from here and not be limited like I am."

He added, in the most charming and disingenuous manner, "I know I am an attractive man, but where am I to go? I am limited. My father, my grandfather, his father, and his grandfather before him have all lived in Bethlehem. I must live there, too. That is not right. A man should be able to move. I speak English, Arabic, Hebrew—but what good does it do me?" He explained that as an Arab Christian, he was viewed with suspicion by Moslem Arab officials, and said that he could not get visas to foreign countries such as the United States and West Africa, such as thousands of Christian Arabs had done at the beginning of the century. He could go to another Arab country, if he wished, but "I am afraid my life would be even more difficult, sir, to make." He did not rail against a fate that prevented him from living a full and better life: he was describing a fact which he accepted, a situation which he found hopeless. He saw himself always as a taxi driver from Bethlehem.

"Do your friends read about politics?" I asked. "Do they know what is happening? Are they interested?"

"It is not easy to say, sir, that they are interested. We

sit in the coffeehouse and we hear what the radio tells us, and we talk about what is taking place, but we have no power, my friends and I. The common man here, he is not important. He does not vote, no one asks him anything, and no one will listen to him. He can do nothing. He has no say in anything. A wise man does not become deeply caught in matters in which he can do nothing."

Michael possessed a natural dignity of his own. He enjoyed himself where and how he could. He was not above becoming pleasantly intoxicated on Palestinian brandy, which he obtained in Richon-le-Zion, a Jewish village. As a Christian, alcohol was not forbidden him, and Michael gratefully accepted this privilege.

I found it interesting to discuss morals with him. In this he was as fatalistic as in other things. "You know, Jerusalem is a pure city, sir," he told me. "We do not permit any houses of women within the boundaries of the city, but we know that when men have this desire, it is foolish to pretend they do not. We do not have such places within the boundaries of the Holy City, sir, as in Jaffa: here, sir, they are on the outskirts."

As we drove through the country, I became aware of a strange physical phenomenon. Many of the Jewish children I saw were blond and blue-eyed, a mass mutation that, I was told, is yet to be adequately explained. It is the more remarkable because the majority of the Jews of Palestine are of east European Jewish stock, traditionally dark-haired and dark-eyed. One might almost assert that a new Jewish folk is being created in Palestine: the vast majority almost a head taller than their parents, a sturdy people more a throwback to the farmers and fishermen of Jesus' day than products of the sons and daughters of the cities of eastern and central Europe.

I attempted to see Jewish and Arab life both in the whole and in detail; upon its average economic level and among its poor and its rich. I visited many Arab villages with Michael as my translator.

On one trip Crick, Sir Frederick, and I entered the town of Beisan (associated in the Bible with the death of King Saul) and were guests at a reception given in an ancient Turkish palace. Apparently, the Arab Higher Committee had been there before us, for placards in English, reading "Bring the Mufti Back" and "Support the White Paper," greeted me. Photographs of the Mufti, wreathed in leaves and flowers, decorated the village cafés.

Numerous sheiks welcomed us in their colorful robes, and there was much gracious and ceremonious bowing. We found these village Arab leaders extremely nationalistic. An Arab Roman Catholic priest was also present, and he expressed in strongest terms his opposition to the Jews. I told him that I, too, was a Roman Catholic, and recalled to him the clear stand of our Church on anti-Semitism.

On other trips, I saw Arab citrus groves, and cities like Nazareth and Jericho, which I remember as two of the greenest and loveliest Arab towns in all Palestine. Bethlehem, however, disturbed me. The commercialization, particularly that centering about the Church of the Nativity, I found offensive. At least half a dozen Arab Christian souvenir shops are to be found directly opposite the entrance of this great basilica, and tourists are literally buttonholed and taken inside to buy olivewood and sheepskin souvenirs. The road to Bethlehem from Jerusalem was desolate, and I could understand the significance of Christ's story about the good Samaritan. It was easy to see why no one had stopped on that lonely road.

I traveled throughout the country. I visited a banana

plantation on the Sea of Galilee; orange groves near the Mediterranean coast; vineyards and dairies in the hills; truck farms, co-operative markets in Haifa, factories, stores, the beginnings of a steel industry, and the growing shipbuilding industry. I visited monasteries and Biblical mileposts of the centuries; the fields where David is said to have vanquished Goliath, and where Ruth stood amid the alien corn; I followed the stations of the Cross in Jerusalem, and for a while stood on the Mount of Olives, thinking of all the overwhelming human history that had been written here.

I visited Hadassah Hospital on Mt. Scopus, not far from the Hebrew University, and was impressed by this institution, whose medical staff and nursing corps are unquestionably among the finest in the world. Later, at the hospital's out-patient clinic in the heart of modern Jerusalem, I saw Arab mothers bringing their children for treatment. Here, I felt, was a real tribute to the work of the late Henrietta Szold, founder of Hadassah, and to thousands of American women of Jewish faith.

I was eager to see Tel Aviv, the only all-Jewish city in the world. In Jerusalem I met George Backer, president of the Overseas News Agency, and he in turn introduced me to Yaakov Shiffman, the municipal engineer of Tel Aviv and the man who had planned most of the city's development. The three of us, together with Moshe Brilliant, the Tel Aviv correspondent of *The Palestine Post,* drove to Tel Aviv one sunny afternoon—a distance of perhaps forty miles from Jerusalem.

CHAPTER 13

Tel Aviv: "We Are a Good People"

MY GATEWAY to Tel Aviv was through Jaffa. Thus, all the greater was my surprise when I saw the youngest metropolis of the world, whose name means "Hill of the Spring." I had expected to find, of course, a modern city. An American soldier had told me of his pleasure at seeing the shadow of a tree outlined on a white sidewalk and realizing that this tableau meant civilization. Jaffa, in contrast, reminded me of Cairo. Vegetables and decayed fruit lay in the streets, whitewash scaled off the fronts of shops and buildings, and the city had the air of an overgrown Arab village. Then, at the edge of Tel Aviv, I saw the first Jewish houses. There was a marked improvement. I thought to myself: *Here before your eyes is proof that Palestine Jewry is bringing civilization to the Middle East.* You didn't need to have streets of squalor and a population diseased and beaten by life. From the Colonial Office and the Arab hierarchy you got the impression that such things were destined to be in this part of the world, that such was the way of life in the Middle East and nothing could be done about it. At least one Colonial official had told me, "Oh, well, they prefer to live that way, you know." But here the Jews proved it was not necessary to live so. Driving into Tel Aviv, you saw the houses become more habitable, the streets grow wider and tree lined; the green of grass and trees, planted to beautify, begin to take the place of the ever-present gray of mud and silt, and you realized that the Jews had done this because they wanted wide streets, they wanted trees and green places for the children to play in. The earth had been blighted for centuries, and of all who had passed this way, these were the first people to remove that blight. They had built a thriving city of nearly 200,000, a thoroughly civilized community, with tree-shaded boulevards, with opera and theaters, with playgrounds and modern schools, with busses and apartment houses. I had no idea that in Tel Aviv you could stand on a street corner and say: "This might be any modern American town." But you could.

"I want to give you as clear a picture of Tel Aviv as possible," said Shiffman, and we drove first through the old section of the city. Here was Jaffa again: the streets were narrow, the houses clustered together as fortresses behind brick and plaster walls.

"This was originally a suburb of Jaffa," he said. "When the first European Jews came to Palestine, some settled here. Later this was incorporated into Tel Aviv, when the city was founded in 1910." He told us how the city's character had changed from that of a residential suburb in which trade was barred to that of Palestine's commercial center, following the 1921 Arab riots, when Jews were compelled to move their shops out of Jaffa. In 1936, an Arab general strike, which paralyzed port activities in Jaffa, led the Jews to develop a port of their own.

We drove through Lilienblum Street, Tel Aviv's first thoroughfare, then past Herzliah College on Herzl Street, one of the older secondary schools of Palestine, and then through the busy industrial section of the town. Here were hundreds of modest workshops, small entrepreneurs, employing from two to three workers. We drove down Rothschild Boulevard, a wide tree-lined double thoroughfare, similar to New York's parkways, with traffic flowing on either side of an island of green lawn. White-capped nurses were pushing perambulators, children were playing in sand boxes, and elderly couples sat peacefully on green wood benches.

At one intersection, Brilliant pointed to a large, white building of classic architecture graced with enormous white columns. "That is our latest theater, the new home of the Habima players," he said. "It is as splendid as anything I have ever seen in the States."

Curious, I asked when he had been in the States.

Brilliant smiled. "I was born in West Hoboken, New Jersey, Mr. Crum," he said. "I came to Palestine with my parents when I was eighteen and I've been here since."

"Have you ever wished you were back?" I asked. We were walking across the richly carpeted foyer of the theater. "For a visit, yes," Brilliant said, "but otherwise—well, I think I live as full and rewarding a life here as any newspaperman with a comparable job in the States. I married here. My children are here, and we're all quite content. Besides, I have a very definite sense of taking part in something pretty big and exciting. Take this city—thirty-five years ago there was only a sand dune where we stand now. This was plain desert and yellow sand running down to the sea. I am thirty-one, and in these last thirteen years I've seen Tel Aviv grow amazingly and I've been a part of that growth." He said it was not easy to explain, but he thought perhaps that what he felt must be akin to what the early settlers in the Western states must have felt: a sense of ever-expanding horizons, a challenge of worlds to conquer.

We had entered the theater during a rehearsal of a Hebrew play, and though, of course, I could not understand the language, I listened to it and was surprised how much it sounded like Italian, at once liquid and musical. Now there was a break between acts, and the actors came out into the foyer to meet us. I had heard much of the Habima players as one of the finest repertoire groups in the world, and I was interested to meet them. They gave us autographed copies of the last Habima yearbook and told me something of the theater and their organization. The theater was obviously their pride, and they spoke of its moving stage, its modern theatrical facilities, and the fact that it seated one thousand persons. Shimon Finkel, one of the Habima artists, told me how eagerly he was looking forward to the next *première—Hamlet,* in Hebrew —in which he would play the leading role. He was not to be considered a "star," he hastened to add. "We have no such system here," he said. "All of us receive equal billing and the most renowned artist in the troupe receives no more in salary or privileges than the least known."

Another artist, Abraham Meskin, said, "We are a co-operative organization, Mr. Crum, and we live up to what that means. I, myself, play Shylock in *The Merchant of Venice* one night and the following evening may be one of a dozen persons in a mob scene."

Back in the car again, we drove to the Yarkon River, which marks the northern boundary of built-up Tel Aviv. We stood on the bank. Before us stretched a vast reach of undulating sand dunes.

"What you see before you is equal in area to all Tel

Aviv," said Shiffman. "We have just incorporated it into the city. Tel Aviv, up to now, has literally been bursting at its seams. Now at least we have room to expand."

"If you were to get 100,000 refugees into Palestine, how long would it take before you could provide housing for all of them?" I asked.

"If we can get the building materials, we could have them all housed in a matter of months." He added that in 1933 nearly 60,000 Jews came to Palestine and were housed in short order.

During the war an American rest camp had been established at Tel Litwinsky, about twenty minutes from Tel Aviv. Here thousands of American soldiers from Italy and from the Middle East and Persian Gulf Commands came for two weeks of relaxation. They swam in the Mediterranean, dined in the cafés, were invited to various homes for parties and dances. It was the only oasis in the Middle East where they could enjoy fresh fruit with impunity and spend hours gazing into shopwindows reminiscent of their own home towns.

Behind the city's façade of restless activity, one sensed stability. Here in Tel Aviv were published seven daily newspapers and a score of weekly newspapers in Hebrew; new translations of Shakespeare, Sinclair Lewis, and Thomas Wolfe were pouring off the presses; and I saw bookshops everywhere. Rarely had I come upon a city with such abounding vitality.

Tel Aviv apartment houses are built of cement or brick and white plaster; the roofs are flat; and scarcely any building is above four stories high. Each apartment has its terrace, however tiny; and each apartment house has its plot of green. And what, I thought, was a delightful characteristic of this brave new world of Palestine Jewry was the discovery that nearly every street had been named after men and women, both Jew and gentile, who had distinguished themselves in law, medicine, science, literature, and statesmanship. We drove down Allenby Road, named after the British general who had liberated Palestine from the Turks, through Ben Yehuda Street, named for the late Eleazer Ben Yehuda, a Palestine scholar known as the "father of modern Hebrew," and on to Bialik Street, honoring the Hebrew national poet.

I found the people friendly. Many of those with whom I spoke knew English: it is the second language in the schools. Others spoke German, which I managed haltingly on the strength of my college German. Some had come from central Europe shortly after Hitler rose to power; some had come to Palestine before the turn of the century, convinced by the Zionist prognosis of the Jewish problem that there was no real hope for European Jewry, that the solution for them as a people lay in the establishment of a state of their own with a return to the land, to productive rather than service occupations. They seemed to me generally to possess an inner security of their own: it came from their realization that they were on Jewish soil—Jews proudly and simply Jews—relieved of the ever-present anti-Semitic pressures they had known in Europe. They had achieved a normalcy, I felt, certainly lacking in the Jews I had seen in Europe.

On this visit Brilliant suggested that we take tourist's license and drop in at random upon a family. We did so. The apartment in which we found ourselves might have been an apartment in San Francisco. A radio stood in a corner; a piano in the other; there were Viennese etchings on the wall; a mantelpiece with a few personal photographs; a sofa with end tables, on which were two modern lamps; a coffee table with copies of *Parade* and a copy of *Palestine and the Middle East,* a trade and economic publication.

We discussed this vibrant, growing Palestine and the generation of men and women who were growing with it.

"Yes," said our host, a roly-poly little man who had been born in Berlin and had as his guests that day his grandchildren and a small nephew recently rescued from the concentration camps. "Yes, but it is our children whom you must see. They are growing up blessed above all. They are self-reliant, at home, without any sense of apology for being alive. This is their world; they feel they belong; the word Jew to them is not an accusation, or a badge of shame, or a secret to be concealed; here all are Jews, and what of it? We are a good people, with great traditions and distinguished men among us; we feel ourselves as the salt of the earth, as all other peoples should feel. That is normal and that is the way it should be. So our children grow up and we are grateful."

His nephew was buttering a piece of bread, and his arm, just above the wrist, showed the same purple brand I had become so familiar with in Germany and Austria. He was a thin, peaked child who appeared about twelve, and having seen such children in Europe, I was not surprised to be told he was actually fifteen years old. His face was narrow, his arms and legs were thin, but his eyes had lost that haunted look, that unsmiling, unchildlike look which I had found so characteristic in the camps.

"And how do you like Tel Aviv?" asked his uncle, as we sat around the table, sipping tea.

The boy said nothing, but he looked at the roly-poly little man, and there was that in his face—gratitude, peace, a trembling on the edge of tears—which held us silent for a long moment.

CHAPTER 14

Kibbutzim: "Back to the Land"

IF TEL AVIV was an impressive example of what urban Jewry, given the opportunity, could achieve, the collective settlements of Palestine were a revelation to me of what could be done by the men and women who had gone back to the land. Long before I came to Palestine I had been eager to see these *Kibbutzim,* not only because I had seen young people in the DP camps training for this kind of life, but also because I knew the history of collective agricultural settlements in the United States, begun with idealism and best intentions. Nonetheless, few if any had succeeded.

One afternoon, I was driven to an agricultural *Kibbutz* where perhaps 350 men, women, and children lived. My guide, furnished by the Jewish Agency, was prepared to translate German, Yiddish, French, Italian, Serbian, and Polish. This agricultural settlement seemed to present an excellent example of how smoothly Palestine Jewry fits into the life of Palestine. Near by was a monastery, and not far was an Arab village. The secretary of the *Kibbutz* was about thirty, wearing khaki trousers and a shirt open at the neck, and spoke English with an accent.

"I came from Yugoslavia ten years ago," he told me. "My wife came with me. Our family believed that the

Jews had no future in Europe: that we must return to the soil; that we must make a nation or be lost. We studied together in an agricultural school near Belgrade, learning Hebrew. One of the courses was on the topography and geography of Palestine. We married upon graduation and with a group of half a dozen fellow graduates we came to Palestine."

The land had been leased to the founders of the *Kibbutz* by the Jewish National Fund. A secretariat, elected by the members, was in charge of the settlement, and although any member could leave when he wished, none had done so in the last eight years.

I asked him if they had experienced any trouble with the Arabs.

"Our problem here is clear," he said. "We must get along with our Arab neighbors. We do get along with them. They get along with us. When we drilled our well, the first to take water from us were the Arabs who live near by. Let's go there for a moment," he said.

In the bright sunshine, we strolled toward the village. As we walked he showed me what had been done. Here they had planted a grove of trees chosen because they created humus and helped conserve the soil. It was part of a long-range program to reforest land which the Crusaders, the Turks, and Napoleon's armies among them had denuded and which had remained neglected ever since. We passed the dairy shed, where more than a hundred cows waited to be milked. "We made many investigations to determine what breed of cow would thrive best and produce the most milk on the kind of grass we grow here," the secretary observed. "Finally, we found a cross between Damascan and Frisian cattle that did very well; we tried Holsteins and Jerseys, but ours seem to thrive better. As a result, I think our butter-fat percentage would be considered high even in Wisconsin."

As we passed a large lumber shed, I peered in. Two boys about sixteen were working with an electric buzz saw. They were making wooden marionettes in preparation for a children's show they were to give a few days later.

"You are surprised?" my companion asked, smiling.

I said I was. Somehow the thought of a marionette show in the heart of this "troubled" country seemed bizarre.

"But why not?" he demanded. "Our children are our future. There is no reason why they should not enjoy the same pleasures as children in any other country." And he added, almost sharply: "Because we are Jews, must we always be associated with tragedy and despair?"

Once in the Arab village, we came upon a *Kibbutz* member adjudicating a dispute between two Arabs, and I was gratified to learn that he had been a lawyer in Berlin.

During the Arab disturbances of 1936–39, the secretary told me, many Arab villagers warned their Jewish neighbors of attacks. More Arabs were killed by Arab raiders than were Jews, principally because Arab villagers refused to give up men, donkeys, and food requisitioned by Arab mercenaries.

We lunched in the large communal dining hall. The waitresses were women of the settlement, sturdy women, most of them in plain blue dresses, with white aprons, and a white kerchief about their heads. I was told every woman spends a period of time serving tables and working in the kitchen, although a trained dietitian was in permanent charge. The large, wooden tables, seating eight, had already been set when we arrived; and the women were kept busy replenishing the food as the *Kibbutz* members, men in work shirts open at the neck, and women, many in slacks and shorts, came in for lunch. This consisted of barley-and-bean soup; peppers stuffed with rice and macaroni; a salad of cooked eggplant; porridge with jam; coffee and, for dessert, oranges.

The secretary observed a bit ruefully: "If you were to stay here for the next month, Mr. Crum, I imagine you would tire of this dessert."

"Not I," I said. "As a Californian I'm strong on fruit."

"Ah, yes, but not if you had oranges for dessert three times a day every day for weeks on end," he said. "We must be practical people. We pay low rent for our land —about two per cent of its value—but we must pay it and amortize our loan. We are not a charitable enterprise. We must be able to live from the land. And we are happy that we have been able to show a profit. Our settlements belong to a co-operative marketing organization to which we sell our excess milk and butter and the produce of our truck farms, as well as eggs and fowl. Sometimes we must sacrifice because when certain fruits or vegetables are too plentiful and have no value on the market, we use them as much as possible at our tables. Oranges are plentiful now—and so we are being given oranges without mercy. If you were to visit us at some other time, you might get your fill of watermelon."

The coffee was strong and had something of the flavor of the coffee we had had in Vienna. "It's made of barley," he said. "We grow our own barley, roast it, grind it, add coffee to it, boil it in water and milk, and there you have it."

Their bread was baked from their own flour. Australian

and Moroccan wheat seed had been brought to Palestine four years ago and thrived.

"Our baker used to be an electro-technician," he said. "Three years ago our regular baker changed to another job, and this man—his name's Cohen—volunteered." He looked around. "He's sitting over at that other table, grinning at us now." Cohen came over—a slim, shaggy-haired, studious-looking young man. "I didn't have a full-time job as an electrician here," he said. "I wanted a steady job. So now I combine baking with electrical work. I came here in 1938 with my wife, Lillian." He turned about. "Here!" he called. A chubby little girl with a red clip in her brown hair came to us. "This is my little girl, Esther," he said. "She's four and a half." They had another child, two years old, he said. His wife woke each morning at four o'clock to take the cows to pasture and remained there until nine A.M., when she brought them back because they grazed badly in the heat.

He baked 110 loaves of bread daily, he said, and twice a week baked an extra 110 loaves.

Lunch over, we began to stroll through the *Kibbutz*. We passed by two low cement barracklike buildings. "Those are our showers," he said. They were very conscious of the needs of sanitation and health, he went on. A nurse was always in attendance, and a physician came from a near-by *Kibbutz* three times a week, principally to check the health of the children. "Most of our diseases here are sore throat," he said, "and occasionally dysentery."

Remembering the children I had seen in Europe, I asked whether they had received any here.

"Ten boys and six girls arrived a week ago," he said. "As you can imagine, we treat them in a very special way. Some at first trust no one. But we have teachers who speak their languages—German or Polish or Rumanian—and who were also in concentration camps. That is the first calming influence: the children know their teacher is one of them." He added that the youngsters came here after Jewish Agency social workers interviewed them and decided they would be more easily rehabilitated on a farm than in the city.

He introduced me to one of the male instructors, a heavy-set, slow-speaking man, who explained some of the psychological questions involved in his work.

"Our problem is to implant in these children from Europe the understanding that after their bitter experiences they have finally reached a haven. They come to us suffering from a great melancholy and nervousness. We wish to create in them the feeling that they are at home and in their own land: this is permanent. From here there is no chance of being sent away.

"In this the study of Hebrew is very important because since they come from many parts of Europe and speak many tongues, when they learn Hebrew it becomes a bond bringing them all together. We find that in two months they can learn enough Hebrew to talk quite well with each other."

As an instructor, he said, it was necessary for him to be on the closest terms with the children. Some were still sullen and suspicious, distrustful of everyone. Some of the older boys and girls spent much of their time writing letters to lists they had obtained of persons who had names similar to theirs. "When they are all alone, they are almost desperate to find a relative in the world," he said.

The older refugee boys and girls had duties about the *Kibbutz,* so they divided their time between work and study.

We moved on and found ourselves in a large Children's House, which held sixty of the smaller children of the *Kibbutz*. I was told there were two other Children's Houses, each holding from fifteen to twenty youngsters. Here the children lived, as far as I could determine, in modern progressive nursery-school fashion, under the care of young women. The parents lived in their own quarters, but were with their children at intervals throughout the day. They fed them at dinner, played with them in the evening, tucked them into bed at night. I think one of my pleasantest half-hours was spent in this child world in the heart of Palestine. Here were rows of hooks on which to hang their clothes—hooks at just the right height for a five-year-old child to reach. Basins to wash in—at the right height for a five-year-old to manage. There were swings, sand piles, teeter-totters, and little gardens.

I was impressed by the care with which talent was encouraged. In one *Kibbutz* a ten-year-old girl pianist was introduced to me with much excitement because the *Kibbutz* had promised to send her to America to study music.

Down at the Sea of Galilee, where I found a *Kibbutz* with banana plantations, a youngster wanted to know all about the University of California, where he expected to go to study soil cultivation. I thought of the orphans I had seen in Europe and the aimlessness of their days; of Dr. Grinberg's words: "Our children have learned nothing for six years"; and I thought of these youngsters here. In my heart I could not blame any Jew for taking whatever steps he thought necessary to bring children from the misery and anti-Semitism of Europe into Palestine.

I asked about wages and salaries. Or did members share in the profits?

The secretary shook his head. "We have abolished the

system of individual wages, Mr. Crum. What we own we own collectively, and the profits go into the pool of our common resources.

"As for money, it has no value here within the collective. We have food, we have lodging, we have clothes. Each man has one leisure suit of clothes and accessories, and two sets of working outfits and accessories. We have a communal laundry, and everyone turns in soiled clothes on Friday and receives a laundered set. If clothes become worn out we request new clothes. If they can be repaired, we have them repaired. We each receive such items as soap, toothpaste, and razors. We are all mature here. We do not ask for more than we need. We do not take advantage of each other."

"But what about your young women? Do they wear identical dresses?" I asked. "The girls wouldn't stand for it back home."

He laughed.

"Yes, we recognize that, and so we have a few different styles of dresses. The women choose what they like, and, of course, they can sew or decorate it according to their own wishes."

"And courtship and marriage?"

The secretary said thoughtfully, "I should not be surprised if we haven't a record of more successful marriages in these collective farms than the cities have. For one thing, many of the usual tensions are removed. Because a woman takes her place with the man in the work of the collective, she is not confined to the job of rearing children and housework. I think this makes for a healthier relationship between parent and child. Again, we think a far greater percentage of our marriages are marriages of love. If two men court a girl, since neither man can

offer more in material possessions than the other—since
they have only themselves to give—she isn't so likely to
be confused by extraneous pressures to make a decision
that runs counter to her heart. That," he said, "is why
I think our marriages are more permanent. And things are
very simple. When a man and a girl decide to be married,
they notify our housing secretary. After the ceremony,
the housing secretary makes a shift; one double quarters
now occupied, two single quarters now empty."

Members of the *Kibbutz* are entitled to a two-week
vacation annually and are given a modest amount of
pocket money for the period. It is sufficient to take them
to Haifa or Tel Aviv or Jerusalem, if they wish to spend
their vacation there, although many take a busman's holiday by visiting another *Kibbutz*.

Frequently groups of young people commandeer a
wagon and drive to Tel Aviv for a day's swimming at the
beach, or to near-by villages for dances, debates, harvest
bees, and similar rural pastimes.

"If they wish to go to a cinema in town, they ask for
ticket money and we give it to them," the secretary said.

"Doesn't anyone abuse that system?"

"We feel that anyone likely to take advantage of this
would not be likely to be found in a *Kibbutz*," he said.
"Make no mistake, life here is not easy for many people.
Some could never manage it. Yet we have had members
who have gone into the cities—who have gone abroad and
lived abroad—and have returned to *Kibbutz* life again."
What had particularly gratified them was that the second
and third generation remained in the *Kibbutz*. There had
been some fear that ultimately the less vigorous life in
the cities would win back the Jews and retard the return
to the soil.

There were from fifty to twelve hundred people in each settlement. Nearly all required a probation period to determine if newcomers would be content with collective life and could fit into it without friction. In one settlement two men had settled a personal argument with their fists, and both were expelled on the ground that once a quarrel reached physical violence it must sooner or later prove a source of friction.

In the early days of this *Kibbutz* out of 102 members, about fifty worked outside the settlement, at various jobs in towns and villages, helping support the colony with their earnings. By the fourth year the colony became self-supporting, and no members found it necessary to work outside.

It was growing late. We dropped into the social hall of the settlement. Two men and a woman were working over papers at a table near the door. "They're making assignment for tomorrow," the secretary told me. "We have to shift people about as the work piles up seasonally—sometimes in the truck farm, sometimes in the orchard, sometimes in the barley fields."

The hall itself was simply furnished. There were maps on the wall, with typewritten digests of the day's news. There was a radio and record player in one corner, and, in another corner, two boys were lost in a game of chess.

"This is the center of our intellectual life," the secretary said. "The Palestine Orchestra visits us now and then on its tours, and professors from the Hebrew University drop in on us to lecture. Here we have our discussions and debates and entertainments."

There was a small bookcase, and he read the titles of half a dozen books which had been translated into Hebrew: Balzac's stories, Ernst Toller, Tolstoi's *Resur-*

rection, Léon Blum's speech before his judges at Rouen, Knut Hamsun, *In the Northern Forests* by Jack London, Sinclair Lewis' *Babbitt,* Shakespeare's *King Lear,* and a book of Chekhov's plays.

In the quiet darkness of the Palestine night, with the stars gleaming in a velvet sky, I was driven back to Jerusalem. Somewhere, far away, cowbells sounded, and off in the distance I saw the lights of the Holy City.

It is always difficult to draw conclusions on the basis of a brief study, but the *Kibbutz* movement seemed to me a striking contribution to modern life. In addition to privately owned farms, there are more than three hundred collective and co-operative settlements, the oldest dating back to 1908. New ones are being founded constantly. These men and women, I felt, were genuine pioneers; they built their settlements on desert and swamp, on mountain peaks, on barren plateaus. Behind them lie memories of Hitler's Europe and preceding that the ancient story of Jewish persecution. They derived deep satisfaction from what they were doing, these Jewish farmers, Jewish poultrymen, Jewish husbandmen; they saw a new generation of Jews rising free from the stigma of the ghetto, free from the self-consciousness of "differentness." I arrived back in Jerusalem feeling inspired by all I had seen and heard.

In my admiration for them I was not alone. I remember being seated several days later in the Café Régence of the King David, when Buxton entered. He had just returned from a visit to a *Kibbutz,* and his eyes seemed welling up with tears. "I felt like getting down on my knees before these people," he said. "I've always been proud of my own ancestors who made farms out of the virgin forest. But these people are raising crops out of rock!"

CHAPTER 15

Haganah: "We Are Not Anti-British"

As I LEFT the King David Hotel one morning, I was accosted by a man I recognized vaguely as having been a spectator at the hearings. He had an armful of manuscripts.

"Please take these," he said, giving me several copies. "They are for the committee."

I accepted them almost automatically and did not examine them closely until I was in the hearing room. Then I realized what I had.

They were mimeographed copies of a long statement addressed to the Anglo-American Committee of Inquiry, signed "Head of Command, Jewish Resistance Movement."

I placed them on the great table.

Manningham-Buller read his with mounting indignation.

The memorandum warned that virtually every Jew in Palestine belonged to the resistance movement and that every Jew therefore would have to be crushed before the *Haganah* could be disarmed.

"To prove the authenticity of this document," an attached note read, "the Voice of Israel, the radio station of the Palestine Resistance Movement, will announce this afternoon that this memorandum has been presented to you."

The document declared in part:

"Our path is not the path of terror. If there is terrorism, it is practiced by the authorities. If, against unseaworthy craft carrying a few hundred refugees, the British government sends reconnaissance planes, destroyers, operates radar stations, builds special police posts, uses air-borne troops, that is terrorism—when we attack these things, we do nothing more than defend ourselves from government terror."

The Jewish Resistance Movement, the document went on, is "not anti-British. We have devoted ourselves to a struggle against a hostile policy, pursued against us by Great Britain, but we have no interest whatsoever in weakening the British position in the Middle East or Palestine. We have no connection with any undermining activity, as goes on against Britain elsewhere. The sole conflict between us is created by the British government's repudiation of the mandate.

"Our struggle has just begun. Thus far we have confined ourselves to defense against hostile assaults and a few warning actions. We have resolved not to interfere with the work of the Inquiry Committee, although we know in whose hands lies the actual decision and how the decision will be reached.

"If the solution is anti-Zionist," the warning continued, "our resistance will continue to spread and increase. We will not acquiesce to the carrying out of a solution which consigns the last hope of the Jewish people to the grave. Our resistance is liable to result in the creation of a new problem—a problem of British security in Palestine—and this problem will be resolved only by a Zionist solution."

215

To many of the British members it was, of course, an infuriating document. Lord Morrison, particularly, was most bitter. Some of us tried to point out that the *Haganah* did in fact represent a Jewish Home Guard Movement, established for self-defense, and that such acts as the assassination of Lord Moyne, British Minister Resident in the Middle East, in 1944, were perpetrated by members of the tiny Stern Group, which repudiated entirely the discipline of the Jewish leaders in Palestine.

I went further into the subject of the Jewish Resistance Movement. Some of the story was told me by Gershon Agronsky. Some of it was told by others.

As I got the story of the *Haganah*'s beginnings, the first Jewish pioneers coming to Palestine from eastern Europe at the turn of the century found that neither person nor property was safe under Turkish rule. Highway robbers, plundering Bedouins, brigands from the mountains—all in the ancient tradition of raid and spoliation—roamed the country. The European Jews, with their farm implements, their cattle and livestock, were made-to-order prey. It was not a question of anti-Jewish feeling.

As a result, the younger generation of Jews organized themselves into a body called *Hashomer*—the "Watchman." They determined that since it was impossible to farm without carrying a gun, they would carry guns and become as expert as the Arab raiders. They succeeded in repelling attacks, and within a few years Arab raiders began to have a genuine respect for the new Jewish settlers.

Then the British conquered Palestine. At first, the Jews were relieved at the thought that security was now in the hands of the British, but they found that raids continued. Anti-Jewish riots, aimed at annulling the Balfour Declaration, took their course unchecked in 1920 and 1921. Haj

Amin el Husseini, one of the major ringleaders in these riots, became Mufti. Troubles continued. The British either could not or would not protect the lives and property of the Jewish community in Palestine.

Inevitably, the *Hashomer* became the *Haganah*—"self-defense." It became a citizens' reserve army, in which virtually every able-bodied man and woman took part, prepared to go into action to defend themselves and their property. The riots of 1936–39 tested their capability, morale, and discipline. Not a single Jewish settlement—even among the most exposed—had to be abandoned. Attack after Arab attack was beaten off. Yet, I was told, in that period there was not one act of reprisal on the part of the Jews. They practiced *Havlaga*—self-restraint—based on the conviction that Zionism was a movement of the highest moral quality and that in its consummation no harm should come to innocent people.

When the war isolated a hard-pressed Britain in the hostile Middle East, members of the *Haganah*—the bulk of Palestine Jewry's 30,000 volunteers—fought with British forces on every front from Dunkirk to Italy; and members of the *Palmach*—the inner striking force of the *Haganah*—were trained by the British for special Commando jobs behind enemy lines in Africa, Asia, and Europe.

The war ended with the White Paper of 1939 still in force. V-E Day meant only increasing bitterness to the Jews. The doors were shut in the faces of the survivors in the displaced-person's camps. What the British termed illegal immigration seemed to the Jews perfectly legal, on the ground that the British owe their position in Palestine to the mandate bestowed upon them by international authority, which specifically obligated them to facilitate Jewish immigration and the establishment of the Jewish National

Home. This the British now were actively opposing, not facilitating.

It became the chief postwar job of the *Haganah* to assure and protect continued immigration. For the *Haganah,* as I realized fairly quickly, was not an independent organization and did not decide matters of policy. *Haganah* organized its activity in accordance with the policies set by the elected representatives of the Jewish community in Palestine. To disband *Haganah,* as some of our British friends wanted, would have meant disbanding the Jewish community of Palestine.

Each time I returned to Jerusalem from my trips about the country, the sense of being watched, which had first made itself felt in London, grew stronger. In London I suspected I was being trailed and my mail opened. Here, I knew it. Toward the end of our stay, whoever it was who was opening my letters did not even take the trouble to reseal them. They arrived opened. Of course, on my trips I was seldom left by myself. If I traveled in company with other members of the committee, it was not unusual to find ourselves either trailed or preceded by armed cars, and on at least one trip we were forced to wait half an hour for our military escort to catch up with us. It had gone down a side road by mistake, following the wrong car.

Since this pattern of surveillance had been general since Washington, I was not too deeply concerned. But one incident made me furious. George Polk, Columbia Broadcasting System correspondent in the Middle East, suggested that I make a nonpolitical broadcast from Jerusalem for CBS. We decided that I should make a transcript of my speech, and Polk would ship the record by air to

Station KYA, in my home city of San Francisco. I proceeded to the local British Broadcasting System studio, made the recording, and promptly forgot about it. A few days later Polk, obviously angry, stopped me in the lounge of the King David.

"Bart," he said, "the Palestine government has censored you off the air. You're evidently a dangerous, subversive character."

"I don't understand," I said.

"That recording," he said. "I had it wrapped and sealed, and sent it on, but the government authorities in the post office opened it, played it, and refused to ship it. I asked them why—and they told me that they couldn't send it because it was inflammable and would be a 'fire hazard' on the plane."

Later I discussed with my colleagues whether we should not take up the question of the Palestine government and its excesses in denying civil liberties and in policing the people. Lord Morrison interpolated to say that we ought to take a firm position as to the arms which the Jews possessed. I said, on the contrary, the Jews had to keep their arms and that any attempt to take away this protection would lead to bloodshed. I had an opportunity to go into the matter of Jewish arms earlier than I expected.

One morning, after a very brief session, we were driven to a well-guarded building some distance from the YMCA. Here we were ushered ceremoniously into a high-ceilinged room, where a slender, very British, very precise military figure waited for us. This was General J. C. D'Arcy, the General Officer Commanding Palestine. I cannot report our conversation verbatim, but the substance of General D'Arcy's evidence to us, without question the most authoritative military information we could obtain, was as follows:

1. Speaking purely from the military point of view, he could enforce a pro-Jewish solution without much difficulty.

2. In enforcing such a solution, the *Haganah* could be most helpful.

3. In the event of a pro-Arab solution, he would have to contend with a "highly efficient" military organization (the *Haganah*). He estimated the budget of this organization to reach four million dollars a year. He would require three army divisions and from four to six months to break the back of the opposition. Even then, some measure of underground resistance would persist.

4. In enforcing a pro-Arab solution, Arab support, he was afraid, would be of no value.

We discussed with him what would happen if British troops were withdrawn from Palestine. "If you were to withdraw British troops, the *Haganah* would take over all of Palestine tomorrow," General D'Arcy replied flatly.

"But could the *Haganah* hold Palestine under such circumstances?" I asked.

"Certainly," he said. "They could hold it against the entire Arab world."

One of my British colleagues asked: "Are you implying, sir, that it is impossible for His Majesty's government to disarm the *Haganah*?"

General D'Arcy said: "You cannot disarm a whole people. I rather think the world will not stand for another mass murder of Jews."

Sir Frederick turned to me. "Suppose the British left and the *Haganah* took over. What would the United States do?" he asked rhetorically.

"I shouldn't be surprised if the United States would recognize the Jewish provisional government the very next day."

Sir Frederick snorted. "Then the United States is worse than I thought."

Before we adjourned, I wandered over to a table upon which General D'Arcy's aides had displayed photographs with rifles and ammunition uncovered during a raid on Byria, a new collective settlement. The photographs were described as "of extreme military importance." I looked at the back of one. It was a commercial postcard, the type on sale in any Jerusalem shop. Without comment I showed it to General D'Arcy. "Well," he said, surprised. "That is odd, isn't it?"

On another occasion, with the same panoply of guards, we were led to an unpublicized meeting with the then Chief Secretary, John Shaw, now Sir John Shaw. Shaw, expressing the point of view of the British Administration in Palestine, asserted that the Jewish Agency must either become the government of Palestine or be dissolved. That it should be dissolved had been, of course, the feeling of Sir John Singleton and others as early as our *Queen Elizabeth* meetings. If the Agency were liquidated, and the *Haganah* disarmed, Shaw indicated that he would be ready to recommend the admission of the 100,000 into Palestine over a three- or four-year period.

In the light of what the British military had told us, disbanding of the *Haganah* appeared virtually impossible. Crossman and most of the American members of the committee had no doubts on this point. "We're dealing with a genuine Maquis movement," Crossman argued. "History shows that no government has been able to disband an underground resistance movement backed by the people."

An event occurred about this time which vividly underwrote his words. Four Jewish young men, members of the resistance movement, were killed in a clash with the British near Tel Aviv. Nearly the entire adult population of Tel Aviv—over 150,000 persons—attended the funeral.

I was not in Tel Aviv to witness this, but friends who were returned profoundly impressed with the sense of unity: it was evident that the people and the resistance were one.

CHAPTER 16

Arab vs. Jew: "On the Top Level"

LIEUTENANT GENERAL Sir Alan Gordon Cunningham, High Commissioner for Palestine, is a slim British gentleman of the old school, his cheeks ruddy and crisscrossed with the fine lines of a man who has lived an outdoor life. Sir Alan certainly has no enviable position as His Majesty's highest executive in Palestine. Part of this derives from the troubled situation within the land itself, and part from the fact that Palestine is a mandate and all decisions relative to it are taken in the Colonial Office in London rather than in Sir Alan's office in Government House, Jerusalem. The High Commissioner for Palestine, therefore, has responsibility without corresponding power, and must carry out Colonial Office policies whether he likes them or not.

Sir Alan had succeeded that doughty old warrior, the late Field Marshal Viscount Gort, who had resigned his position in Jerusalem in 1945, shortly before his death. Gort had given illness as the reason then for his resignation, but there were many in Palestine who said that Gort had been unwise enough to let his heart rule him: he had become pro-Jewish, and he simply could not carry out policies, particularly after the war ended and thousands of Jewish refugees pleaded to enter Palestine, which he knew would only add to the bitterness and anguish of Palestine Jewry. Whatever the cause, there was no doubt that Gort was one of the most popular High Commissioners Palestine had ever had. In contrast to Sir Harold MacMichael, who preceded him, Gort took an interest in Palestine—its people, its Arab villages, its Jewish collective settlements. I was told that Sir Harold, in his years as High Commissioner, had not once visited a Jewish farm.

Sir Alan struck me as a worthy successor to Lord Gort. Possessing an air of great gentleness and kindliness, he was not at all military in manner. If he had a free hand, I am convinced the Arab-Jewish problems in Palestine would be enormously simplified. He was one of the few British officials I met in whom I found a sympathetic understanding of both the Arab and Jewish positions.

"I have tried hard to get both Arab and Jewish leaders together," he said. "I have attempted it at government receptions, which you might say are really command performances. But"—he smiled wryly—"within a short time you'd discover the Arab and Jewish leaders on opposite sides of the room, afraid to speak to each other in public, especially in front of British officials.

"Yet I know from my own confidential reports that in day-by-day activities the Jews and Arabs of course see each other and get along well."

We discussed the many charges against the Palestine administration that men and women were arrested on suspicion and imprisoned in camps in Eritrea without trial, and that in Palestine the writ of habeas corpus had been suspended. Sir Alan admitted this was true, but added, "I look forward to the time when civil processes will be restored in Palestine. The subject is now pending before the Palestine High Court."

I put a fundamental question frankly to him: would American troops be needed in Palestine if 100,000 Jews were admitted?

Sir Alan shot a sharp glance at me.

"No, sir," he said. "But I should not mind having a token squad of American troops here to show everyone that the United States is behind Britain in such a solution."

And he gave us a piece of advice. "Whatever you do," he said, "I would suggest that you make a bold and forthright recommendation and then see that it is carried out with boldness and determination."

I asked Sir Alan about the Jewish Agency. Repeatedly since we first had discussed the subject aboard the *Queen Elizabeth* the wish of many of the British members to dissolve the Jewish Agency had come up in our discussions. What was Sir Alan's opinion?

He shook his head.

"No, I shouldn't want to see the Agency disbanded. I am not one of those who underestimate it. The Palestine government may not like it, but it cannot ignore it: it is a force to be reckoned with, and my own feeling in the matter is that it really cannot be destroyed—even if the government should wish to do so."

I left Government House with the feeling that Sir Alan himself favored partition as a solution, not partition along the lines of the Peel Report but with a far more generous territorial allowance to the new state of Judea.

It was at Sir Alan's residence that I met Brother Anthony, a Franciscan monk, and other priests, who gave me more testimonials to Jewish-Arab relations.

Wearing a short Vandyke and in his flowing brown robe, Brother Anthony looked anything but a product of

New England, yet he had been born in Vermont. He invited us to Terra Sancta, the Franciscan monastery near Jerusalem, and there mixed for Buxton and me the best Manhattan cocktails we had had in Palestine. You could not mistake the American touch. "As an American whose ancestors fought in the Revolution, I sympathize with the Jews in their struggle for freedom," he said.

I remembered, too, the comment of another priest, who observed with a twinkle in his eye, "If an Arab state were set up here I am afraid it would mean the Crusades had been in vain." He spoke with much pride of a school which he and his colleagues conducted. "You'd be delighted to see how Jewish and Arab children study side by side. They study and work and play together." The Jewish-Arab hostility was synthetic and inspired—at least among the people themselves, he asserted.

"Would you say then that the struggle between Arabs and Jews is at the top level only?" I asked.

He nodded. "On the top level," he said. "There is no question of it."

Into my mind flashed the words of Viscount Samuel, first High Commissioner of Palestine, as he sat before us in London, quiet, informed, his hands folded on the small table before him, and summed up the problem:

"I think if you could get a political settlement at the top, things would shape very differently at the bottom. I do not think the bottom people wish to quarrel; at the top they do rather like it."

In London, critics of the Jews in Palestine had charged that Arabs were paid far less than Jews and that this caused difficulties among the two peoples. I had heard the testimony of Mrs. Goldie Meyerson, spokesman for the *Histadruth,* the General Federation of Jewish Labor, who told us that from the first day of Jewish work in Palestine, the *Histadruth* had never ceased to work for mutual aid and co-operation with Arab workers.

"Yes," said Mrs. Meyerson, who had grown up in Milwaukee and become the first woman in the Palestine labor movement, "we recognize two different standards of wage levels in Palestine. It is not a happy situation and the record will show that we have worked constantly to raise the Arab level to the Jewish, or we face the possibility of bringing the Jewish level down to the Arab. We don't want this. We are building a country, a civilization, a way of life, and we don't want to be a master race, with a people of a much lower standard among us. We want our young people to grow up in an environment of high cultural standards, not only within the Jewish communal settlement, but in the neighboring Arab villages, in the streets of Jerusalem, in the streets of Haifa—everywhere."

In the twenties, the Jewish employers and workers urged the Mandatory to establish minimum-wage legislation for all workers, Arab and Jewish, in Palestine, she testified. This was not granted. The Jewish Agency repeatedly requested blanket wage increases to Jewish and Arab policemen and to Jewish and Arab civil servants. This was refused.

I myself learned that much of the difficulty in raising the Arab standard of living lies in the opposition of the Arab effendi to having Arab workers reach the same wage levels as the Jewish workers. This policy has been recognized by the Mandatory itself; even in government work a wage differential is maintained by the Mandatory between Arab and Jewish workers.

I built up my conclusions slowly. Walking through the

streets of Jerusalem, I would come upon an Arab having an English letter read to him by a small Jewish school child. I found that Arabic was taught in all Jewish secondary schools and even in many of the elementary ones, while every agricultural settlement had at least one teacher of Arabic. Down at the Dead Sea, Arabs and Jews worked in harmony. The Arabs received almost double the wage paid Arabs in Egypt performing comparable work. In Haifa, Jews and Arabs are together members of the town council and the mayor is Jewish; and both Jews and Arabs collaborate on numerous government boards, committees, and trade and commerce organizations. In the citrus industry, for example—one of Palestine's great industries—Jewish and Arab orange growers co-operate.

I discovered that basically their common success depended upon their common efforts. In Jerusalem, for example, if Jews were to patronize only Jewish shops, and Arabs only Arab shops, both would suffer.

Arab governments invite Hebrew University professors to formulate schemes of improvement, and officials and students from the neighboring Arab countries work in Jewish research institutions and laboratories. I thought it paradoxical to learn that the very Arab leaders who attack the Jews send their wives and families to Hadassah Hospital, an institution made possible only by Zionist endeavor.

In the rural areas of Palestine I found the Arabs looking upon the Jews with great respect. Farmers themselves, they regarded with approval these people who worked the land so earnestly, who were ready to stay up all night with a sick lamb, and whose sense of values toward the simple things of earth—planting, harvesting, irrigating—was like their own. These Arabs might be told time and again by political leaders that the Jews were a foreign people, alien to Palestine and its ageless way of life: but they saw the evidence of their own eyes that these men and women were ready to endure the greatest hardships, live in malarial country, fight nature with all their energy—and they understood this.

The basic truth of Arab-Jewish life in Palestine is that political conflict on high levels does not affect the relations among the men on the street

I could find no conflict of interests. The nearer an Arab village was to a Jewish colony, the better its economic, social, and health conditions. There was no question that the Arabs of Palestine are better off than those of any other Arab country. The birth rate of the Palestine Arab is higher, the death rate lower; an Arab laborer in Palestine is paid higher wages and lives a better life than his opposite number in Egypt or in Iraq, although they have no problem there of Jewish immigration or of "Zionist invasion." It is precisely because of this better life in Palestine that tens of thousands of Arabs from neighboring Arab countries have been attracted to Palestine, crossing the border from Syria, Trans-Jordan, and Egypt—and they are still coming.

Yet, despite this lack of conflict of interests, despite this lack of hatred and animosity in everyday life, in spite of the signs of neighborly friendship I had seen myself, apparently a feud does exist on the higher levels.

I became almost obsessed with this question of Arab-Jewish relations. Left alone, I was told by both peoples, they would get along. And slowly this same conviction grew in me, and slowly it became definite truth to me that at every turn, whether covertly or overtly, whether by design or through ignorance, pressures were at work upon both peoples to keep them if possible at each other's throats.

It was obvious that there were vested interests militating against a Jewish-Arab understanding. Two distinct groups, each for reasons of its own, are opposed to a Jewish Palestine. The Arab kings and effendis form the first group. British imperialism represents the second—and both, in that "passive alliance" cited by Dr. Einstein, were now acting as one against the common enemy. This, then, was the role of imperialism in the picture.

Pan-Arabism as a solid, united force of the Arab world was more myth than truth. The community of interests of the kings, sheiks, and effendis in the various Arab lands is unquestionably the main factor behind the seemingly united front of the Arab states in their fight against Zionism. And in this united front, the Arab masses are unprotected. What we have is a class interest of state rulers, landowners, and officialdom. To them, as distinct from the multitudes of the Arab peoples, Zionism's social and technical innovations are a threat because they mean lifting the masses from their ignorance and serfdom.

But why, one might ask, should the British Labour government enter into what was little less than an alliance with reactionary Arab political leaders? Even Harold Laski's "long-range" explanation—that there were those who thought that the Labour Party would require at least twenty years of continuous power to complete the needed reforms at home, and therefore, they believed, nothing should be done to upset the Middle East applecart—could not adequately cover this. It was incredible that Labour leaders had any illusions as to the sociological and political character of the Arab League. Nor could they be overestimating its military potential. British officers, after all, had trained most of the Arab armies in the Middle East, and the British knew how limited Arab military strength and equipment were. The Jews of Palestine, we knew, were our only ally in the Middle East during the war. Nonetheless, the Labour Cabinet seemed determined to support reactionary Arab leadership against progressive Jewish leadership. Why?

In years past, I thought, one might agree that the Middle East was crucially important to Britain's existence as a great power. One might then grant that if Britain wished to maintain her status in the world, she must also maintain her predominant position in this area that links three continents and guards the main waterways of the world; that Britain's strength rested on her control of international trade and communications through the Middle East. One could understand why safeguarding that controlling position seemed essential to all British statesmen, whether Conservative or Labour.

But this was the fifth decade of the twentieth century. We were in the Atomic Age. With atomic warfare, was not this a rather antiquated approach? So it appeared to me. Yet perhaps it was from this point of view—a point of view valid a century ago and still subscribed to—that one was forced to view Britain's Middle East policies. For assuredly the British know there is little substance in such political formations as the Arab League: they know that for more than half a century they have successfully controlled Arab leaders; they know the price of each one of them, whether it be paid in unofficial salaries, political subventions, oil royalties, or any other form of bribery. They, therefore, feel that by backing Arab political leaders they do not risk losing the Middle East to a rising local nationalism, or, for that matter, to a competing power. They realize that the Moslem potentates would never align themselves with Communist Russia, the only competitor of Britain now in sight.

The British are playing safe, or, I venture to say, *they think they are playing safe*. Their assumption is that they will be able to control the Arabs indefinitely and thus keep Russia out of the Mediterranean and the Middle East. What the British may actually bring about by such a policy may be a most tragic loss; they may eventually lose the only friend they have in the Middle East—the Jews of Palestine.

CHAPTER 17

The Sweet Waters of the Jordan

PERHAPS ONE of the most challenging schemes for Palestine's future development—and the development of the entire Middle East—was that envisaged in the Jordan Valley Authority as it was presented to us in Washington. My first chance to visualize it came when I visited the great Palestine potash plant on the shores of the Dead Sea, where both Arabs and Jews are employed. Not only are the mineral-laden waters of this ancient lake utilized, but Palestine Jewry also has been able to take the salt- and mineral-filled land and transform it into fertile plantations with the help of chemical fertilizers developed at the Sieff Institute.

Standing on the shores of the Dead Sea, its bitter metallic breath in my nostrils, I looked about me on this floor of the world, 1300 feet below sea level, and tried to see the challenging JVA plan as Dr. Lowdermilk had described it to us that day in Washington. There, in his charts, we caught something of the magic of his dream. Here, in the Holy Land, standing where the waters of the Jordan flowed into the Dead Sea, its daring caught my breath.

What is the plan?

Here is the Dead Sea, a huge evaporating pan, into which daily pour thousands of gallons of precious Jordan

233

River water, flowing wastefully away. If this water could be spread both east and west through Palestine, it would revive earth that has lain arid for centuries. All that the soil of Palestine needs is water, and, given water, hundreds of thousands of acres of land which have been unproductive since Roman times can be reclaimed.

The valley of the Jordan is a natural reservoir which could be utilized for the benefits of both sides of the Jordan and become as valuable to Palestine as the Colorado River development project has been to our own West. The Lowdermilk plan would transform the vast undeveloped desert—the Negev—into the Imperial Valley of the Middle East.

This use of the Jordan to make the desert bloom and to bring a bountiful supply of water at low cost to sections of Palestine now yielding at best only one crop a year is one half of the project. The other half is equally challenging.

If a channel were cut from the Mediterranean at sea level eastward until it met the river, which drops down to the Dead Sea—1300 feet below sea level—the waters of the Mediterranean would roar down in a power-generating cascade. This would bring a source of cheap hydroelectrical power for all Palestine, similar to our Tennessee Valley Authority.

The complete plan, as described to us, has another great advantage. The Jordan's own sweet water would be diverted into canals to irrigate and make fruitful now barren areas. Today less than 100,000 acres of Palestine are under irrigation; with the Lowdermilk plan, more than seven times that amount—750,000 acres—would spring to life again. And this land, as Dr. Lowdermilk stressed, had not always lain waste. It had once been fertile, but through neglect and misuse had been allowed to erode. The Lowdermilk plan calls for completion in eight stages; but each stage of the great project would come into operation independently.

If this could be carried out, it would mean the development not only of Palestine, but also of neighboring Arab states. Trans-Jordan, on the east shore of the Dead Sea, would share equally with Palestine, and Syria and the Lebanon could enjoy as well the fruits of this bold plan. Thus, this entire area, which in Roman days constituted the granary of the East, would become a new great economic unit bringing a higher standard of living, prosperity, and peace to the Middle East.

The JVA would weld together the entire area, eliminate the insularity of the Arab states. It would compel cooperation. It would make peace exciting. What impressed me, too, was that the plan had even taken into account the most delicate religious problems involved in the sacred and holy places. These included keeping the water of the Sea of Galilee at its customary level and arranging dams in the Jordan River around the bends where they would be out of sight of tourists.

But I found discouraging the attitude of the Palestine government officials. They sniped at the JVA. They made snide attempts to undermine our confidence in Dr. Hays and Dr. Savage, the two eminent American engineers associated with the Lowdermilk plan. When I spoke enthusiastically about the JVA, the reaction of colonial officials was: "It can't be done—it's a waste of money—it will never be done."

The difference of approach between the British and American members of the committee with regard to the project was epitomized for me in the meeting which four members of the committee had one evening with Hays and Savage.

Hays had formerly been associated with the planning of the Tennessee Valley Authority and it was he who had worked out the detailed proposals for a Jordan Valley Authority which were placed before us. Savage, probably the world's foremost irrigation engineer, was the genius behind the construction of Boulder Dam. He was on his way to China, where he had been invited for consultation on a vast new irrigation scheme, and had arranged to stop off en route for the specific purpose of appearing before us. The session merited more attention than it received. An hour was set aside at the end of an already long day for four of us—Crick, Leggett, Buxton, and myself—to hear what these experts had to say of this grand-scale proposal for revolutionizing the economic life of Palestine and its neighbors. I had an advantage over the others, for having seen the Boulder Dam, the Colorado River project, and the Central Valley project now in progress in California, I was familiar with what had been done in our own country and could more readily envisage the JVA's tremendous possibilities. Buxton had no expert knowledge, but he, too, had a largeness of vision in a matter of this kind which I felt was characteristically American.

Sir Frederick asked few questions and seemed to me to regard the whole thing as largely talk. He left before the session ended. Crick, as befitted a banker, asked detailed questions on costs and financing. The entire project, as presented to us, would involve an expenditure—recoverable over a period of years, according to the estimates of the engineers—of £50,000,000, or about $200,000,000. It was a large sum, though in terms of what had been expended in America and elsewhere on similar projects, by no means out of the way. To Crick, I believe, it seemed, in the circumstances, astronomic. I felt that he was skeptical about the whole proposal.

Finally, he turned to Savage. "Supposing you were given fifty million pounds to be used on an irrigation scheme anywhere in the world. With your wide experience of many countries, where would you suggest that that money be invested to do the most good?"

Savage is a very quiet-spoken, round-faced, benign-looking man—almost Pickwickian—anything but the average man's idea of a great engineer, whose business it is literally to move mountains. He listened to Crick's question and sat perfectly silent for over a minute; one could see that in his mind he was revolving various possibilities. Finally he said, in the quietest of tones, but with a firmness born of conviction, "I would invest it right here."

The hearing of these two engineers was not even recorded in the minutes of the committee's proceedings, but I am convinced that what they had to tell us was of far greater consequence than the political harangues to which we were treated by many of the witnesses whose names were headlines in the press. As against the passions and prejudices of men, the detached and detailed calculations of these two engineers carried with them the promise of a better life for millions in a land where the common man had for centuries known nothing but misery and grinding poverty.

CHAPTER 18

Arab Adventure

WHILE I EXPLORED Palestine, two sections of the committee paid flying trips to the neighboring Arab states. We had been invited to see for ourselves how contented were the Jews living under Arab rule in Iraq, Syria, and Lebanon, and how unanimously all the peoples of the Arab states wished Palestine to become an Arab state. This invitation was accepted by Sir John, Manningham-Buller, and Buxton, who visited Iraq and Saudi Arabia, and by Judge Hutcheson, Morrison, and McDonald, who went to Syria and the Lebanon. This latter adventure proved, I am afraid, a boomerang to the Arab cause, for if it achieved anything, it was to underline the perilous position of Oriental Jewry today.

McDonald found himself figuring in a fantastic episode in Beirut in which he played the role of a good Samaritan. He rescued a Palestinian Jewish youth, Yehuda Hellman, the correspondent of *The Palestine Post,* from the Lebanese Sûreté Nationale, or secret police, in an adventure which might well have been taken from *The Arabian Nights.* Had it not been for McDonald's courageous intervention and assistance, young Hellman might have been interned indefinitely in Beirut under the most distressing conditions. But of that, more later.

In Damascus, capital of Syria, the government chose three Jews to testify as to political and economic conditions of Jewry in Syria. More than a week before, the Palestine press carried charges that the Syrian Jewish witnesses had been warned what to say and what not to say. The government allotted two hours, divided into twenty-minute periods, for the presentation of the testimony by interested groups. These groups included Moslem clubwomen, Moslem spiritual leaders, Moslem political leaders, Moslem merchants, Moslem journalists, and the Jews.

The committee of three chosen Jews appeared. Only one spoke. There had been testimony in Jerusalem before us by Oriental Jews, charging that Jews in the Oriental countries were given only second-class citizenship. Our subcommittee expected the Jewish spokesman they now heard on the scene to need far more than twenty minutes to tell his story. Instead, he used forty-five seconds of his allotted time. He raced through a one-sentence written statement in which he said that the Jews of Syria were happy and not discriminated against; that their situation was excellent under the present Syrian government; and that they had absolutely nothing whatsoever to do with Zionism.

The three presented a picture of terrified men, McDonald told me. Judge Hutcheson, surprised at the brevity of this presentation, asked, "You have nothing else to add?" The Jewish spokesman shook his head. "Very well," said the Judge, nodding his head, and with the dismissal, the three hurried to their seats in the rear of the room amid murmurs of sly amusement from the Moslem audience which said, as clearly as words, "They knew what was best for them."

The facts as to the situation of the Jews in Syria, as I

learned elsewhere, refute this testimony. Once the Damascus Jewish community had flourished. Today, less than three thousand Jews live there, of whom more than half are so poor they must exist on relief funds collected from Jewish organizations outside Syria. There are few Jewish civil servants, and Jews are discouraged from professional pursuits. Most Jews are peddlers and small merchants, with a very few listed as wealthy merchants. They live in a small Jewish quarter, helpless and unprotected against nationalist riots. With the French driven out of Syria under General Spears' machinations, the Jews remain as the sole distinctive "foreign" group against which Syrian nationalists can demonstrate to show their unity. During Balfour Day, in November, 1945, Syrian students surged through the narrow Jewish quarter, shouting anti-Semitic slogans and hurling stones at the windows.

While the plight of European Jewry was well known, hardly any but scholars had looked into the true position of Jews living in the Arab states. Here and there our committee had gained an inkling that Oriental Jewry lived in fear and insecurity. Professor Hitti had admitted to us in Washington that the Moslem law requires Jews and Christians to recognize the superior status of the Moslems. In Jerusalem a Hebrew scholar had pointed out to me a passage in the Koran reading: "Thou wilt surely find that the strongest in enmity against those who believe are the Jews and the idolaters." If, in centuries past, the Arabs had been hospitable to the Jews, this was now the twentieth century, and we were in an era of growing nationalism and xenophobia in which the Jew, the perennial stranger, was the first and most helpless victim. The result of Arab nationalism today was to denationalize the Jews and break any connection they had with Jews elsewhere—

particularly in Palestine. At the same time, Arab nationalism did not permit the Jew to become assimilated in
the Arab states, so that he was, as it were, ground between two stones. In Iraq, for example, Zionism was high
treason. Every Iraqi Jew's passport was stamped "Invalid
for Palestine." No Hebrew publication, if printed in
Palestine, was permitted into the country. If the Jew, thus
shut off from his own, sought to assimilate, he found the
door barred. Government posts were closed to Jews in
most Moslem countries. The differences of religion, a
much more important factor in Oriental countries than
in the West, further isolates the Jews, so that they are
able to take little or no part in the cultural life of their
Moslem neighbors. Thus, everywhere the Jew in the Arab
Middle East remains the eternal scapegoat.

The situation is made no happier by the imposition of
the Arab boycott against Zionist products. Signs posted on
the customs building at the Palestine-Lebanon border
read: "The importation of Zionist goods is strictly forbidden." Zionist goods are any products made by Palestine
Jewry. The Arab authorities claim they are anti-Zionist,
but not anti-Jewish, but no distinction is made. As of
today, any Arab who carries a can of Zionist orange juice or
Zionist peas into the Lebanon or Syria can be arrested. The
average Arab is inclined to laugh at the boycott; how seriously he takes it may be seen from the fact that invariably
he asks any foreign fellow passenger to carry across the
border such Jewish-made products as chocolate bars, clothing accessories, and other "Zionist" products.

The situation of the Jews of Yemen is perhaps the most
lamentable. Here Jews are, *ipso facto*, third- and fourth-
class citizens. They must get off a sidewalk and into the
street when an Arab passes; like the untouchables of India,

they live in a state of constant persecution. They are forced to live in ghettos which are locked at night; yet they are not legally permitted to leave Yemen.

These facts were brought back to us by some of my colleagues. Additional data on the Jewish situation were reported by correspondents Ruth Gruber, Gerold Frank, and AP man George Palmer, who accompanied the subcommittees. McDonald's personal experience in Beirut, the capital of the Lebanon, gave us some idea of what we might expect in Arab treatment of Jewish minorities if we recommended that Palestine become an Arab state.

The story related by McDonald went something like this.

The Lebanon is the only Arab state with a Christian majority. Most of its Christians are members of the Maronite Church, which owes allegiance to the Pope. The chief Christian religious figure is His Beatitude the Patriarch Arida, now in his eighty-fifth year, who resides in Bkerke, near Beirut.

In the Lebanon, as elsewhere, the hearings were arranged by the government, so that only government-sponsored witnesses appeared. Significantly enough, neither the Patriarch Arida nor his spokesman, Monsignor Moubarak, Archbishop of Beirut, had been invited to testify, though they represented the majority of the citizens of the Lebanon. The government, it was obvious, took no chances of any discordant note sounding in the prearranged Arab symphony.

This conspiracy of silence was known to newspapermen. But in a police state such as the Lebanon, the press is controlled. No word leaked out to the committee that they were being deprived of the opportunity to hear recognized Lebanese spokesmen.

At this point of the story, *The Palestine Post* sent twenty-three-year-old Yehuda Hellman, a former student at the University of Beirut, to Beirut to cover the committee hearings. Hellman registered at the Hotel Normandy there a few hours before the committee arrived from Damascus. A few hours later he was suddenly arrested by the Lebanese secret police, his luggage searched, and his passport, identity card, his press credentials, and all other papers taken. He was ordered held incommunicado in the hotel, his telephone was disconnected, and he was prevented from sending any dispatches to his newspaper. McDonald told me he was unable to determine precisely on what charge Hellman was arrested. Apparently, the Lebanese took the position that since Hellman was a Palestine Jew, *ergo* he was a spy and possibly a terrorist assigned to assassinate the three members of our subcommittee.

"A secret agent was set to guard Hellman, and the boy wasn't permitted to speak to anyone," McDonald told me. "No one, that is, except the three members of the Anglo-American Committee, because, I suppose, we had diplomatic immunity. The result was bizarre: young Hellman spent most of his time drinking tea with his intended victims, usually in my room." McDonald chuckled. "I questioned him for hours and gained an invaluable insight into the feelings of Jewish youth in Palestine."

That evening Hellman was sitting morosely in his room, his police guard on duty in the corridor outside. Suddenly the hotel manager burst into his room. "The Prime Minister has invited you to attend the government reception for the committee at the palace!" he announced excitedly.

"He has sent his car for you. It is waiting downstairs. Please hurry, sir."

Hellman immediately dressed and was ushered ceremoniously into the limousine and driven to the palace. His police guard commandeered a taxi and followed him. There Hellman was greeted cordially by the Chef de Protocol, who introduced him to the Chief of Secret Police, who took his arm in paternal fashion and introduced him to the British Minister, Terence Shone. "I am delighted to see you here, young man," said Shone. "I know it was all a mistake, but such things do happen. Let's all forget it, shall we?" They raised their glasses and drank a toast to Hellman's health. A moment later the Prime Minister himself entered. "Well, well!" he exclaimed. "So this is Mr. Hellman." He shook hands warmly. "Make yourself at home. You are our guest."

Young Hellman, dazed but thankful, dined sparingly. He caught a glimpse of Judge Hutcheson and Lord Morrison, wandered about the palace, and finally proceeded to return to the hotel. As he strode down the street, whistling, he glanced behind him. He was being trailed by the same police agent who had been guarding him from the beginning. When he reached the hotel, and sought to leave to send a dispatch to his newspaper, his guard stood in his way, apologetically but doggedly. He was, it appeared, still under arrest.

It seems that Judge Hutcheson earlier that evening protested to a Lebanese government official against the house arrest of a young newspaperman, and added that he, Hutcheson, had met the young man and hardly thought him a dangerous character. Hellman's invitation must have been an *opéra-bouffe* attempt to soothe Judge Hutcheson.

The following morning the Judge, who evidently was not amused, called Hellman to his room. He placed his hand on the youth's shoulder.

"Mr. Hellman," he said, "many times before I have been happy that I was an American. But I tell you now, I thank God that I am an American citizen."

Gerold Frank, the newspaperman who had accompanied our committee from Washington, and who was sharing Hellman's room at the Normandy because the hotel was full, was arrested with Hellman but released a few minutes later. That night Frank obtained a revealing interview with the Archbishop Moubarak in which the latter charged that our committee "heard only spokesmen selected by the government who said what the government wished them to say." The Archbishop asserted that President El Khoury of the Lebanon "did not give his true views on Zionism because he fears the Arab League."

Development of the Lebanon was tied up with that of Palestine, he went on, and added: "We Christian Lebanese know that. We realize that Zionism is bringing civilization to Palestine and to the entire Middle East. I am very much in favor of Zionism because I have the good of Palestine at heart.

"You can be sure that in this country the great majority of the Christians—and that is the majority of the population—are against the reactionary Arab anti-Zionist opinion and support the Jews because they have the best relations with them and know that together with them they will work out the best solution."

The Archbishop charged that Moslem Arabs in Palestine, Damascus, and Beirut had sold land to the Jews at high prices; that they now wished to regain those lands by ousting the Jews. He added that he had been invited to the Prime Minister's dinner and reception the night before, but refused to let his presence give the impression that he agreed with the opinions expressed before the committee.

As a result of this interview, McDonald and Stinespring, of our staff, called upon the Patriarch and the Archbishop and received their testimony, which paralleled Frank's interview; this evidence later was incorporated into the official record of the committee hearings.

The denouement of this story came on the third day. McDonald, preparing to leave for Palestine (he had been indisposed and had remained after Hutcheson and Morrison had left), discovered that young Hellman was still held incommunicado in the hotel and was by this time a very troubled young man. McDonald announced that he would not leave Beirut unless Hellman accompanied him. A Lebanese government spokesman explained regretfully that the Hellman matter was in the hands of the Sûreté Nationale and nothing could be done about it.

"Very well," said McDonald. "If he stays, I stay."

One hour later the government found it possible to release Hellman. McDonald's car waited outside the Hotel Normandy. Hellman hurried down with his luggage, climbed in next to McDonald, and thus, under the protection of the former High Commissioner for Refugees, Hellman departed from the tender hospitality of the Lebanon.

Something like a page out of *Othello* were the experiences of Sir John, Major Manningham-Buller, and Buxton in Baghdad and Riyadh, the capitals of Iraq and Saudi Arabia. Beeley, who had once said he would rather live in Jerusalem than anywhere else in the world because there he could enjoy the society of the most cultivated

Arabs, accompanied them because he wanted the thrill of meeting King Ibn Saud.

The committee examined perhaps a score of witnesses in Baghdad. There had been a massacre of Jews in Iraq in 1941, and the committee was eager to learn their situation now. As in Damascus and Beirut, the Jewish witnesses who testified publicly declared that all was well. Their lot was not hard, the handicaps to which they were subjected were not serious, there was no danger of another pogrom, and their economic status was generally similar to that of the Arabs.

The committee then flew to Riyadh, where they were ceremoniously welcomed by King Ibn Saud in his palace. He received them seated in a thronelike chair at the end of a great room hung with tapestries. Near him was a small table on which there was a telephone. A push button on the table also was suggestive of that industrialized society which some Arab witnesses appeared to scorn.

Through an interpreter—the King speaks only Arabic— he suggested that they rest the remainder of the day and speak with him the following day. After breakfast the next morning—made notable by the fact that two boxes of Kellogg's Corn Flakes were on the table—they were received again by the King. He spoke freely, impressively, and at some length. He showed remarkable vigor, and the committee felt they were definitely in the presence of a man who had qualities which are usually ascribed to a masterful leader of men.

Buxton told me: "Listening, detecting the working of his mind, studying his mannerisms, and trying to learn how he had obtained such a strong following in his own country and throughout the Arab world, I am afraid that I succumbed to him. I think that if I had been a young Arab in the days when he was carving out his destiny, I would have followed him over the walls and even ventured to assay the first jump over if he had so commanded."

So far as the Jews were concerned, it became evident that Ibn Saud thought of them in premedieval terms. The question of the Jews in Palestine concerned him, he said, because he was an Arab; and this question, he said, "was not the product of modern times but an ancient enmity going back thousands of years." He said that the Koran declared that "Thou wilt surely find that the strongest in enmity against those who believe are the Jews and the idolaters; and thou wilt find the nearest in love to those who believe to be those who say, 'We are Christians.'" He told the committee: "I say that the Jews are our enemies in every place. In every country to which they come they create trouble and work against our interests. I am convinced that the Jews strive to create difficulties between the Arabs and their friends, Britain and America, and this is what the Arabs do not want and seek to avoid." He asserted that the Jews in Palestine were being given every help, every resource, while the Arabs were "homeless or refugees or penalized."

In Cairo and Jerusalem Manningham-Buller had asked Arab witnesses whether they would object to the admission of helpless old men and women, and the reply was invariably in the negative. The same question was asked of Ibn Saud. "Not a single Jew," he replied, although later, in a transcript made of the conversation, in which the King's words were translated by H. St. John B. Philby, British writer and convert to Mohammedanism, who was present, the King is quoted as replying that he could not answer this question until the Arabs agreed on it among themselves.

No Jewish witnesses were interviewed in Saudi Arabia, for there are no Jews in the country. Buxton later told me he had the feeling while King Ibn Saud was speaking about the Jews that he was talking "mainly for the record—Arab shorthand men took down what was said during the audience"; and that "the King would have pooh-poohed the idea of violent resistance to large-scale Jewish immigration."

Likewise, I gathered, one might look doubtfully upon threats that the Arabs would withdraw American oil concessions if the United States continued to press for the admission of Jewish refugees into Palestine. In the course of my discussions on the subject of oil I came to a number of conclusions. Ibn Saud, as well as the other Arab potentates, were more dependent upon the revenues from American and British oil concessions than we were dependent upon them. They needed our capital, our industry, our experience, and our commercial protection. I felt, too, that the growth of American oil interests in the Middle East—we now own forty per cent of the oil reserves in that area—had been accomplished with the consent of Great Britain rather than despite her. It appeared to me that Great Britain valued our political and strategic partnership with her in the Mediterranean area too greatly to let commercial rivalry with us work to either her or our detriment. As for the bogey of Ibn Saud and the others withdrawing their oil concessions to offer them to the Soviet, this seemed to me altogether untenable. There is too great a gap between the economic socialism of Russia and the economic feudalism of Saudi Arabia and Iraq. It seemed highly unlikely to me that Ibn Saud and the other Arab rulers would be able to maintain their privileged status if they permitted Russian economic expansion into their countries.

CHAPTER 19

"We Are Here to Stay"

WHEN THE HEARINGS resumed during our final week in Palestine, they took on new meanings for us against the background of what we had seen and experienced.

Black-robed bishops and scarlet-turbaned dignitaries of the Arab Christian Church and the ministers of the Anglican Church appeared to testify for the Arabs. The Arabs, they said, were the rightful owners of the land; Zionism was a political invader threatening the social, political, and religious rights of the people of the land, they declared.

One witness—the Reverend Mr. H. R. A. Jones, of the Church Mission to the Jews—urged us to issue immigration certificates to "Christian Jews."

"Our mission cannot continue to staff its schools and hospitals if such people are not admitted," he asserted. The Jewish Agency refused to recognize these persons as Jews and withheld certificates from them, whereas such Jews, converted as they had been to Christianity, "still consider themselves as Jews and better Jews."

"Can you give us some idea of the scope of this problem?" asked Crossman. "How many such Christian Jews are there in Palestine?"

"A Jewish doctor in Tel Aviv told me fully two per cent of the people of Tel Aviv secretly believe in Jesus Christ," he said, and added that these Christian Jews had not been baptized "for fear of ostracism and boycott."

The Moslem religious leaders who appeared were dignified and remote. Jewish immigration, they maintained, had not really helped the country, regardless of what statistics we had been given; in reality it had harmed Palestine. The Jews sought to destroy Arab holy places. The Jews were Communists who would communize the country, capitalists who would industrialize the country and "profoundly shock" the sensibilities of all religious peoples, atheists who would irreparably destroy the religious significance of Palestine.

If the Zionists based their claim to Palestine on the Old Testament, that claim was no longer valid because "the Old Testament has been superseded by the New Testament," the Archbishop Hakim, Greek Catholic Bishop of Galilee, told us. He added that Archbishop Moubarak of Beirut had spoken falsely when he said that the Christians of the Lebanon were sympathetic toward the Jews; that there was a strong possibility that such a statement had never been made. Since we had in our files the testimony given by the Patriarch and the Archbishop, these words were less effective than the witnesses might have believed.

Another witness asserted that the Jewish National Home was already created and that the Zionists' real design, cleverly hidden though it was, was manifestly clear. It was to set up a giant Land of Israel, reaching from the Tigris to the Nile.

Now came Dr. Judah L. Magnes, president of the Hebrew University. Long before we arrived in Palestine we had heard of him. A native of San Francisco, he had given up his pulpit as rabbi of Temple Emanu-El in New York during the First World War because of his pacifist convictions and had come to Palestine. He was well known for his advocacy of the bi-nationalism plan for Palestine, which proposed that immigration should be controlled to allow the same number of Jews in Palestine as Arabs, and that each then should have equal representation in the government of the country. He had written widely on the subject and his following, the *Ichud,* though very small, commanded respect.

A tall, spare man, he had not altered his pacifist views when he appeared before us as one of the last Jewish witnesses. He made it clear that he was opposed to force of any kind.

"Our view is based on two assumptions," he declared. "First, that Jewish-Arab co-operation is essential for a satisfactory solution, and, second, that it is possible. The alternative is war, but the plain Jew and the plain Arab do not want war."

He added that the real problem was trying to establish an equilibrium between two forces. "What is it that most Jews want? It is immigration. Give us the chance of an ample immigration, and many of the sincerest advocates of the Jewish state will forgo the state. What is it that most Arabs want? It is self-government. They are certainly not behind other Arabs in their capacity for self-government. Give them a chance of ample self-government, and many of the sincerest opponents of Jewish immigration will acquiesce."

The immediate problem was the DPs. "We pray you to help these 100,000 come back home to this Jewish National Home, and this without further delay.

"They are not a threat to Arab numbers, for they would constitute a net gain for the Jews of not more than 33,000. According to government figures, the Arab natural increase during five years of war was about 150,000, or 30,000 a year. The Jewish increment was only about 83,000, including natural increase and all immigration. Thus, there is a net Jewish gain of not more than 33,000. This is not such a frightening number. It is a smaller number than was envisaged during discussions between some Jews and Arabs. In 1936, after the outbreak of the Arab revolt, they agreed that after ten years, this very year 1946, the Jews would constitute forty per cent of the population, that is, 800,000 persons."

Sir Frederick asked whether it would be right to bring in young children from the DP camps if the only way determined upon by either side was to fight.

Great pacifist though he is, Magnes replied, "I am going to give you an extreme answer. Even though that were the only way, I would bring them, but that is not the only way."

Sir Frederick questioned him about the "fighting spirit" of the Jewish youths in DP camps.

"What do you expect of these boys?" Dr. Magnes replied. "They underwent the same militaristic excitement as the whole world. Is not the American youth being given military training? Nevertheless, I recommend bringing these youths here because they will not fight."

This testimony by a man whose judgment was based not only upon years in Palestine, but on American background, was most impressive, and particularly to Judge Hutcheson.

"You are not denominated a Christian, Dr. Magnes," he said, "but you talk as I should like Christians to act. I am not ready to assess your proposals, but I am a fairly old man, and I recognize moral power when I see it."

The last spokesman for the Arab side was Albert Hourani, Mrs. Antonius' outstanding protégé, Director of the Arab Office in Jerusalem, a friend of Beeley and one of Crossman's former students. Hourani made an extremely competent summation of the Arab case. The Arab nation was "unalterably opposed to the attempt to impose a Jewish state" upon it. His solution was that presented by other Arab leaders from Washington to Damascus: establishment of Palestine as a self-governing state with an Arab majority, but with full rights for its Jewish citizens and with further immigration to be determined by the majority of the population.

"Either one must attempt to establish a Jewish state with all the risk involved," he declared, "or else one must attempt to put into practice the Arab proposals. All intermediate solutions are illusory."

"I propose to examine as briefly as I can three such solutions," he said. "First, partition; second, a bi-national state; third, the proposal that a certain number of immigrants, let us say 100,000, shall be brought in with the least possible delay, and a certain amount of self-government should be established, but that the final solution of the problem should be postponed until the future."

Partition: "If the Arabs object to a Jewish state on the grounds of principle in the whole of Palestine, they cannot accept it in part of Palestine." Establishment of a Jewish state in part of Palestine, he said, would not satisfy the great majority of Zionists, but would encourage them to ask for more.

Bi-nationalism: As with partition, the basic Arab objection was one of principle, since bi-nationalism would mean further Jewish immigration. In addition, this plan of Dr. Magnes would satisfy only Dr. Magnes and his supporters, who represented a very small section of the Jewish community in Palestine. It would not satisfy the vast majority of Zionists.

Bringing in a certain number of Jewish immigrants: To this again the Arabs objected on the grounds of principle. The Arabs could never acquiesce, he said, to further Jewish immigration, and the number of immigrants to be brought in was irrelevant. It was unfair for Palestine to bear the burden of the European refugees.

Jews should not fear living as a Jewish minority under Arab rule, he went on. The Arabs had been traditionally friendly to the Jews. They were not offering them "ghetto status," but "membership in the Palestinian community."

He concluded by asserting that if the problem were not solved now, the situation would grow steadily more serious.

When he paused, Crossman said to him: "Please don't misunderstand me, but let me ask: who are you? What right have those who speak for the Arabs to do so? On the Jewish side, I know that there are elections and the spokesmen before us have been elected."

Hourani replied that though the Arab Higher Committee had not been elected, he was certain it represented the people in Palestine. He added that he himself was speaking as a private individual.

He had been most persuasive, and I asked him:

"Mr. Hourani, is it part of your case that in the establishment of an Arab state force might have to be used?"

"Yes," he said, "if you do not broaden that with the conclusion that I welcome it."

"No," I said, "but you feel that the establishment of an

Arab state or any other conclusion might result in the use of force?"

"I feel there is no solution of the Palestinian problem, not even refusal to solve it, which does not involve the risk of using force."

He made it clear that if military forces were withdrawn from Palestine he felt that the Arabs, with the help of the Arab League, could establish a state against any activities on the Jewish side.

Judge Hutcheson engaged in a rather lengthy discussion with him on what I felt was perhaps the essence of the Arab case against the right of Britain and the United States to take action on the Palestine problem. The Arabs had urged that Palestine become an Arab state, with assurances to the Jews that they would be given minority rights and be enabled to live side by side with the Arabs.

Had not the Arabs' basic assumption been that the problem was one for them and the Arab League, Judge Hutcheson observed.

"No," said Hourani, "rather that foreign intervention, even if it is undertaken in order to protect the minority, may do more harm than good."

Was it not true, Judge Hutcheson went on, that a nationalistic Arab world was almost an entirely new phenomenon? That therefore the treatment of the Jew in the old Arab world was not a measure of his potential treatment by the new Arab world? Might not one question what kind of tolerance an Arab state, with its present spirit of nationalism, would extend to persons of other religions and faiths?

"I think there are great risks involved, but I do not despair," Hourani replied.

"You feel you can take the chance because you have

nothing much at stake except trying to achieve your nationalism," Judge Hutcheson observed. But was not Hourani overlooking the fact that the Jews in Palestine were there on the guarantee of the Christian nations of the world? And since the nations of the world had been responsible for creating the present situation, had they not the responsibility of seeing what they could do about it rather than saying simply, "Give it back to the Arabs and let them both fight it out"?

Hourani replied that the Arab proposals were justified not only on grounds of justice "but also because they are the only proposals which offer the slightest chance of avoiding some dreadful catastrophe to the country."

Major Manningham-Buller observed that it would take time to set up Arab self-government, and there were old, sick people in Europe today. They could scarcely wait until Arab self-government was set up, if it were to be set up, and then continue to wait to see what the Arab government decided to do about them. As a humanitarian measure, would the Arabs be prepared to open their doors to those elderly Jews who might have relatives in Palestine?

Hourani thought for a moment. It wasn't fair, he said, to assume that the only choice before these refugees was Palestine. They could be assigned elsewhere.

But assume, said Manningham-Buller, that the only relations these elderly Jews had in the world were in Palestine. Great Britain had opened its doors to Jews with relatives there. Would he be in favor of keeping these old people, in their last few years, away from the one relation who perhaps might give them help?

There was silence. Hourani, in the presentation of his case, had presented most understandingly the points of view on both sides. Yet this question crystallized, as it

257

were, the substance of his testimony. Was he less intransigent than Jaamal Husseini, the same Jaamal who was conspicuously absent today? Hourani looked about him and finally replied slowly, "In view of all that has happened, and in view of the political aim of the Jewish Agency, I am afraid there is no alternative. But I insist the Arabs are not responsible."

One heard a sigh through the room.

Sir John continued to be troubled by Jewish resistance. He recalled Ben Gurion to the stand and asked many questions about the *Haganah*, finally demanding, "Who is the head of the *Haganah*?"

"I don't know," Ben Gurion replied. "I represent the Jewish Agency. If you ask for someone to appear to speak for the *Haganah*, I am sure that they will appear."

Sir John brought up the question which had been troubling Manningham-Buller. Was Mr. Ben Gurion really powerless to halt extremism? "I have tried many times, but if I try now they laugh at me," Ben Gurion replied, choosing his words with care. "There are outrages against us. There is a record of how we have tried to stop our youth, but it is futile now."

Sir John leaned forward. "I ask you again," he said. "I beg you to raise your voice in the interest of peace."

Ben Gurion was silent for a moment. Then he said, "I appreciate your words and I ask you to reciprocate. Your voice is mightier than mine."

He left the stand.

The Jewish case was finally concluded by Moshe Shertok, head of the Political Department of the Jewish Agency, who summed up for us with great skill what we had heard from scores of Jewish witnesses. Shertok, Russian-born, had grown up in an Arab village in Palestine, had managed a Jewish farm in Palestine, had studied in a Turkish university, had been an officer of the Sultan in the Turkish Army, and spoke eight languages fluently.

The basic fact that had to be recognized and accepted was that the Jews had come to Palestine to stay: they were here. The essence of the Balfour Declaration was the recognition of the Jewish right to their homeland. The Mandatory's weakness of purpose had proved futile to the success of that policy.

He disputed charges that the Jews had not attempted to seek conciliation with the Arabs and cited a long list of attempts at Arab-Jewish co-operation, beginning with Dr. Weizmann's agreement with Emir Feisal in 1918. He charged that the attitude of the British Administration in Palestine contributed to the failure to reach an accord.

"The government is sensitive to Arab criticism," he charged. "It apologizes for anything it does for the Jews. The Arabs are treated as true sons of the country, while the Jews are treated like stepchildren." He declared that the Jewish Agency must have control over immigration, so as to be enabled immediately to bring in and settle on the land distressed Jews of Europe; that the restrictions on the sale of land should be abolished, and that the Mandatory should proclaim as its ultimate aim the establishment of a Jewish state as soon as a Jewish majority had been achieved.

And thus, quietly, on a note almost echoing the first words we had heard in Washington so many days and so many countries away, the hearings of the committee officially came to an end.

"We thank the witnesses," said Sir John. "We thank the police for their protection of us. I now announce the completion of our hearings."

We were to leave Palestine in a matter of hours. Before dusk fell, I revisited the old city of Jerusalem. I felt I was back in the Middle Ages as I walked through the narrow, cobblestoned streets filled with the pungent odors of spices and peered into the dark, cavelike interiors of the tiny shops in which Arabs and Jews sold wares ranging from shoe polish to olives, from gas stoves to Turkish sweets. I found the Via Dolorosa and proceeded through it slowly.

These were my last hours in Palestine. I thought to myself, this was the city of Jesus Christ and through these very streets He walked. Now, more than 1900 years since His time, we had just concluded the most terrible war of all time. We could not condemn His principles, because in truth they had not really been tried in all these nearly twenty centuries.

I realized, as I had realized subconsciously before here in Palestine, how sound were the principles Jesus had laid down: the brotherhood of man, the community of work by all for the good of all. Here, in Palestine, I had seen them put into practical use, paradoxically enough—or, perhaps, appropriately enough—by the Jews of Palestine.

It seemed to me that we were perfectly ready to accept Jesus' principles as long as there seemed to be no chance to put them into practice, but that we shied away, symbolically and physically, when the opportunity came. Now, going through old Jerusalem, I thought that just as the Jews, because of their tortured centuries, had achieved the ethical concepts of Jesus, so the world must find its way to that same achievement. The Jews living in the settlements of modern Palestine were living according to Jesus. He saw that community good must come before all else. Just as He so deeply loved children, and His most touching words were those about children, so it was here in Palestine, where the immediate and deepest concern of Palestine Jewry was their children, the generation to come.

I felt that in Palestine I had peeled off all the accumulated layers of mystical tradition and legend that had been built up about Jesus. Now I saw Him as Jesus the Man. I realized how relentlessly the facts of the modern world were driving us to accept His economic principles, the only principles that could work in the modern world; and I realized, too, that the very things for which He stood were coming true in Palestine with the Jews, and by the Jews and because of the Jews—the people from whom He sprang.

CHAPTER 20

Lausanne: The Great Debate

WITH OUR INVESTIGATIONS in Palestine completed, we waited to fly to Lausanne, Switzerland, to write our report. Some of us earlier suggested that we remain in Palestine and write our report on the spot; others felt that pressures here would make our task difficult. Switzerland, as a neutral country, remote from the *Sturm und Drang* of Palestine, seemed a logical choice.

It was still dark when we were driven one morning to Lydda airfield, not far from Tel Aviv, and were on our way to Switzerland. It was time to consider what was in our own minds. The report had to be written in less than twenty-eight days. I summarized some conclusions apparently reached by certain members of the committee—conclusions of a rather surprising nature:

(*a*) One should not pay too much attention to the pleas of Zionist spokesmen. Such persons were in reality office-holders in a great political hierarchy, and they made their living out of a continuance of the problem. (Later I learned that the members of the Executive of the Jewish Agency for Palestine were paid ridiculous salaries, averaging $4000 a year, and that a political secretary of the Jewish Agency in London, an attorney who had been graduated with distinction from Cambridge University and who might well have earned $20,000 a year in private practice, had been putting in sixty hours a week for years at a salary of $66 a week.)

(*b*) Since the Jews of Germany had made an immense contribution to the civilization and intellectual advancement of Germany, their elimination would be a calamity for Europe. I thought it pretty grim to force the few German Jews surviving to remain in Germany against their will in order to fertilize Europe's intellectual life.

(*c*) Jewish schools in Palestine are turning out ultra-nationalists of the Hitler *Jugend* type.

(*d*) Many ill-informed people, rather anti-Semitic in belief, thought it might be a good idea to send the Jews to Palestine. *Ergo*, was not all this emphasis on Palestine merely giving a new impetus to anti-Semitism?

(*e*) It was understandable why no country wanted to receive the survivors of European Jewry. All the best elements had been killed off. It would take a generation or two to restore the stamina and quality of what remained.

Some of these conclusions seemed to me to be rationalizations based on the inarticulate major premise of the individual's unconscious hostility to the Zionist idea.

We would have to thrash out the fundamental issues in Lausanne.

Our headquarters in Lausanne, forty-five minutes from Geneva, were at the Beau Rivage Hotel on Lake Leman.

From the beginning, there were differences of opinion. The British, conscious of their government's status as the Mandatory Power, found themselves at once the judged and the judging. We Americans had no such responsibility, and I could understand how annoying it might be for those charged with responsibility to be the recipients of constant advice. Yet our advice had been asked for, and we felt an obligation to speak forthrightly. What all of us sought was a key to peace for Palestine. Our own American record, which I regarded as double-dealing, certainly did not put us in a very strong moral position either. But facts are facts. *The basic law of the mandate had been violated by the agent entrusted with carrying it out.* Our problem was to bring to contemplation of this fundamental fact those of our British and American colleagues who were inclined to overlook what was the very nub of the situation.

The divisions of opinion naturally sharpened now, yet, surprisingly, the alignments did not always find all the Americans on one side and all the British on the other. Crossman, for example, found himself quite frequently, in our debates, on what might roughly be called the American side, while Aydelotte and Phillips, with similar frequency, found themselves essentially in agreement with the majority of the British.

But it was not a question of personalities: fundamentally, the stumbling block was that many of the British saw Britain's life at stake in this problem. Weary after six years of struggle, embarked at home on a policy of nationalization and socialization of major industries, fearful of liquidating the empire, the British found themselves in a most difficult situation, for the *equities* were clearly on the side of the mandate and its terms. The real question was whether the *realities* were also. I am not at all sure that we Americans would have behaved half so well in the same situation. But we felt that it would be giving renewed strength to Britain, as well as to the world, if we could work out a joint and unanimous solution which would conform both with our conscience and with the needs of the situation.

In the end, it was the leadership of Judge Hutcheson which kept us all together. He would not permit our initial differences to result in a breakup of the committee into American and British groups. It is not an overstatement to say that had it not been for him, the final report would not have been unanimous. He labored from twelve to sixteen hours a day, drafting proposals and trying to reconcile points of view without yielding on basic principle. Many matters were extremely delicate, such, for example, as the desire of powerful forces in the Colonial Office—and of similar elements in the United States—to set up an Arab state.

Suggestions to this end were always cloaked in terms which could be described as the purest of democratic doctrine. The argument ran something like this: it was immoral in the first place to set up a Jewish National Home in Palestine; the Balfour Declaration was wrong; the mandate was superimposed upon the indigenous Arab inhabitants of Palestine without their consent; in any event, the Jews had been given a sufficient opportunity since the mandate to come into Palestine, and any attempt to continue to develop a National Home for the Jewish people in Palestine would be a negation of the principles of the Atlantic Charter. This, of course, was to ignore both the legal question and the unique position of Palestine not merely in Jewish but in world history. Nor could I forget the way in which the Catholic Church had summed the matter up: "No Christian can in fairness deny to the Jews the sympathetic support of their humanitarian efforts to make a spiritual and temporal place of refuge for oppressed Jews—a place which they could truly regard as their homeland." *

Manningham-Buller, being an excellent lawyer, knew that the 1939 White Paper was illegal because it was an obvious departure from the mandate. Yet he believed a case could be made that the Jewish National Home had been completed. What he objected to about the White Paper were the procedures. He felt that the forthright way to handle the matter would be for the British government to go to the League of Nations and ask for a judgment that its obligations concerning the Jewish National Home in Palestine were fulfilled. Beeley, of the Foreign Office, went further. It was his contention that to admit a single Jew to Palestine beyond the quota agreed upon or set out by the White Paper of 1939 was for Britain to break her word—to the Arabs.

Our discussion was not made any easier by an intensification of British surveillance brought on as the result of a leak to the press. How it occurred, we never learned. In any event, a Captain Ayers, of the British Criminal Investigation Department of the Palestine police, who had been charged with our security in Jerusalem, suddenly appeared in Lausanne and took a room at our hotel. To the press he explained that he was "on a holiday." To us he said he had come for our "security." This security took the same strange and annoying forms already familiar to me. He asked permission to go through our rooms, look through our papers, and destroy any documents we weren't going to use. Frequently, when I made telephone

* *Catholics and Jews*, by Gregory Feige, published by the Catholic Association for International Peace, 1945, p. 45; *Nihil Obstat*, John A. Ryan, D.D., censor deputatus, imprimatur, Michael J. Curly, D.C., Archbishop of Baltimore and Washington.

calls I found him on the other end of my wire, and when persons outside the hotel attempted to call me, the concierge (who, I learned later, was paid for this favor) turned them over to Captain Ayers. Captain Ayers would demand to know who was calling Mr. Crum and from where. This forced me to make my telephone calls elsewhere.

Mail and cables addressed to the American members of the committee seemed to have the greatest difficulty reaching us. Even when the President of the United States cabled Judge Hutcheson at Lausanne, expressing his pleasure at our safe arrival and the hope that we could come to a unanimous decision, his message was first delivered to the British consul in Geneva. A second cable to Hutcheson from President Truman was delivered to the British consul and was opened before it reached the Judge. McDonald, equally harassed, complained to me that his mail was being opened and that he could not take a taxicab without the concierge learning where he was going.

Our meetings began to have real substance after Judge Hutcheson made a statement which helped greatly to clarify the problem before us. He stressed the following points:

(1) "I could not turn away from the history which had been made since 1917 and particularly since 1922, and, therefore, I could not support as just the view of the White Paper that Jewish immigration had to stop and the whole plan for keeping open a place to which Jews could go must, unless Arab consent be secured, be frustrated.

(2) "I have been struggling to find a way out, which, recognizing the real, the substantial, rights of both peoples, denied their unjust claims, and have finally found it in the establishment in Palestine of some form of bi-national state.

(3) "I know that something has been and is to be said in favor of partition. I feel that such a solution is a solution of despair: it will satisfy neither the genius of the Jews nor that of the Arabs."

In his opinion, the general future policy as to Palestine should be determined as follows:

(a) The White Paper is out, and there shall be no Arab state;

(b) The question of forced colonization to produce a Jewish majority and ultimately a Jewish state is also out;

(c) We affirm that the development of the Jewish National Home must go on with the fullest protection to Arab and Christian in that Holy Land through some form of bi-national arrangement which will protect all interests. For the success of this plan a trusteeship under UN will be necessary. As to immediate immigration, we should announce as a part of our plan the largest possible immediate immigration, if necessary up to the 100,000 figure. If we agreed on some such plan, we would break the deadlock of the White Paper. By making it clear that the Arabs would not be made subjects of a Jewish state, we would allay the fear of the Arabs that they would be placed under Jewish domination, and we would have furnished a basis for firm and definite action for the future.

He now saw our problem in perspective, he said. The White Paper was a great injustice; it could not stand. There should be substantial continuing immigration under the Jewish Agency. After what he had seen in Syria and the Lebanon—the precarious position of Jews under Arab rule—he realized that it was impossible to put Jews into an Arab state. Palestine could, therefore, be neither an Arab nor a Jewish state.

Actually, as we went from country to country, Hutcheson's point of view had undergone a considerable development. He was evidently influenced also by Judge Proskauer's argument in Washington, by Dr. Magnes in Jerusalem, and by a publication of *Hashomer Hatzair*, a young left-wing Jewish labor organization which stood basically for bi-nationalism.

He had clearly done a great deal of soul searching. He was not only convinced of the legal validity of the Jewish case, but he felt that a people who had suffered so much should be compensated. He told us very honestly that he favored the immigration of the 100,000 this year and then free Jewish immigration under the Agency. The Jordan Valley Authority project, he was convinced, was a most desirable thing. As a Texan with great faith in the land and its potentialities, he saw the Jordan Valley Authority as a contribution to the social and economic well-being of all the peoples of the Middle East. As to the political solution, he believed bi-nationalism might be the answer, but he was open to conviction.

I did not underestimate the significance of the Judge's point of view. I had long since regarded him as a key figure in our final decision. I felt that four of us—McDonald, Buxton, Crossman, and myself—would definitely fight for immediate admission of the 100,000 and for abolition of the White Paper, which we regarded as cruel, iniquitous, and legally unsound. With the Judge joining us, I was sure that both Ambassador Phillips and Dr. Aydelotte would not remain outside our fold. The question now, of course, was whether the Judge would be as forthright when it came to the actual crossing of the swords with the Sir John-Manningham-Buller majority of the British section, and would he remain firm in the subsequent maneuvering?

The Judge's statement was received with mixed feelings. I felt he had made a real contribution which sought to reconcile the just aspirations of both Jews and Arabs. If carried out, it would have meant freedom by 1947 for those in the DP camps, and would have established a yardstick for the future. Sir John, to put it mildly, was shocked. He apparently had expected the Judge's support for the Colonial Office point of view. Manningham-Buller, too, felt that the Balfour Declaration had been fulfilled and the time had come to release Britain from her obligations and set up a Palestine state, which meant, of course, an Arab state. The other British members, save Crossman, supported Manningham-Buller. We Americans sided with Judge Hutcheson, but with variations.

I doubted whether a bi-national solution was workable. Nor did I accept the Judge's characterization of partition as a solution of despair. I wanted abolition of the White Paper, immediate immigration of 100,000, the enlargement of the authority of the Jewish Agency to enable it to meet the increased demands upon it, the establishment of the Jordan Valley Authority, and, as a political solution to the Palestine problem, partition of Palestine into separate Arab and Jewish states.

Buxton was perhaps the most militant. He objected to partition and looked to an eventual Jewish state in an undivided Palestine. As an immediate step he wanted to see 100,000 Jews admitted immediately.

"To do that you'd need six divisions," said Sir John. Buxton retorted: "Legalize the *Haganah,* and you'll have three right there." Sir John said that it was intolerable that the blood of British Tommies should be shed in behalf of this National Home policy. Someone retorted: "Take the Tommies out and let the Jews take care of themselves. That is what they want."

In our discussions we concluded that President Truman's repeated request for 100,000 was not unreasonable; actually, McDonald, Crossman, Buxton, and I were convinced that Palestine could easily absorb more than that number. We were convinced that the primary way to resolve the whole unsettled condition in Palestine peacefully was by doing precisely what the President of the United States had suggested. We felt that this was not merely an act of human decency. Without a firm decision in favor of Jewish immigration and freedom to settle anywhere on the land of Palestine, we did not see how the tragic struggle in the Holy Land could be stopped.

Since all evidence attested that 100,000 immigrants could be quickly absorbed, an obvious question was whether they could be quickly transported to Palestine. Judge Hutcheson and Sir John Singleton cabled to Colonel Stanley R. Mickelsen, Director of the Displaced Persons Division of the U. S. Military Government, and Colonel D'Arcy Stephens in Germany and invited them to Lausanne to testify on this. They appeared before us the next day. Colonel Mickelsen told us that because we had the necessary ships and our troop redeployment to the United States had slowed down materially, 100,000 could be moved in by rail to Marseille or to Bari within one month. Colonel Stephens was even more emphatic. The camps in Austria could be cleaned out in two weeks' time, he told us. This meant the entire 100,000 could re-establish their lives in Palestine within the year.

Sir Frederick and Manningham-Buller had both worried

271

whether this immigration would constitute an invading Jewish Army, as General Spears had charged. Neither of the two witnesses thought so. Mickelsen said that the DPs were "peaceful citizens outside of the centers" and were "obstreperous" only when "German policemen or others come in to disturb the tranquillity."

Manningham-Buller asked: "Would you say that anti-Semitism is being conquered in Germany, decreasing, or about the same as it was?"

"I don't think there is any change among the Germans," Colonel Mickelsen replied. "Outwardly, yes, but inwardly, no. Inwardly, anti-Semitism is still strong."

From all points of view, therefore—humanitarian and military, peace in the Middle East, the re-establishment of the moral integrity of Britain and the United States in the eyes of the people of the world—the course of wisdom was to give these battered human beings their chance to live.

But what about the Arabs? Would we be sending the DPs from the comparative safety of the camps into a fight for their lives? The Arabs had spoken with such vigor, had threatened such violence. I had concluded that a good deal of this Arab opposition was synthetic and exaggerated. It was evident that the opposition to further Jewish immigration stemmed primarily from self-appointed Arab nationalist "leaders" (not without the assistance of certain British colonial officials), and ill-will was fomented from the top down and not vice versa.

We had seen average Arabs and average Jews by the thousands living in peace and harmony in Palestine. We saw their establishments side by side in Jerusalem. We saw Arab farmers tilling their fields next to Jewish *Kibbutźim*. We had seen evidences too numerous to cite to prove that Arab and Jew could live together. The average Arab knew that with the Jews had come a far better life for him and his family.

It had been obvious to us that these plain Arabs could not speak out with freedom; we had had to get at the facts rather indirectly in our journeys throughout Palestine. In the informal discussions we had had at the King David Hotel with the young Arab leaders, it had been stressed to us, time and again, that it was quite impossible for an Arab to be anti-Semitic because the Arabs, too, are a Semitic people. These young Arab leaders had told me that they felt that even the Arab leadership was making a great mistake in not recognizing that the Palestinian Arabs and the Palestinian Jews share a common destiny. If the Arab leadership were convinced that the Jews were not part of a creeping invasion engineered by England to destroy their position, the Jews and the Arabs even at the top would be able to reconcile their differences.

Thus, we were faced with a state of mind which had been imposed on the overworked, uneducated, and illiterate Palestinian Arabs—a political interpretation which had no validity in fact and which was being refuted in the day-by-day activities of the Palestinians themselves. It was quite possible, for instance, for an Arab to hold to this false political view even while he would select as the judge of an inter-Arab dispute a former Jewish lawyer from Lithuania. A visit to Palestine was sufficient to give the lie to the proposition that Arabs and Jews do not and cannot get along together. Yet this charge was constantly repeated.

In the midst of our deliberations we received a note from Yussef D., who, I learned, had also seen Beeley and Aydelotte in Jerusalem. Whether he was as frank with them as he had been with me, I do not know. But he had sworn me to secrecy. If his views ever were made public it might cost him his life, he said. I was surprised, therefore, to receive his note, copies of which were sent to all of us. He warned us not to accept at face value the greater part of the Arab testimony in London and in Jerusalem. He charged that the British Foreign Office wished to keep the Middle East in its present feudalistic condition—first, to prevent the possibility of a social revolution which would topple the landholding aristocracy, and, second, to offset any possible outside influence. The purpose of Yussef D.'s note was to urge what had been broached to us in private conference in Jerusalem: the setting up of a Greater Syria, with King Abdullah at its head. This would embrace Syria, the Lebanon, Palestine, including a semiautonomous Jewish sector, and Trans-Jordan. Setting up such a state under Abdullah would not only serve to satisfy the nationalistic aspirations of Syrians who maintained that Palestine had never ceased to be South Syria, but would restore the Hashimite dynasty to power throughout the whole area.

The discussion of Mr. D's proposal led to consideration of the entire problem of partition. Despite public demands by Arab spokesmen that all of Palestine must be declared an Arab state, some of the younger intellectuals—including Mr. D., the Nashashibis, and others, as against the Mufti, Jaamal Husseini, Auni Abdul Hadi—were not too unfavorable toward partition.

Partition had been proposed by the Peel Royal Commission of 1936. It had been turned down by both Jews and Arabs at the start, although at the Zionist Congress in 1937, after a fierce debate, the Zionists had agreed to authorize their representatives to negotiate a better proposal than that contained in the Peel Report. Weizmann, as he told me in London, felt very strongly that had partition gone through in 1937 a great number of European Jews might have been saved. But shortly after, the British withdrew their support of the Peel proposal.

We knew that many different partition plans had been offered. One plan, to which some of the younger Arab intellectuals would not have objected, contemplated annexing to Trans-Jordan the purely Arab section of Palestine adjacent to Trans-Jordan. Thus, a greater Trans-Jordan would be created, and the remainder of Palestine could be established as a Jewish state.

But finally, our committee rejected partition. I felt with Crossman that this was a mistake. Both of us realized the possibility that neither the Palestinian Arabs nor the Palestinian Jews would accept any other solution we would propose. We both, therefore, reserved the right to inform our governments fully as to our favorable views on partition, and we obtained the permission of the committee to write such a communication, Crossman to Ernest Bevin, and I to President Truman. We debated for some time whether or not our views on partition should be included in the report itself, but finally agreed that to stress the issue over partition would serve only to weaken our unanimous recommendations. Crossman, I think, was less optimistic than I that the committee's recommendations would be carried into effect. All parties, he felt, would ultimately be compelled by circumstance to accept the principle of partition.

The words "Jewish state" were a source of constant difficulty for the committee. There was no doubt in our minds that the intention of the Balfour Declaration and the mandate was to enable the Jews to make Palestine a country which would be predominantly Jewish—a Jewish

National Home to which Jews could go as of right and not on sufferance. This meant, as Lloyd George put it, that if the Jews ultimately constituted a majority there, then— and only then—the purpose of the mandate would be achieved. For then there would be set up in Palestine a democratic commonwealth with equal rights to Arab and Jew alike. How, then, were we to resolve our dilemma? We determined not to delimit the intent of the mandate. Yet we had to make it plain to the world that we rejected the notion of Palestine either as an exclusively Jewish state or an exclusively Arab state. We sought to return to the intention of the framers of the Balfour Declaration; namely, to provide an opportunity for free immigration and close settlement on the land of Palestine. If these two major British commitments were discharged, we were convinced that the ultimate political organization of Palestine would take care of itself.

We rejected the narrow, almost sinister interpretation of a "Jewish state" as a chauvinistic or racial state, in which only Jews could be first-class citizens and only Jews could hold office. This was the meaning placed upon the words by the Arabs and by Lessing Rosenwald and the American Council for Judaism.

But this, we concluded, was in no sense the type of state desired by the Zionists themselves. What the words meant was that through the immigration of large numbers of European and other Jews, the Jewish people should be enabled to attain a majority in Palestine and thus guarantee an open door for others who might follow. In that "Jewish state" the Arabs would participate on the basis of equality of citizenship. The development of the country as a whole would be ensured in accordance with the purposes of the mandate, including, of course, raising the Arab standard of living side by side with the development of the Jewish National Home. Obviously, this could be achieved only with governmental powers, which the Jewish Agency lacks. It cannot freely choose land upon which to settle people; it cannot determine the rate of immigration, or go ahead with irrigation plans to open up large areas of land, or bring into Palestine the machinery to make that land productive.

This authority, this freedom to make decisions, to draw up blueprints and carry them out—this was what the words "Jewish state" were written to mean. They were not intended to imply dictation or domination. "All we mean," Ben Gurion had stated, "is simply safety, simply security."

I recalled an episode in London. There had been testimony before us dealing with a Jewish state. Judge Hutcheson had looked askance on the Jewish Resistance Movement.

"You remember, Judge," I had told him one afternoon as we were having tea in our offices, "that about a hundred years ago the people of Texas were in almost the same situation as the Jews in Palestine." The Judge cocked his head to one side and raised his eyebrows.

"Absolutely," I said. "The Americans were then under Mexican rule. The Mexican government got tough with them. It halted all immigration into Texas. It attempted to take away the arms and ammunition of the Texans." I paused. "Well, Judge," I said, "you know what happened. The Texans kicked out all the Mexicans and set up a state of their own."

The Judge put up his hand and shook his head and said seriously: "Oh, yes, but we were prepared to fight for our liberty."

Now, as we sat on the spacious veranda of the Beau

Rivage, I brought it up again. This time the Judge agreed that the Jews, too, were prepared to fight for their liberty and recalled that it was traditional for the American people to be permitted to carry arms in their own defense and that, in fact, the United States Constitution guaranteed this right to every citizen.

Some of the British, returning to what they had suggested four months earlier, aboard the *Queen Elizabeth,* wished us to recommend the disbanding of the *Haganah* and the withdrawal of recognition of the Jewish Agency. I was one of those strongly against this. The British High Command in both Cairo and Jerusalem had warned us of the difficulties involved, and we knew that no government had succeeded in disbanding a Maquis movement backed by the entire population.

If one viewed the Jewish community of Palestine merely as a willful group of rebellious subjects resisting lawful authority, one might agree that the government would be compelled to try to disarm the *Haganah* and to relieve the official representatives of such people from any position of authority. I am afraid that is how some of our British associates saw it. Sir John's indignation over the death of a British Tommy in Palestine was genuine, but I imagine his counterpart in the eighteenth century would have felt equally strongly on American patriots killing redcoats in Boston. My point of view, and that of many of my American colleagues, was that illegal armies were certainly to be deplored: that the death of British Tommies was an infinitely tragic chapter in the history of Palestine and no doubt a painful one for the Jews, who had such a warm feeling of gratitude to Britain for the Balfour Declaration. But we pointed out that if British soldiers or Palestine police had lost their lives in defense of the high purpose of the mandate rather than in destroying that very purpose, then we would have felt that the point of view of Sir John and other British members was well taken.

The discussions on this subject were extremely warm, Sir John feeling that it would be improper and unjust to permit any further Jewish immigration into Palestine so long as the *Haganah* remained a force in Palestine. Sir Frederick Leggett sided with Sir John in this. He pointed out that we Americans could have no concept of the feeling of indignation in Britain whenever a British Tommy was injured or killed in Palestine. This, he said, was creating anti-Semitism in Britain—a matter which he viewed with alarm. I know that Sir Frederick had been concerned with this because as early as our crossing from England to Paris, he had said that if conditions did not settle down he was fearful that the onus would be borne by the Jews of Britain. Lord Morrison had similar convictions, and so, too, did Manningham-Buller. Crick, also, had strong feelings upon the subject, and naturally all of us deplored violence.

The difference in our point of view can be summed up by saying that the Americans and Crossman felt that the way to end violence was by removing the cause for violence. We knew from the questions we had asked in the camps of Germany and Austria that no Jew was willing to purchase his freedom upon the terms suggested by Sir John and—as events were to show later—by Prime Minister Attlee. Further, our position was bolstered by the repeated statements from the highest military quarters that it would be virtually impossible, in any event.

Judge Hutcheson was particularly firm. Finally he said, "I will not, under any circumstances, be a party to any recommendations which would strip the Jews of Palestine of their right to defend their lives."

Similarly Crossman was firm and articulate on the subject. The issue was resolved our way.

From the decision on the *Haganah* it was natural for us to pass to a thorough consideration of its relationship with the Jewish Agency. There were some things in relation to the Agency which both of our chairmen found distasteful, such as the reported requirement imposed on all young Palestine Jews to volunteer for a year of "national service." While this service consisted, in the first place, of work wherever required in the agricultural settlements, it was also alleged to include, in some cases, guard duty in the settlements and training in the use of arms. Even if this were true, it would be difficult to demand that the Jews of Palestine not be allowed to learn how to protect themselves. After a rather lengthy debate, however, the Agency's position was reaffirmed, with the cautioning note that the Agency must resume relations with the Mandatory Power.

And so it went from point to point, each side arguing for its position, yet ready to modify and conciliate for the sake of the unanimity which, we all clearly understood, was the price that Bevin had exacted for putting our conclusions into force. The report then was a compromise, divided into immediate and long-term recommendations. If omissions were made necessary by this laborious process, if one or another of us was not wholly satisfied by some sections, at least there was nothing from which any of us felt compelled to dissent, and, on the whole, we could say that the report fairly represented the convictions of all twelve members of the Committee of Inquiry

For the present, we were agreed that there was no hope of assistance for Jewish emigrants from Europe in any country except Palestine and that 100,000 certificates of entry should be issued immediately. For the longer range, we recommended as principles of government for Palestine neither an Arab nor a Jewish state, but a return to the basis of the mandate, pending execution of a trusteeship agreement under the United Nations; revocation of the land and immigration regulations of the 1939 White Paper; and—for the distant future—a standard of economic and cultural equality which would assure to Arab and Jew alike a life of peace in Palestine.

When we concluded our report and our recommendations we held a dinner. Everyone was happy. It is my opinion that our British colleagues were as pleased as we were; first, that we had been able to come to unanimous recommendations, British and Americans alike—this augured well for the future relationship between England and America; secondly, we were pleased because all of us believed we had found the solution to this vexatious problem by the direct method of keeping our word. Such a conclusion may seem simple or naïve to some, but it heartened us and we believed then, as I believe now, that the moral prestige of the Western world would have been restored in large measure by this simple device of doing what you say you will do.

Since we felt that there had been enough words about Palestine and that it was action and deeds that counted, Judge Hutcheson prepared to fly at once to Washington, to lay the matter before President Truman, and Sir John also prepared to leave at once for London, to present our joint report to Mr. Bevin. So convinced were we that our unanimous recommendations would be carried out that Manningham-Buller undertook to see Mr. Anthony Eden, and Sir Frederick Leggett—an old friend of Foreign Minister Bevin—agreed also to talk with him.

What happened between the time we signed the report and the subsequent actions of the British government, I do not know, but certainly all of the American members of the committee were greatly surprised and disappointed when Mr. Attlee said in the House of Commons that before any immigration into Palestine could be permitted the *Haganah* must be disarmed. The subsequent, and to me almost incredible, statements of Mr. Bevin cannot be explained except in terms of high imperial strategy. I breach no confidence when I say that among those in very high positions in England there are others similarly baffled. Here was a unanimous report by a joint commission representing two great nations and set up at the invitation of the British government. The manner and the matter of that government's refusal to act in fulfillment of its recommendations were hardly such as to foster international amity or to give hope for a happy outcome of the Palestine problem. Not least disturbing were the cavalier references to the Jews. Never in her long history of empire, I believe, has Britain had more loyal friends than the Jewish community of Palestine and the Jews of America.

I may say that I never dreamed that when we finally produced our report urging that the 100,000 be allowed to enter—I never dreamed that after this slow and arduous day-by-day argument—our entire report would be so cavalierly discarded by Mr. Bevin and Mr. Attlee. Yet, I suppose I should have suspected that there was more truth than fiction in Beeley's casual observation to me toward the end of our stay in Lausanne. He made it with a twinkle in his eye—an offhand remark—"Well, after all, we certainly won't implement any such program as this." And I remember now Sir John's repeated warning given with the hesitant cough and clearing of throat: "You know, Crum, these are only recommendations."

BOOK FOUR

Conclusion

CHAPTER 21

What of Tomorrow?

THE DUTY of the advocate is to reduce the complex to the simple. I believe that the problem posed by Palestine is, in essence, less complicated than many of us make it. Indeed, is there any international problem today, in the fifth decade of the twentieth century, that does not have its difficulties? But I am convinced that if we approach Palestine with common sense, decency, and a desire to find the greater justice, we shall achieve a lasting solution.

I came home convinced that it was in the best interests of the world that this great Jewish experiment in Palestine should succeed; convinced, too, that the best way to help there, as elsewhere, was to urge the formulation of an affirmative American policy geared to the advancement of genuine political and economic democracy throughout the world.

Writing now in San Francisco, I think of many things: the hearings in Washington, London, Cairo, Jerusalem; the intrigues, the pressures, and implied threats; the extraordinary maneuvering of men and events; the faces of the men and women in the displaced-persons camps; anti-Semitism and bitterness; mass misery in the Middle East; and then—Palestine. Palestine was the lodestar of our trip; that was the center around which all else revolved.

I think of the strong, sun-tanned people in the busy, tree-lined streets of Tel Aviv; of the desperate and successful efforts of the farmers of the *Kibbutzim* to make trees grow on the granite hills about Jerusalem, where nothing had grown for a thousand years; of the overnight building of compounds by young pioneers in the desert country of the Negev. These and a hundred other sharp memories of Palestine crowd my mind. A new and valid civilization—a "one world" in microcosm—has been born in Palestine, a civilization in which the hopes of the Jews and the rights of the Arabs will be reconciled.

The Jews of Palestine realize that the whole world is an indivisible political and economic unit; that their future is inextricably bound up with the future of all people everywhere. But they are not making the mistake of waiting for the world to recognize this truth, to give up its self-destructive militant nationalism and its power politics. They are going forward with their own co-operative society, creating economic conditions under which all Palestinians, Arab and Jew alike, can improve their standard of living. The cry out of the hearts of all men for what Sherwood Anderson called "a new birth of belief" has been answered by them in the planting of the new Judean forests; in the building of the new cities, the university on Mt. Scopus, and the hospitals; in the creation of new art forms, of new forms of social and economic organization. They are building a society which recognizes and emphasizes the fundamental dignity and significance of the individual. In such a society, derived from a people drawn from all nations and all cultures, it is impossible for a narrow, self-limiting nationalism to flourish.

I found these people pursuing their task with tremendous devotion. I spoke with many young men and women

who had fought and worked in the Allied armies. When
the war ended they could well have remained abroad. The
world outside beckoned to them. Many, such as the brilliant assistant of Dr. Weizmann at the Sieff Laboratory at
Rehovoth, had fantastic offers to remain in the West.
Most of these young men and women represented the second and third generations, and I was familiar with the disappearance of the pioneering spirit in our own West after
the first generation. Still, without compulsion, they went
back to Palestine to help in the hard life of building what
they call simply *Eretz*—the land.

No one who has been in Palestine can fail to realize that
the Palestine Jew is a free man, spiritually and psycho-
logically. It is true that Palestine is a police state; that its
citizens can be arrested without warrant, imprisoned without trial, and deported without explanation; that the
streets of its cities are lined with barbed wire and patrolled
by tanks and machine guns. It is true that the Jews of
Palestine live under an administration which looks upon
them essentially with disfavor. I trust I will not shock the
reader if I say that fully seventy per cent of the British
colonial officials whom I met in Palestine either were, at
worst, openly anti-Semitic or, at best, completely unsym-
pathetic and even resentful toward Jewish hopes in Palestine.

The British should long since have recognized that the
Jews in Palestine are not a depressed, native people; they
should have realized their error in placing Palestine under
the Colonial Office, with administrators taken from the
ranks of the colonial and Indian services, where their experience had been almost totally that of overlords dealing
with subservient and illiterate natives. The British should
have placed Palestine under the administration of men

with vision and ability, eager to develop new territories and untapped resources.

But in Palestine the Jew, though living in a police state, has freed himself from that greater bondage of nearly two thousand years; in Palestine he stands before the world, the shackles of the ghetto cast from him, a people like all other peoples, "neither better nor worse," in Weizmann's words. It is the British, not the Jews, who do not feel free in Palestine, who are afraid. For Palestine Jewry represents the power of a collective and unbreakable moral decision which, short of a massacre of the entire population, is bound to prevail.

I did not fully comprehend the great positive influences of this moral decision until I had seen the Middle East and compared the poverty, the disease, and the humiliation of Egypt with the cleanliness, the well-being, and the dignity of the people of Palestine. Then I understood how much the unfettered development of the Jewish people in Palestine could mean to the whole of the Middle East, for it could bring to the Middle East the good in Western civilization—not by domination, but by example. I do not say that the Jews have returned to Palestine for the purpose of conferring benefits upon the Arabs in Palestine. They have come to build up a national home for the Jewish people. They are proud that in doing this they have tremendously benefited all the people of Palestine.

The great experiment in Palestine began nearly a century ago. It has been a success comparable to no other experiment, save our own Union. There have been difficulties, of course: and there will be difficulties in the future. But writing now, I recall Wendell Willkie's words to me when he returned from his round-the-world trip. We discussed what he had seen East, North, West, and South, and we spoke of Palestine. He said, "Bart, the Arabs have a good case in Palestine. There is only one thing wrong with it. The Jews have a better case."

What, then, should be our approach, as Americans, to Palestine?

If my experiences in the days and weeks devoted to this problem have taught me any one thing, it is that everywhere the need is felt for an *American* foreign policy—a foreign policy so firmly embedded on principle that it will hold equally for United States troops in China, or the atom bomb, or Palestine.

To determine this foreign policy, we have one of two paths before us. We can throw our lot in with the forces of reaction who prop up feudalistic regimes in the Arab states in the hope that these will serve as what Mr. Beeley called a *cordon sanitaire* against the Soviet; who believe they can successfully continue the same processes of exploitation in the future which have proved successful in the past. Or we can throw our lot in with the progressive forces in the Middle East. We can recognize that there is a slow rising of its peoples, and that we must place ourselves on the side of this inevitable development toward literacy, health, and a decent way of life. I say to my fellow Americans that not only for the sake of the masses of the Middle East, but for the sake of world peace, we must encourage this development, a development of which Jewish Palestine is thus far the outstanding example, holding great promise for the future of all its neighbors. Therefore, it follows that support for the Jewish National Home is the first and logical step to take on this path toward the advancement of a democratic way of life in that area of the world. Colonel T. E. Lawrence—the fabled Lawrence of Arabia, devoted friend and adviser of the Arabs—saw this more than a quarter of a century ago, when he said, "I am decidedly in favor of Zionism. Indeed, I look on the Jews as the natural importers of that Western leaven which is so necessary for the countries of the Middle East."

It is tragic that Great Britain today seems to have forgotten the original intent of her own men of vision who knew well what they were building, and why. But we must be careful, in judging Britain, to remember that here we Americans, too, have compromised with the basic principle of freedom for reasons of expediency. We have taken our cue from those British statesmen who have based their policy in the undeveloped regions of the earth upon cooperation with local potentates rather than upon promotion of the genuine interests of the masses.'Our course has been one of duplicity, with conflicting public and private pledges. I am certain that our policy-makers have been able to do this only because of lack of clear popular understanding of the issues involved.

It may be that one of the chief by-products of our committee's investigation has been to bring to the American people much greater knowledge of the true situation in the Middle East and Palestine, and much greater awareness of American responsibility and American interest in the solution of the Palestine question. Our country should now be ready to play its role in the Middle East with more intelligence and more justice.

Perhaps the most heartening symptom of our growing national maturity with regard to Palestine is the forthright letter written by President Truman in November, 1946, to King Ibn Saud. In this letter to the man whose oil power has been cited as a principal stumbling block in the path of American support of Jewish aspirations in Palestine, Mr. Truman declared that the United States has a legitimate responsibility for the solution of the Palestine problem, and that his statements urging entry of displaced Jews into Palestine and support of the Jewish National Home can in no sense be considered acts "hostile to the Arab peoples."

The President's words were unequivocal:

"The government and people of the United States have given support to the concept of a Jewish national home in Palestine since the termination of the First World War, which resulted in the freeing of a large area of the Near East, including Palestine, and the establishment of a number of independent states which are now members of the United Nations.

"The United States, which contributed its blood and resources to the winning of that war, could not divest itself of a certain responsibility for the manner in which the freed territories were disposed of, or for the fate of the peoples liberated at the time. It took the position, to which it still adheres, that these peoples should be prepared for self-government and also that a national home for the Jewish people should be established in Palestine. I am happy to note that most of the liberated peoples are now citizens of independent countries."

But, he added, the Jewish National Home had not yet been fully developed, and it was "only natural, therefore, that this government should favor at this time the entry into Palestine of considerable numbers of displaced Jews not only to find shelter there but also to contribute their talents and energies to the upbuilding of the Jewish national home."

This principle enunciated by President Truman, and supported by the great majority of the American people, must guide us if we are to have peace in the Middle East and if we are to carry out the solemn obligation of Western civilization toward the surviving remnant of Hitler's chief victims. It is true that we have made great progress in our understanding of the Palestine problem; but we must still guard against the danger that the President's word may once more be sabotaged by secret diplomacy on the part of the middle levels of the State Department. We must call for a reorientation of our State Department toward the realization that we are embarking on our own American foreign policy in the Middle East. We must make clear, too, that our administration bears a further responsibility: it must match its words with parallel action.

Therefore, I suggest that the following be the immediate objectives and the immediate program of American policy toward Palestine:

A. Stand upon the unassailable legal grounds that the terms of the Mandate for Palestine are absolutely binding upon Britain until she is relieved of her duties as the Mandatory Power. There is no question that the mandate was framed primarily in Jewish interest; the Balfour Declaration was given to the Jews, and I am convinced on the basis of my studies that those rights which the mandate guarantees for the non-Jewish peoples of Palestine have been safeguarded by the Jews.

B. Demand the revocation of the British White Paper of 1939. The Permanent Mandates Commission of the League of Nations found it in violation of the terms of the mandate. This was also the finding of our committee.

C. Make it unmistakably clear that the Arab states have no special position in relation to Palestine.

D. Recommend that, pending a solution of the political future of Palestine, the United States oppose the admission of Trans-Jordan to the United Nations. There is no question that the removal of Trans-Jordan from the terms of the mandate was a violation of its original purpose. All of Palestine, east and west of the Jordan River, was set aside by the framers of the mandate for Jewish immigration and settlement. The setting up of Trans-Jordan as an independent kingdom, moreover, is a violation of Article V of the mandate, which forbids Britain from ceding or placing under the control of any foreign power any Palestine territory.*

E. Insist, as an earnest of good faith, that the British government should authorize the immediate issuance of 100,000 certificates of entry to Palestine. This number can and should be moved immediately. The balance of European Jewry which wishes to or must emigrate to Palestine should be given Palestinian citizenship until they can go there. These Jewish survivors of Nazism who have no other nationality and only await the day when they will reach Palestine are, at the very least, entitled to legal status and protection.

F. Urge legalization of the *Haganah* under Article XVII of the mandate.† This, in conjunction with Jewish immigration, would immediately end extremism in Palestine

---

* The full text of Article V is: "The Mandatory shall be responsible for seeing that no Palestine territory should be ceded or leased to, or in any way placed under the control of, the government of any foreign power."

† Article XVII reads in part: "The Administration of Palestine may organize on a voluntary basis the forces necessary for the preservation of peace and order, and also for the defense of the country, subject, however, to the supervision of the Mandatory, but shall not use them for purposes other than those above specified save with the consent of the Mandatory. Except for such purposes, no military, naval or air forces shall be raised or maintained by the Administration of Palestine."

and make possible the withdrawal of virtually all British troops now in Palestine.

G. If Great Britain persists in her refusal to carry out the terms of the mandate as our committee recommended, she should be brought before the new Permanent Court of International Justice under Article XXVI of the mandate * for calculated and deliberate violation of her trust.

What I have suggested is, I think, a realistic approach to this problem. In achieving a sound basic foreign policy for the United States, we shall point the way for Great Britain. She needs our help. Her burdens are many. It is our duty, for our own protection and hers, to contribute our thought and our strength toward the achievement of a policy which will put an end to these constantly recurring crises in Palestine, as in India, Burma, and elsewhere. Britain's fear of the Soviet is making progress synonymous with Communism, and making Communism attractive to the exploited peoples of the Middle East. The obvious answer to this is to make social and economic democracy work in the Middle East.

If America allows itself to be led by the British down the fatal path of maintaining the *status quo,* of supporting the feudalism of the past instead of the progress of the future, both we and Great Britain will ultimately lose, economically, strategically, morally.

We cannot have peace, I am convinced, with a Middle

* The full text of Article XXVI is: "The Mandatory agrees that if any dispute whatever should arise between the Mandatory and another member of the League of Nations relating to the interpretation or the application of the provisions of the mandate, such dispute, if it cannot be settled by negotiation, shall be submitted to the Permanent Court of International Justice provided for by Article 14 of the Covenant of the League of Nations."

East divided, half Fascist, half democratic. Palestine symbolizes the crossroads, not only for our foreign policy, but for the world.

Which way shall we choose?

About the Author

BARTLEY CRUM *has said, "I take free speech pretty seriously and do not think that the Republic will totter because somebody says what he thinks."*

He is forty-six years old, a liberal Republican, and has been a practicing corporation lawyer for some twenty-two years.

In 1940 he was aboard the Wendell Willkie train for about two months, and in 1941 he became western chairman of Fight for Freedom, helping in efforts to revitalize and make progressive the Republican Party. Mr. Crum was appointed special counsel for President Roosevelt's Committee on Fair Employment of Negroes in the Southern Railroads in 1942. In 1944, he became national chairman of the Independent Republicans for Roosevelt, and in 1945 was named consultant by the State Department to our delegation at the United Nations conference, where he worked on the United Nations Charter.

In December, 1945, he was named by President Truman to be a member of the Anglo-American Committee of Inquiry on Palestine. He has written occasional articles for The New York Times, The Christian Science Monitor, *and* The Nation.